The Impact of
Victorian Children's Fiction

J.S. BRATTON

CROOM HELM
London & Sydney

BARNES & NOBLE BOOKS
Totowa, New Jersey

© 1981 J.S. Bratton
Croom Helm Ltd, Provident House, Burrell Row,
Beckenham, Kent BR3 1AT
Croom Helm Australia Pty Ltd, First Floor,
139 King Street, Sydney, NSW 2001, Australia
Reprinted 1984

British Library Cataloguing in Publication Data

Bratton, J.S.
    The impact of Victorian children's fiction.
    1. Children's stories – History and criticism
    2. Literature and society I. Title
    823'.8   PN1009.A1

    ISBN 0-85664-777-2

First published in the USA 1981 by
BARNES AND NOBLE BOOKS,
81 ADAMS DRIVE,
TOTOWA, NEW JERSEY 07512

ISBN 0-389-20210-X

For my mother, who taught me to love reading, and never chose
my books.

Printed and bound in Great Britain by
Antony Rowe Ltd, Chippenham, Wilts

CONTENTS

ACKNOWLEDGEMENTS

I would like to thank the British and Bodleian Libraries, the staffs of
the Bedford College Library and of the Burnham, Bucks, Public
Library, the Charlotte Yonge Society, Mr Barker of the SPCK, Jeanette
White and M.J. Levens for their help in finding books for this study;
Shropshire County Library, the Lutterworth Press, the GLC Record
Office and the National Society for Promoting Religious Education for
permission to consult and refer to manuscripts; and Marjorie Traies,
Margaret Campbell and Carol Harrington for typing various drafts.

1 INTRODUCTION: EDUCATIONAL BACKGROUND AND CRITICAL APPROACHES

It is the business of this book to describe and to attempt to evaluate the flood of fiction for children which was written during the nineteenth century with the intention of conveying moral instruction. It will deal as far as possible with the questions of who wrote such books and why, who published them, who sold and who bought them, whether anyone read them and, if so, what they learnt. Certain preliminaries are necessary for such an investigation, for it is fraught with difficulties of definition and of methods of analysis. If these tales are to be seen in proportion, they must be set against the background of educational and publishing history which gave rise to them; but such a presupposition immediately raises questions about literary evaluation and the nature of appropriate analysis. While it is to be hoped that the methods employed will explain and justify themselves in operation, the problems presented will perhaps be the clearer for being set out in advance, with an indication of the means which have been employed to tackle them.

The concept of childhood, as a special and important state setting the child apart from adults in respects other than this obvious physical inferiority, was one of the fruits of the age of revolutions.[1] Subsequently millions of books were printed for people who had previously been lucky to get hold of a broadside ballad or a Bible, if they could read at all. For some new readers literacy was the gateway to huge changes, and even for those whose station ensured that they would have been taught to read, the coming of fiction for the young opened pathways for the imagination which had previously been disregarded by educators. With the coming of these changes, however, the experiences of children in reading remained various; books were so numerous partly because education through the printed word was thought of as highly specific, and different books, containing different kinds of information and fiction for moral instruction, were produced for each group of children. By 1850, when the machinery for teaching reading and providing reading matter was already monumentally large, individual experiences of schooling and literature would still differ greatly even for children of the same age and status. Generalisation is made all the more difficult by the fact that for each child the theories, dogmas and attitudes which went to the making of the pattern of education at an organisational level were probably always less important than quite unquantifiable matters such as the personality of a teacher or even a monitor. In 1850, for example, a village girl might have attended the Church-controlled National school from the age of six to thirteen, with long gaps in which she stayed at home to tend her mother or younger children, to help with the harvest, or do any other temporary, paid work in the fields; at school she would have spent her time in a class of mixed ages reading from a few ancient primers, or a Testament, and doing a great deal of mending and sewing for the lady of the manor. She would probably have gone to the Church Sunday school and learnt her catechism, attended church services with her class, and even stayed on at Sunday school after she went into service, if she was employed near enough to home. There would not be much inducement for her to stay unless getting a good character reference depended upon it. During her schooling she might have received two or three sixpenny prize books, published by the Society for the Propagation of Christian Knowledge, (SPCK), but since her attendance was poor, she might have nothing but a Bible on leaving day. At the same period a boy in Stockport might have spent a much shorter time in a day school, going to work in a factory at the age of nine, but attending the Stockport Sunday schools, and experiencing the elaborate orderliness and efficiency of thousands of scholars marshalled by the sounding of bells from ABC to Bible study and on to arithmetic and even training as a teacher. He would have looked to the school as his way out: in immediate terms, offering him the chance to parade with a banner on anniversary day and stand up and receive his handsome prize, to go into the country on a train and feast in an aristocratic garden; in the longer term, his teacher would have attended at his bedside as he passed over to a better world, or found him a post as he attempted to progress in this one. If such satisfactions seemed tame, he could defect to the socialist or Owenite Sunday school, and make a different use of his acquired skills.

There were other widely dissimilar experiences. A London child of the period might well have got no schooling at all, or have played an expert game of milking a series of ragged schools and philanthropic organisations of the benefits they offered to tempt him with, departing from each with pennies, soup, blankets and boots, and learning to read from the shop windows and roadside theatre bills; the son of a small tradesman in the Midlands might have sat in line under a monitor's eye and chanted hard facts, his whole energies absorbed in beating his

neighbour to a higher place and winning tickets and medals, and
reporting his progress nightly to his father, who was paying for it all. While
these children struggled on, their betters were also schooled in new
ways; farmers' daughters acquired obnoxious manners and bad
French in tiny boarding schools, the sons of gentlemen studied and
worshipped earnestly under the successors to Dr Arnold, while families
who were committed to Evangelical ideals or to those of Rousseau
kept their many children about them and read improving tales about
death and Resurrection, or looked on while they learnt to turn a lathe
and take cold baths. Two decades later, after the Acts of the early
1870s dictated that all children should be educated to a certain level,
the actual experience no doubt still differed greatly between the rural
National school run on the old lines and still dominated by the vicar
and the squire's ladies, the brand new London Board school staffed
by hard-working teachers trained up from the schools themselves, and
the Liverpool Industrial school which captured homeless children and
treated them like convicted criminals, refusing to let even the inspectors
see them alone. Gentlemen's sons were by this time falling into the
grip of public school curricula framed around the primacy of
compulsory games; their sisters, if they were lucky, had escaped from
haphazard governesses and become customers of the Girls' Public Day
School Trust, founded in 1872.[2] For all of these children books were
being written throughout the century which were supposed to suit their
level of literacy, their stations in life and their expectations of the
future, and to reflect their present experience so as to mould through
their response to it their moral and social attitudes. The books respond
very closely, therefore, to the varieties and changes in educational
provision throughout the century; and the most important aspects of
education from this point of view must therefore be borne in mind
when attempting to understand the development of children's fiction,
while we may look to the books to enrich our understanding of the
aims of education, and so of Victorian society.

In the first half of the nineteenth century the most important
educational changes to bear in mind were in the teaching of children
under the age of eleven or twelve, and particularly in the elementary
education of those who might previously have had little or no tuition
outside their families or their work. The revolution in consciousness
of the child took place alongside industrial and social revolutions which
also focused on his potential as an instrument of change; a sudden
urgency, therefore, came to the consideration of education. Around
the turn of the nineteenth century many different people felt an

unprecedented concern for children, especially those of the poor. A huge and rapidly growing army of new citizens who should shape the nation's future were suddenly brought to everyone's notice, as they rioted about the streets in the intervals of their work in the factories and mines. In 1805 this awareness reached the highest possible level, and George III pronounced that 'It is my wish that every poor child in my dominions should be taught to read the Bible.' Previously every child's teaching had been a parental responsibility, with each family training its members to take on the occupations which membership of that family destined them for, whether it was international diplomacy or straw-plaiting. Now this system, for a long time less than effective at any level, had obviously failed in respect of the lower orders. Schooling had to be provided for children at work outside their families, with their need for new skills and, more important, the likelihood of their imbibing new ideas about themselves and society.[3]

The first wave of schooling for these children was the Sunday school movement. Its importance for almost three-quarters of a century cannot be too strongly stressed; for the poor child who read and took in ideas, it was probably a stronger influence than any other attempt at education during the period. The reason for teaching on Sundays was at first simply that children were workers, in some areas often the main wage-earners for a family, and so had no other free time. The conscious desire to teach them was, however, religious in its origins, an aspect of the Evangelical revival which affected English life profoundly in the period from about 1780 onwards. There was always, therefore, a potential conflict between the desire to educate, the pupil's desire to be educated, and the religious motive of the education, directing and chanelling the instruction; but there was no disagreement about the first objective, that of reading. Protestantism is based on Bible study and therefore upon literacy; to save one's soul, one needs to read. It was also strongly felt by many of the ladies and gentlemen who are regarded as the founders of the Sunday school movement, men like Robert Raikes of Gloucester, that the real believer must also testify to conversion by converting others, and that a good method was to teach the malleable children who were to be found everywhere in a heathen state. Indeed, as has been recently pointed out, 'educational humanitarian work became a form of cultural definition for some of the middle classes, an activity akin to participation in a literary and philosophical, anti-slave trade or prison reform society'.[4] Far more teachers in Sunday schools, however, were working men or women who were earnest Christians and who gave up their only free day to help their neighbours' children. In many places, especially the industrial towns of the north of England, the Sunday schools became centres of working-class life and the focus of the powerful Victorian drive for self-help and self-improvement.[5]

The effectiveness of Sunday school teaching undoubtedly owed much to the sense of purpose with which it was undertaken, and all later writers within the movement stressed their religious motivation; the Sunday School Union Report of 1861, for example, states that 'the Sunday school . . . has for its object the evangelizing the mind of the rising generation'. W.H. Groser called the teaching of reading and writing a 'drudgery' which had to be undertaken before the main business could be approached.[6] The obligation to teach reading first was nevertheless taken entirely seriously, and reading was probably better taught because it was a means to an end, for which an imperfect or pretended understanding would not suffice. The independence of the volunteer teachers and their pupils alarmed many churchmen, who believed with some justification that they were a bridgehead for lay invasion of priestly authority. The schools were indeed often centres of religious feeling, and there are many reports of fervent piety and even mass conversions during periods of strong Evangelical revivalism; but for many pupils, and also for some of their instructors, the main objective was education, first in the reading of the Bible, and then in writing, arithmetic, and any other available subjects.

The strength of the inducement offered to working children through the opportunity of learning to read and write was very great. The first Sunday schools spread like wildfire across the country. Reliable figures are not to be had, but the optimism inspired in the founders can be judged by Raikes's claim that there were 250,000 children in Sunday schools by 1787. Overall numbers continued to rise until after the end of the century. When Queen Victoria died '2 millions of Sunday Scholars' sent a wreath to her funeral, and there were 22 million of them scattered across the Empire.[7] However, the proportion of the child population of Britain attending Sunday school dropped after about 1880, when compulsory elementary education and a proliferation of other youth organisations began to take over some of the Sunday schools' functions. This led to urgent reassessments of their role: religious teaching for all children, not simply the poorest, was now said to be their aim and, increasingly, secular activities were used to reinforce the community life of the school, spreading their moral effect into social areas so that the ethos penetrated and affected, in theory, the whole outlook of the participants. In this process literature played its part alongside Bible reading circles, picnics, cricket teams and lantern slide lectures.[8]

Many other new schools were founded as various groups perceived the challenge and potential influence of education. Old-established day schools, which were often no more than child-minding establishments where old or infirm persons earned a few pence, were no longer felt to be sufficient by any parent who could possibly afford to give his child a better start in the race for progress and self-improvement. By public subscription, Church patronage or philanthropy, new school systems were set up. Children at the bottom of the scale, below even the working patrons of the Sunday schools, were drawn into ragged schools, patronised from 1843 by Lord Shaftesbury. Most planners of the reformation of society included schooling: there were Owenite Sunday schools and infant classes, and Benthamite projects for the technical and business training of the rising generation of industrial entrepreneurs. These schemes impinged upon the established bastions of education and contributed to the reformation of all schools and colleges, eventually affecting even Oxford and Cambridge. In the first decades of the century, however, the fiercest competition was over the elementary education of the children of the poor.

In 1811 the National Society for Promoting the Education of the Poor in the Principles of the Established Church took over the schooling previously managed by the SPCK, and embarked on massive expansion; in 1812, the school enterprises which had been begun by Joseph Lancaster were reorganised into the less powerful British and Foreign School Society, under non-conformist control. These societies, working in competition, operated similar monitorial systems of teaching, which seemed to offer the same advantages as the newly-established factory system, mass-producing scholars cheaply and efficiently; competitive rote-learning under the instruction of an older child does not seem to have been as effective as the personal instruction of the Sunday schools, and the system was soon modified or neglected, especially in county schools. The inefficiency of most day-schooling, and the resentment which was fostered by the fact that it gave the established church a near-monopoly of influence outside large towns, eventually led to a gradual and reluctant state takeover.

The first meagre grant to schools was made in 1833. The commitment of funds led to the demand for public accountability, and thus to the establishment of the Inspectorate; this in turn led to dissatisfaction with the standard of existing provision, and so to the Elementary Education Act of 1870 which set up the Board schools.

In the closing decades of the century a pattern of compulsory, free
and essentially secular state education was built up from this basis.
The teaching provided inevitably had a moral element, and also an
element of social control in a wider sense, but the articulation of this
through religious teaching and its relation to the operations of
philanthropy were subsumed in new social requirements and ideas.
One element in the change was that the close links between literacy
and morality, basic education and social control which had led to the
development of children's literature in the early part of the century
were either broken or redirected in a way which is clearly reflected in
childrens' fiction.

These books were given a formal and often very prominent place in
the schemes of education operated by the various organisations. From
the earliest days of the Sunday school movement goods had been
distributed to the children: Raikes gave money to those in need, and
the schools continued to be used as channels for philanthropic
benevolence, partly because it was felt that they selected the deserving
poor who were trying to improve themselves. Early tracts about Sunday
scholars, for example Mrs Sherwood's *The Little Sunday School Child's
Reward*, stress material benefits -- in this story a little girl is given a new
set of clothes so that she will be presentable enough to go to the school.
This mere benevolence was rapidly organised in most schools into a
reward system to induce and maintain attendance and good behaviour,
and as such had to establish less costly but still attractive ways of
marking approbation. Printed material was the obvious choice, since
the children came to the school to learn to read. The second volume of
the *Sunday School Repository*[9] reprints from the minutes of the
quarterly meeting of the Sunday School Union the question, 'What
system of rewards is best adapted to Sunday schools?' The answer
suggested is the presentation of reward tickets, which the child collected
and then exchanged for a tract or saved up for a larger book. This
remained a popular system for many years, despite the misgivings which
were already being voiced in 1815 about the barter and trading (as
practised by Tom Sawyer and his friends) to which it could lead.

In the 1815 debate speakers stressed the danger of exchanging tickets
for cash, or for objects begetting pride, such as medals and ribbons,
especially on Sundays, which amounted to Sabbath-breaking. One
speaker deplored the whole idea of rewards as 'a very great evil', and
thought it just as bad if it was based on examinations rather than simple
attendance and behaviour; his own system was to reward Sunday
attendance by admission to evening classes in useful subjects like writing

and cyphering. These remained the spectrum of Sunday school attitudes and possibilities for most of the century, and the reward book accordingly came to occupy an increasing place in the system, especially as counter-attractions multiplied and the day schools invalidated the Sunday schools' primary inducement, that of learning to read and write.

The National schools also gave books to their scholars. The National Society found it necessary to debate and resolve upon prize systems in the 1850s since, according to a letter from Nash Stephenson read at an 1857 meeting, 'a network of secular and latitudinarian prize-schemes is fast covering the country'.[10] These were often complicated sets of rules involving achievement in school-work and in examination as well as certificates of attendance and conduct; the certification of results was soon to become a much more vital matter under the Revised Code, but at this stage examination was used to reward children. At first the prizes were Bibles and prayer books, but by 1867 the society's depositories were distributing the latest juvenile fiction, as published by Thomas Nelson.

When the London School Board, which may be regarded as the pioneer amongst the boards set up by the Act of 1870, began to debate its policies, reward systems were soon launched. They were complicated and employed the power of emulative and competitive instincts in ways which would have shocked the Sunday school organisers in 1815, giving, for example, attendance cards and certificates embossed with the seal of the board in bronze, silver or gilt paper. In 1875 the system was further refined, awarding cards for attendance in progressive degrees of merit, the lowest being rewarded at the end of each quarter with a book valued from 1s to 3s according to the standard of the recipient.[11] Similar systems can be found operating in private schools at every level throughout the century. A random example is the academy for young ladies attended by Elizabeth Sewell on the Isle of Wight before 1820: there the little girls won a series of tickets leading up to one made of red or purple leather, with gilt letters, exchangeable for half a crown.[12] Cash rewards were soon superseded by books at this level, as they were for Sunday school children; and the prize book, that compendious symbol of the purpose and satisfactory achievement of learning, and reminding the scholar of his teacher and continuing that teacher's work in influencing him, took over.

There was another system of book distribution which also played a part in the attempt to extend the influence of schooling, and that was the lending library. These were set up in the early years of the

Sunday schools, on the assumption that the pupils had no access to good books and that lending them 'serious interesting and instructive works' would give them and their families 'employment for that leisure which would otherwise expose them to temptation . . . calculated to influence their future life, and become a blessing to their descendants'.[13] Accordingly, 'juvenile Theological libraries' and others with slightly less forbidding names were established, often with borrowing rights used as rewards. In 1836 the Sunday School Union instituted a system of grants to supply them with suitable works, while the religious publishers invented package deals to furnish them at cut prices. Elementary schools also regularly set up libraries and in well-served parishes there were reading rooms for general use, which included juvenile sections. Despite, however, enthusiastic reports of little faces looking eagerly to the librarian, in many places they were only half-heartedly kept up and supported. The recommended cure for this was usually the inclusion of lighter and easier books, and especially more stories, until by 1886 C.M. Yonge was making a case for the library as the proper place for childish fiction, 'read in a week and passed on', while prizes should be more solid and lasting.[14] She was aware that her idea about prizes was not popular: by the time that she suggested it children's fiction was a nearly universal tool of educators.

I have tried in the ensuing chapters to trace the rise and development of this form of fiction, and to say something about its qualities, intentions and effects. I hope it will make the picture which I am endeavouring to paint clearer for the reader if I outline the critical and the methodological problems of such an attempt, and the means by which I have tried to overcome them. I do not mean to make the customary apology for the contextual treatment of fiction; nor, however, do I wish to assert that this or any art is explicable in terms of market forces and social pressures. But the liberal humanist tradition of literary criticism offers no effective approach to the material with which this study is concerned. E.M. Forster found that the novels of Sir Walter Scott failed to meet his highest standards, and where the giant of popular story-telling is too slight, his innumerable Victorian progeny writing tales for lads must seem immeasurably puny. On the other hand, the sort of ferreting after origins which T.S. Eliot dismissed as 'embryology' may be essential for the understanding of the peculiar but vigorous and influential hybrids which were born of the Victorian boom in children's fiction.

If we wish to understand the experience of reading as it was introduced to the majority of the British in the nineteenth century it is necessary to remember such things as the revolution in printing, brought about by the introduction of steadily improving steam presses from 1811 onwards, and the progress in the binding and casing of books which led to the development of publisher's pictorial jackets. The juvenile publishers were amongst the first to use these new methods of production, and the cheap but gorgeous Sunday school prize book was in some measure the direct result of technological advance.[15] The changing attitudes to children and their education outlined above account for the devotion of so much energy and capital to a kind of publication previously left to hack printers: the providers of children's fiction were responding to a powerful market demand springing from complex sources.

The books are meaningless to us without these considerations because they are unlike most other fiction in that they were neither written nor purchased under the impulses which govern the relationships involved in the novel, with which existing critical theory is concerned. By the people who wrote these books, the novelist's desire to explore and convey his or her own perception of the world was felt rather as an explicitly didactic intention to teach certain moral and social attitudes, which were not even necessarily general truths, but which were specific to the age, sex and social standing of a very precisely defined reader. The other parties in the financial transaction which created the book participated in this, choosing it not for the possible aesthetic, emotional or intellectual sustenance which it offered them — for they did not intend to read it — but for didactic purposes explicitly related to those of the writer. The intended reader had therefore none of the freedom of choice which constitutes the novel-reader's influence upon the adult fiction which is written and published, but could only accept whatever books were offered to him, complete with the lessons they taught.

In discussing these books, therefore, I have placed them as fully as possible in the context of their publication, and considered them in groups based upon the categories writers and publishers set up. The division between evangelical tales concerning waifs and strays saved from sin in the streets of London, and adventures in the South Seas where natives are rescued from the evils of cannibalism and English youths from shipwreck is not strictly a literary one, for the stories may have much in common structurally and expressively, and analysis of them is bound to overlap. They cannot be properly understood, however, unless the powerful distinction between sixpenny reward books for Sunday scholars and 5s presents for private school boys, a distinction which not simply influenced but wholly dictated their production, is also explored. How this strange set of extra-artistic conventions and considerations shaped the development of nineteenth-century children's fiction, how far the reader's needs and desires did in fact influence the books, and what the products themselves are like, is therefore first approached indirectly. The stories are placed in context by attending to the policies not only of the writers, but also of the men and the societies who published their work, the philanthropic and educational organisations which paid for it, and of their deputies who made the choices and gave them away, under constantly changing circumstances and pressures which influenced their selection.

When one has considered the authors' letters to young readers, the publishers' burgeoning lists, the minutes of the prize committees and the books themselves as objects — adorned with gold blocking and inscribed 'to Herbert from his teacher' or stuck with a splendid gilt label from the Sunday school, awarding 342 out of a possible 365 for conduct and attendance — the most important question remains to be asked of them: how and how far did they work? Did the anxiously studied, painstakingly directed child whose moral education was the objective of this elaborate enterprise respond in the way he was intended to? Did he desire to win these books, so that they acted as an incentive to learning and good behaviour? Finally, when he received them, did he read them, and did he learn the lessons they contained? This was the most important question to the originators of the books, just as it is to the modern student; but, understandably enough, writers and publishers tended to assume that their high circulation figures meant that all was as well as could be expected, while we must look beyond those figures for positive evidence.

Few inferences may be made with confidence from external sources. It proves nothing that many editions of, for example, *Tom Brown's Schooldays* or *Eric or Little by Little* were sold, since they were not bought by the young, and indeed sometimes not bought for them but for adult readers; and reviews, also by adults, cannot tell us what schoolboys thought. Famous books like these are often mentioned in memoirs as being recalled from childhood reading, with affection or the reverse, and such testimony to their effect carries some weight, although memory is not necessarily reliable in matters of taste and feeling at a great remove of time and experience. But the bulk of moral fiction for the young seems in any case to have left no trace in memoir and autobiography. This should not surprise us, and does not mean that such books were never influential in the lives of those to whom they were given: only a very few, even of the articulate and cultured, ever write their memoirs, and this was designed as reading not for the literary and exceptional but for the average, humble, basic reader, submerged in the inarticulate majority. Writers of memoirs of working-class lives are even more exceptional than writers within the middle classes, and the testimony of men whose urge to verbal expression was strong enough to burst the bonds of Victorian class conditioning is perhaps the least useful of all in assessing the responses of the ordinary child reader of the time. The observations which writers like Flora Thompson, for example, have offered of the responses of the unexceptional villagers around her are interesting, but no general conclusions may be safely drawn from such scattered testimony.[16] The only sufficient evidence upon which general conclusions may be based lies in the books themselves; and so the final analysis must after all be a literary one, an attempt to understand and assess the effect which reading these books would have upon the audience for whom they were intended.

Orthodox models of literary criticism are variously inappropriate for such a task. Any analysis must take into account the youth of the reader, and it must do so, moreover, in historical perspective, allowing not only for Victorian conventions of writing and feeling, but also Victorian assumptions about the young and the possibility that these represent real differences of perception and response between children then and children as observed by modern psychology. The difference of experience between modern and Victorian children extends beyond such observable matters as diet, discipline and the knowledge of death to less easily imagined questions of literary experience: literacy has always to be considered in analysis of the responses of young readers, but in the historical context its assessment is doubly complex. To be literate may be taken to mean to know one's letters, or even to be just able to sign one's name. For the purposes of a study of literature of any kind, however, basic definitions used in other historical contexts will obviously not serve, and one must consider the many gradations in the capacity to read, from spelling out monosyllables to the comprehension of specialised technical prose or sophisticated verses. The reading of fiction is further complicated by the possibly different rate of variation in the comprehension of literary codes such as story-telling conventions and complexities of style. An adult may be highly literate as a reader of engineering textbooks and less skilled than a bookish teenager at interpreting Jane Austen; a full understanding of Henry James probably requires maturity as well as literacy, yet the measures of the difficulty of vocabulary and sentence structure which are used to assess 'reading age' will be inaccurate in forecasting how well a child interested in a story, especially one constructed according to patterns which he recognises, will cope with and effectively understand language he cannot actually be said to be able to read. This observable phenomenon may be acutely relevant to a Sunday scholar in 1840, to whom simple sentences about his own kind of life could present reading problems while the catechism or the Gospels were recognised and readable text, and the highly conventional manner and material of his prize books made them more rather than less accessible to him.[17]

This matter of the familiarity of the text is connected with another difficulty for the critic. The less fluently literate, the less given to books a reader is, the further his responses are removed from the sorts of assessment usually applied in literary analysis. A familiar, fully-mastered book is a rare thing for such a reader, and the imaginative rewards it offers him may be out of all proportion to any measure of its richness or complexity which may be objectively applied. C.S. Lewis[18] has pointed out the results of this in the context of popular fiction, recording his observation (which is also mine) that some book which seems to him as a skilled reader trivial, thin, even positively ineffective in its literary inadequacy has been treasured by a less advanced reader, and rightly valued very highly by him, since it has triggered for him imaginative and emotional responses which for a more sophisticated reader it simply did not contain, and which Lewis himself would have needed to turn to Shakespeare or Milton to find. In the present context one must add to this the huge difficulties presented by the shift in sensibility which makes it so hard for us to understand the responses of even highly articulate and cultured Victorians to such matters as deathbed scenes, and on top of that the fact that the immature reader compounds these peculiarities by having urgent needs for certain kinds of imaginative or emotional stimulus for fixed periods only. A fourteen-year-old may perhaps be on his way to mature and wide-ranging literacy, but still needs to devour endless repetitions of tales of torture in prisoner-of-war camps, or in an earlier generation the pulp of public school stories and cowboy sagas purveyed by the *Boy's Own Paper*. The need itself may be suspect, but it is a very strong incentive, and its satisfaction gives the writer a power over the reader's imagination which probably surpasses anything the novelist writing for adults may expect. The complexities of these relationships between reader, writer and text in the Victorian children's story need to be elucidated, for all these reasons, by something quite other than the canons of excellence in the novel represented by the Great Tradition.

It has proved to be both impractical and unnecessary to attempt an exhaustive treatment of the thousands of children's books which are extant from the period. Surveys in literary-historical and bibliographical terms of the more conspicuous landmarks already exist,[19] and an attempt to be more comprehensive would swamp any other consideration of the material. The books may be said to fall into patterns for which representative examples may be given, and like all previous writers I am obliged by the bulk of the material to treat them to some extent in this schematic way. I am very wary of the falsification which such generalisations must entail, however, and acutely conscious that the more examples one reads the more variation and even contradiction of the obvious categorisations one finds. I have therefore tried to select representative or influential writers whose works may be considered at some length, and so produce literary judgements and generalisations which may be fully tested at least in the individual case.

I have found an assorted group of concepts useful in this attempt, and hope they will not appear incompatible or inconsistent with each other when applied in various proportions to the consideration of each group of authors and their stories. Pope's injunction that we should first of all 'regard the writer's end' is a widely discredited critical approach to books for adults, but it is still followed, at least implicitly, by some of even the most combative modernist writers about children's books. In the case of so didactic, so intention-ridden a creation as the Victorian moral tale for children, the author's avowed desire to teach is an unavoidable starting point. The story may have several other layers worth exploring, but its surface is more or less entirely covered by the author's moral and educational plan. I am concerned with a peculiar interrelationship of theme, *dianoia,* with *mythos* and *ethos,* in which the balance usual in the novel or story is avowedly reversed, and the author tells his tale illustratively, claiming to concentrate his interest upon the relationship between himself and the reader, which is a teaching relationship. How far this is really the case for each writer embarking upon children's fiction, how far other balances come to predominate, and what tensions may be felt in the relationship each has with his tales and his audience,

are major areas of consideration in understanding these books. In all
the variations of moral tale, however, the reader and hence the critic
cannot but be aware that he is meant to learn. The latter must in this
case be very careful to adopt a more than usually objective position. If
he cries with Keats that he hates art 'that has a palpable design upon
us' he cannot read these books at all; but it is equally unproductive to
respond to the lessons they teach as if they were directed at him, or
at a child for whom he is selecting a book, putting himself in the
position of the original purchaser. The result is likely to be the sort of
judgement which condemns didactic fiction for the young as a dirty
trick, but in fact is really indignant because the lessons taught are
so often contrary to his own beliefs. Such a book as Bob Dixon's
Catching Them Young[20] .may be a guide for like-minded book-buyers
but no help at all in the understanding of cultures, the subtle interactions
of feeling, reading, thought and action. I have tried to consider the
writer's intentions, both overt and subconscious, and to contemplate
the possibility that a moral to which I do not subscribe may be
inextricably linked with, or may itself constitute, the vital literary
ingredient which made a book a valuable experience for its readers.

My first critical question, therefore, has been about the nature of
the writers' intentions and the way that these were related to the
fictions they made. Intention in this case includes both fully conscious
didactic aims, and the other aspects of the transmission of values which
are part of any literary production. A novelist seeks to show his
readers the world from his point of view; when a writer consciously
addresses his inferiors in age, wisdom or social standing, however,
this bias unavoidably becomes a part of his didactic intention, saying
not 'this is a way to perceive and judge' but 'you ought to look
at things like this'. Whether or not he is conscious that his teaching
extends beyond the story and the characters he chooses to show, and
the explicit things he says about them, the writer of such books as
these envisages his influence as benevolent. Often, however, the
author is not aware of the extent of his manipulation of the reader,
has not, perhaps, explored his own assumptions and values. These are
often naive writers, as well as naive readers; their interaction is
mediated by a literary object, a story told according to established
patterns and conventions, which is sometimes more powerful in itself
than either of them understands. I have explored the notion of moral
education throughout my discussion, therefore, by considering the
explicit and the implicit direction of the reader in these stories, and
the way in which moral intention and narrative interact.

In saying that these writers were often naive, I mean to suggest that they were unlearned and unsophisticated in literary matters. There are exceptions to that generalisation. Writers like C.M. Yonge can scarcely be called outsiders to the high culture, though her participation in one of the leading currents of thought in her day did not automatically lead Miss Yonge to the forefront of literary progress. In a minor way, however, she and her fellow writers for the middle-class girl at home were participating in the mainstream of fiction, the serious novel, and in so doing they chose the vehicle for their teaching most likely to interest their chosen readership. But other groups within the child audience were not expected to desire such literary sophistication. Evangelical writers often had little contact with the world of art and literature, the most extreme being scarcely free of sectarian conviction that fiction was no different from lying, and that stories to be good in their effects must therefore be true, or as near to the literal truth as possible, consistent with their being made to point to the required moral. The less extreme, who did countenance fiction, still concurred, usually quite unwittingly, with the dominant mid-century theory of the novel, which held that an idealised realism was a necessary prerequisite for fiction if it was to carry conviction.[27] They also thought, with many mid-twentieth-century theorists, that stories offered to children will only be emotionally and morally helpful to them if they deal with a world recognisably like that of their everyday lives; a world in which their emotional and moral problems may be literally reflected. There is therefore a vein of circumstantial mimetic realism in tract writing which makes it an interesting comparison with the mid-Victorian domestic melodrama, for the details of modern life are displayed within a structure very far removed from the general experience, in a pattern in which moral distinctions are clear-cut, and a benevolent providence operates with absolute justice and predictability. In the boys' adventure stories there is a similar conjunction of 'fact' or 'truth' — scientifically correct geographical, biological or historical information — with story-telling which is shaped by quite different forces, and presents a fantasy world of action. The implications of these uses of the mimetic are explored, therefore, in relation to the expected readers' lives, and also in conjunction with the very formal patterning of the story which the moral purpose of the writer superimposes.

In the analysis of the formal patterns I have found several critical devices to be of use. It is tempting to reach for a structuralist analysis of this kind of material, since structuralist theory is particularly

appropriate to 'infantile or popular literatures, including recent forms
like melodrama and the serial novel' in that it offers ways to deal with
large masses of material whose main interest is not a matter of the
individual author's creative originality.[22] In giving so much weight to
historical context and authorial intention as I have felt necessary,
however, a structuralist model is ruled out; but I have made some use
of the insights afforded by the collation of motifs, and found that
they supply another important contextual link, for they make clear
how often and how closely these authors relied upon story material
which was part of the common stock of popular literature, rather
than the high culture. The difficulty already touched upon of finding
a proper response to some Victorian conventions which are
pervasively present at all levels of writing may also be approached
in this way; certainly the recurring motifs and their relationship to
the stories highlight such areas and may, by attention to how and
where they are used, be found to illuminate them. The same may
perhaps be said of the treatment of formulaic characters in these tales;
I have often found it most helpful to consider these figures as functions
or relationships within the story, following Propp's analysis of the
personages of folk tales.[23] In this light, they assume more significance
than is discovered by an attempt to find interest in them as
representations of pyschologically likely, whole or consistent persons.

More important than either recurring motifs or conventional
character-drawing are the patterns which can be seen to govern the
construction of the stories. It is in these, ultimately, that I find the
means by which I would discriminate between the books, and assess
them as being effective or otherwise in communication with their
readers. In this analysis I have made use of the notion of romance
story-telling as described by Northrop Frye, in particular in *The
Secular Scripture.*[24] My extrapolation from those theories is as
follows. Story-telling is an essential activity of the human mind,
satisfying certain basic needs of the psyche, most simply expressed
as the need to impose order and pattern upon experience in order
to fend off despair about the negation of life's meaning which
death presents. We tell ourselves stories to prove that we are
significantly alive. There are of course other death-defying acts of
mind, of which religious faith is the chief; the link between Gods
and myths, that is between faith and story-telling, is a very deep
one; but there is another story, the secular scripture, which fulfils
a purpose parallel to that of the story of God and faith and
everlasting life.

This story is the romance, which is the most basic tale of human activity, and which best satisfies the need for narrative; its shape is that of a journey or passage or quest, in which the protagonist moves from one level of existence to another and either returns, or passes through, to find a further, final resting-place. The story is the account of movement: outside it there is

> a state of existence in which there is nothing to write about . . .
> before 'once upon a time' and subsequent to 'and they lived
> happily ever after'. What happens in between are adventures, or
> collisions with external circumstances, and the return to identity
> [the state of repose] is a release from the tyranny of these
> circumstances . . . Most romances end happily, with a return to
> the state of identity, and begin with a departure from it . . .
> This means that most romances exhibit a cyclical movement of
> descent into a night world and a return to the idyllic world.[25]

There are various possible designs and directions of movement: the journey may be out from an earthly paradise, up from hell, or even down from heaven; the scenes through which the traveller passes are those proper to whichever of the planes of existence he is obliged to traverse. In these designs nothing is merely accidental or coincidental. That is what design means; all inevitably falls into place, the right people meet, the necessary discoveries are made, the outcome ties up all the ends, and our expectation of the significant pattern is fulfilled. A story may stick very close to the romance outline, using the settings and characters of the oldest stories, or it may displace the events into settings which are, for example, ostensibly realistic, disguising the providential movement as a representation of a series of events motivated and brought about by ordinary relationships, deriving action from character. It will still be satisfactory as a romance so long as the pattern is completed, though we may never be convinced about the attempt to present it as unpatterned, 'natural' events.

Another possibility, one very important in the stories dealt with here, is that the romance's providence, the things that happen because it is a story, may be called Christian Providence, and the romance 'captured' and made to enforce didactic or moral lessons and, on a deeper level, to indoctrinate the reader with the values of the serious mythology of his society, whether social or religious. What happens in practice when such a story is written is that an author,

unskilled in literary displacements of romance or in any other literary
conventions, wishes to tell a tale to illustrate a moral point, and
naturally falls into the use of the pattern most basic to story-telling
in his common culture. I have felt it reasonable to assume that the
child readers with whom I am concerned would be familiar with the
romance story, and would respond to its satisfactions in the captured
form of the moral tale as surely (though I would not insist, as
intensely) as in a less displaced presentation in, say, a gothic melodrama
or a chapbook folk tale of heroes.[26]

There is a mixture, then, of several possible functions in many moral
tales. They may present a set of behavioural rules for the child to learn,
and their adaptation to himself will be clearly indicated in the realistic
description of the characters and events through which they are
demonstrated. Another value system, that of Christianity in some form,
or of the ideal of England or of the Empire, may also be offered,
in which the child, who is pressed into instrumentality by the set of
practical imperatives, is shown a larger scope and purpose which may
be served by his conformity, and give meaning to his life; and the
story itself, as an inevitable pattern, may reinforce these meanings
by the magic of art, whose rightness he may feel and enjoy for
itself. This romance element in the stories also had a force independent
of the message it is made to carry because it passes into the realm of
fantasy, the enactment of possibilities beyond the restraints of direct
experience. At this point its enjoyment becomes part of the
individual's psychological development, and begins to fulfil the
essential function of all literature, not just the specialised roles so far
discussed. To quote Professor Frye once more:

> the journey towards one's own identity, which literature does so
> much to help with, has a great deal to do with escaping from the
> alleged 'reality' of what one is reading or looking at, and recognising
> the convention behind it. The same process exists in the elementary
> teaching of literature, or should. The child should not 'believe'
> the story he is told; he should not disbelieve it either, but send out
> imaginative roots into that mysterious world between the 'is' and
> the 'is not' which is where his own ultimate freedom lies.[27]

According to Bruno Bettelheim,[28] this psychologically healthful
function of story-telling is best served by the special 'otherness' of
fairy tale, and even that must be treated in certain ways to do its
work properly; but I find that there is much that is 'other', a separate

world to be entered free of the self, in these books.

The final theoretical prop which I need to explain and assess the books as reading for the young is provided by James Britton, in 'spectator role' theory. This deals with the relationship of the young reader to the experiences of the story, and modifies the too-simple assumption that the child 'identifies' with one of the characters in his reading; rather, he suggests, there are various stages of awareness of story in the developing child. Before the age of six or seven there is little differentiation between fact and fiction in narrative, and after the age of twelve or thirteen the adolescent recognises empathy in himself for the characters. In between, however, there is a state where fiction is very powerful without being simply 'believed' or regarded as 'only a story', in which the child reader uses an awareness of some sort of separation between the world of the book and the world of his life to help in his understanding of the latter, recognising in fiction patterns of values (expectations about roles and relationships within his culture) which he might be too unskilled and anxious to deal with outside the special world of fiction, where he is a spectator.[29] In this awareness is the possibility of learning about his own responses, to evil and fear as well as goodness and joy; and while it may be made through stories of pirates, cannibals, orphan saints and providential district visitors, it is nevertheless as important a transaction as takes place in the most refined of literary appreciations. The possibility that this is not only present in moral tales but actually well served by their conventions and patterns of narrative is obviously central to the final judgement on how, and indeed whether, these stories affected their readers: whether fiction can be an instrument of education in the direct way these writers sought to make it, or whether its effect should not be seen as very important in the lives of the new readers to whom this was amongst the first fiction they experienced, but important in more complex and ultimately in more, rather than less, influential ways than as a lesson book.

2 THE DEVELOPMENT OF JUVENILE PUBLISHING AND CHILDREN'S FICTION, 1800-1850

The level of literacy in Britain in 1800 remains a matter of debate,[1] but there is no doubt that it was felt by contemporaries to have risen dramatically and with dubiously desirable results. While the importance of controlling childhood reading, providing suitable matter for the moulding and instruction of young people, had been recognised for at least a century, the issue had become much more pressing and more controversial, as it was accepted that it was not only the children of the gentry who would henceforth learn to read. Books for children and reading for the poor became closely-linked and hotly-contended issues. The outburst of enthusiasm for education, therefore, was inspired by no simple desire to spread the art of reading. It was an attempt, variously motivated but united in its assumptions, to direct and control the education of the people and to channel their literacy as soon as, or even before, they attained it. They were to learn to read; but it was felt by each group which interested itself in education that the learning must be for a particular purpose, and so through particular instruments. After literacy was attained, even by means which conveyed the lessons which the educators wished to impress, it remained an edged tool in irresponsible hands. Materials must be provided upon which it could work not only harmlessly, but so as to continue the inculcation of good lessons.

The situation presented itself to one chronicler thus:

It was in the midst of memorable and anxious events that the Religious Tract Society had its rise. In the signs of the times all appeared to be dark and portentous. The revolutionary spirit which broke out in France was still shaking the European nations, and threatened to overthrow the thrones of princes, and to uproot all public order. Insubordination and irreligion almost universally prevailed. Infidelity, taking advantage of the general confusion, assumed an undaunted front, and zealously made the press the means of circulating the most immoral and soul-destroying sentiments. In our own country the writings of Paine and other sceptics had produced a wide-spread spirit of impiety and discontent; yet in 'these days of trouble and of rebuke and blasphemy', when 'men's hearts were failing them for fear', a spirit of prayer and

31

revived zeal appears to have descended on the church of Christ, and various important institutions were formed to promote the spread of religious knowledge both at home and abroad. At this critical period the attention of the Christian public was specially called to the great importance of educating, on scriptural principles, the youthful poor of the country.[2]

This is an Evangelical statement of the case, and therefore presents religious teaching as of paramount importance, but that objective is inextricably entwined here, as in most commentators, with social and moral objectives. 'Impiety and discontent' are coupled, and both are fed by 'the writings of Paine and other sceptics' whose influence upsets not only religious faith but the social order to which that faith was a support. Those who felt the 'revived zeal' of the Evangelical movement were inspired in their wish to convert others, and especially the poor, by motives which mixed fear of change, both industrial change and potential political revolution, and apprehension about their own safety in a world increasingly immoral and regardless of old proprieties and hierarchies, with their desire to save souls. The proportions of these motives differed, various groups deliberately stressing the aspects of their mission which concerned them most and probably each individual philanthropist, from Bishop Whately to the newest village Sunday school teacher, had several conscious intentions and very complex unconscious compulsions to his or her work. But the one thing which all theorists and workers in the field had in common was the conviction that no proper reading matter existed for the use of children and others who were learning to read. Between 1790 and 1830 massive schemes were launched by several organisations for distributing reading matter to the poor. One of the longest-lived and most influential was the Religious Tract Society (RTS), which became the foremost nineteenth-century institutional publisher of children's fiction.

The Religious Tract Society

The RTS was founded in 1799 by a group of men who present a cross-section of Evangelical society. The leading spirit was the Rev. George Burder, a congregationalist minister. His first children's book, *Early Piety*, had been published in 1776; he now felt that there was a need for a publishing organisation issuing tracts which were more explicitly religious than those of the Cheap Repository Tract movement: their tales, by ladies like Hannah More, were largely intended to teach social subordination, while his would contain a 'fuller statement of the great evangelical principles'. With Rowland Hill, the famous Evangelical preacher and founder of the Surrey Chapel, he gathered a group of writers and philanthropists to publish tracts 'adapted, by their variety, to readers whose respective attainments, condition and character, demanded so many different modes of address', with the golden rule that each one must contain '*some account of the way of a sinner's salvation*', that is, of the central evangelical message of conversion. There are many tales recorded of the conversion of hardened sinners by chance perusals of the vital message and each tract, they felt, had to offer that opportunity. Enthusiastic distributors handed out bundles of their new tracts wherever they went, but by 1805 they had decided upon the necessity of copying the Cheap Repository Tract method of distribution, through the existing secular network of ballad sellers who were the book suppliers of the rural poor.

They also supplied most children, who bought from them the 'penny histories' of heroes, wonders, folk and fairy tales that were almost the only story books written especially for the young.[3] The society produced for this purpose what it called the 'second series' of Hawker's tracts, to supplant 'the feculant *dregs* of the "popular literature" of former days' which were still in print. The RTS goods were sold at a lower price to undercut the market and:

> the Committee were obliged, in the first instance, to prepare tracts with striking titles, and in some degree inferior in their contents, to prevent too great a discrepancy from those they were designed to supplant. The titles of some of them fully evince this: 'The Fortune Teller's Conjuring Cap', 'The Wonderful Cure of General Naaman', 'The Stingy Father's Dream', 'Tom Toper's Tale over his Jug of Ale', 'Rhyming Dick and the Strolling Player', all indicate that it was necessary to catch at very uninformed minds . . . In the first year, a quarter of a million were issued . . . Some of the most suitable were put into covers, for rewards in Sunday Schools, and thus caused a demand for a series of children's books . . . it was plain that had not a superior article been supplied, the old wretched tracts would still have been forced upon the Sunday school scholars, and others who were acquiring the ability to read.[4]

The goods found a market; they were actually cheaper to the hawkers than their old wares, and they would have passed as the old tales with the barely literate customer at least until he had handed over his penny. By 1818 twenty-five to thirty million had been printed. Despite this huge figure (which incidentally lends some support to the claims for large sales made by the printers of the ballads, which are usually regarded as exaggerations) it is the nature of such material to disappear, and few copies of each title survive. It is perhaps significant that some of those in the possession of the British Library are gathered into a volume[5] which intersperses them at random with 'real' chapbooks, printed by Pitts. There is little difference of appearance between 'the awful death of Richard Parsons, whose flesh rotted off his bones agreeably to his impious wishes, when disputing at a game of Whist,' and the Pitts' account of 'the murder of Mary Ann Smith, aged eight years, daughter of John Smith, by a former wife, by cruelly starving, beating, and otherwise inhumanly treating her, so that a Mortification took place in her feet which deprived her of life'. Indeed, to the impartial eye there is very little difference of subject-matter or appeal.

Some influential members of the RTS including Legh Richmond, their most successful compiler of narrative tracts, distrusted fiction as lying. He wrote to his daughter that:

> Fully as I can enter into the beauties of works of fiction, yet I exceedingly dread their tendency. The utmost caution is requisite in meddling with them. The novelist I unequivocally proscribe, and many of the poets, and their poems, which are only nets to catch young minds in the maze of Satan.[6]

It was not necessary, however, to invent tales which were sufficiently horrifying to capture the attention of a child reared on chapbook prodigies and superstitions: there was a time-honoured, puritan story-telling method which used lurid physical detail to enforce the urgent religious message. Its model was Janeway's *A Token for Children, an exact account of the Conversion, Holy, and Exemplary Lives and Joyful Deaths of several Young Children* (1671 and 1672). This had been a leading children's book of its time in Puritan circles; its preface asks the child reader 'Did you never hear of a little child that died? And if other children die, why may you not lie sick and die? And what will you do then, Child, if you should have no Grace in your Heart, and be found like other naughty children?' This apparently horrific approach to the young was the result of the Calvinist conviction that only God's elect will escape hell-fire, working upon the observed fact that many children, including some in most families, did not survive to adulthood. It was republished as part of the renewed Evangelical thrust, altered to make it 'intelligible to modern ears', but in no way softened, in at least seven editions between 1785 and 1830. It was much copied, as a striking way of embodying the message, easily reproduced, and combining a specious likeness to the popular broadside formula of the dying confession with the great virtue of truth, or at least the appearance of a true record. The truth of such stories as John Griffin's 'Account of the Early Piety and Happy Death of Miss Dinah Doudney, of Portsea, aged nine years', which he delivered to 'a congregation of Children, in the Orange-Street Chapel on New Year's Day, 1815', is perhaps of a curious kind, for the child and her minister are both intensely self-conscious and aware of the literary models which they are following. We are told that she read Janeway's *Token for Children* 'with much pleasure, and great profit . . . and pointed out the experience of those children she thought most closely resembled her own'. She then asked the preacher to tell other children about her when she died, as he does in the sermon and the tract. The interaction of literary convention and life is so close that it is impossible to disentangle, at this remove in time, what was said and done and what imagined, the fantasies of sick children and those of earnest clergymen.

The earliest children's narratives published by the RTS were of this kind, and when the society set up its first series of books specifically for the young in 1814 it began with Burder's *Early Piety* and two other deathbed tracts. One of these, 'A Recent Instance of the Lord's goodness to Children, Exemplified in the happy Death of James Steven, Camberwell, Near London, who died March 8th, 1806, aged eight years and eight months', by the Rev. John Campbell, is a particularly gruesome example, intent upon every detail of the child's sufferings with a tumour in the eye socket, describing his pain and the bowls of blood at great length.

The writer whose deathbed and conversion tracts were most widely read, and cited more often than those of Janeway in other memoirs and memorials, was the Reverend Legh Richmond (1772-1827). His career and writings can be taken as an exemplar of evangelical activity, a testimony to what he would call 'experimental' religion. He underwent an evangelical conversion, largely as a result of reading William Wilberforce's *A Practical View of the Prevailing Religious System of Professed Christians* (1797), after he had followed the ordinary course through university to ordination as an Anglican clergyman. After his conversion he divided his life between parish work in pulpit, Sunday school, cottage meeting and sickroom, the bringing up of a large family of his own on strictly evangelical lines, touring England preaching for the benefit of mission organisations and the British and Foreign Bible Society, and writing tracts and weightier works for the RTS. During his lifetime he became a leader of the Evangelical movement, and remained an inspiration to it after his death. The parishioners he converted became models to convert others, through his writing and preaching; his family furnished an example of the principles of evangelical education. They were taught at home, since Richmond blamed school for the ruin of his eldest son, who ran away to sea, and they were constantly under his eye, exhorted to search their souls, and seek conversion. In the meantime they were expected to amuse themselves with microscopes and collections, and abjure field sports, games of chance, theatres and secular reading.

Though he was not noticeably successful with his own family, Richmond inspired many others through his writings. His famous tracts were first published in a periodical, *The Christian Guardian*, between 1809 and 1811, and then collected as *The Annals of the Poor*. They included *The Negro Servant*, *Jane, the Young Cottager* and *The Dairyman's Daughter*. They are very circumstantial and personal accounts of his dealings with three of his flock in his first parish, on the Isle of Wight. They are both biography and autobiography: Jane, whose story conforms to the pattern of infant piety and happy death, is presented for her own sake and also as the first of Richmond's converts, who therefore made a great impression on him. The dairyman's daughter was not a child but a young woman of twenty-seven who first came to him with the request that he should bury her sister, and then asked him to visit her when she was herself stricken with consumption. Richmond did as he was asked and recorded in the tract her letters and conversation, by which he found himself most edified. The accounts have none of the hysterical exaggeration the recorded speeches of the dying children often display; she appears rational and sensible, and the reader might reasonably find her piety impressive, as Richmond says he did.

The element of personal confession in the tracts is part of their appeal, both for the humility the clergyman displays in acknowledging his parishioners his equals or superiors in conviction, and for the circumstantial detail he includes, which gives the stories an air of concrete authenticity. The *Annals* are also specifically *of the Poor* and

so nearer than many other accounts of pious infants were to the
situation of the Sunday school child who received them; for their
enormous appeal we have the testimony of many teachers and writers
during the first fifty years of the movement. Wherever he went on his
preaching expeditions Richmond gave away his tracts, and received
in return testimonies to their effect. In August 1820, for example, he
wrote home from Scotland with news of 'three new and distinct
instances of the conversions and happy deaths of children in Glasgow,
Paisley, and Greenock; two, through "Little Jane"'.[7] On a tour of
Scotland and the North in 1818 he recorded an account of the
dissemination of his all-powerful works:

> On Sunday last I visited a school of two hundred children. It was
> the half-yearly day for distributing reward-books. The sixty most
> deserving scholars were to receive 'The Young Cottager' as their
> reward. Three of them had already been blessed some time ago, in
> hearing it read at school. I was requested to present each child with
> a tract, as they were successively brought up to me, in presence of
> about two hundred grown-up persons of all ranks. It was a most
> solemn and affecting scene. The gentleman who manages the
> school offered a most affecting thanksgiving for the good which had
> attended the distribution of my tracts throughout Scotland, and in
> his school in particular, and for the opportunity now afforded
> of introducing me personally to so many children, 'who had long
> loved me with all their hearts'. Immediately all the company and
> all the children sang a thanksgiving hymn. Then followed what
> affected me greatly. The children were drawn up in a triple semi-
> circle, in the centre of which I stood. Each successful candidate
> successively stepped forward, and received from my hand a 'Young
> Cottager', and from my lips a short exhortation and blessing. Not
> an eye was dry, and my own with difficulty allowed me to go through
> the simple and interesting ceremony. One girl, who was two years
> since converted by God's blessing on the tract, as she approached me,
> was so affected, that she dropped on her knees and burst into tears.[8]

No wonder he felt it necessary to insert in his diary such ejaculations
as 'Lord, keep me humble, and show me the real character of myself'.[9]
The deathbed scene, eventually fictionalised and softened, and
becoming sentimental rather than pious, remained a feature of the
majority of nineteenth-century children's stories of an evangelical cast.[10]
  The series of children's books begun by the RTS in 1814 was

cautiously continued along traditional lines, so that in 1824, when the Sunday School Union were already rejecting 'obituaries, unless particularly excellent'[11] as unsuitable for children and likely to lead them into cant and hypocrisy, the RTS brought out an edition of Janeway's *Token*. However, in 1817 and 1818 respectively, William Freeman Lloyd and his close friend George Stokes joined the committee of the society and began its decisive movement into the position in the forefront of children's publishing, which it was to occupy for the middle decades of the century. The field was in fact about to expand explosively: by 1824 the twenty-fifth report of the society was warning that though the RTS had pioneered publishing for children, its 1,688,760 children's books published in 1823 made up only one-fifth of the total number published in the field, and greater efforts were needed to dominate the market and exclude the 'Romances, Novels, Plays, Farces and Tales of a very improper description' which were now menacing the newly literate under an 'insidious garb'.

In 1825 Lloyd left his commercial life to work full-time for the RTS, and devoted his major efforts to acquiring and seeing through the press more books for children. Stokes, whose writings he published, was very prolific, and brought to his work for the RTS an erudition which issued in theological commentaries and selections from and studies of seventeenth-century divines. Like Lloyd, he felt that it was important not to underestimate the capacity and interests of the new readers, and he hoped to offer children's tracts and books that would lead an enquiring mind to larger and weightier works. He was still convinced of the inspiring effects of biography, but saw it in terms of large works such as the 'Christian Biography' series of monographs which told the stories of full and useful lives, rather than tales of infant piety and death. This merged into his historical interests, especially in the Reformation, to produce historical works like *The Life and Death of Lady Jane Grey*, *The Lollards* and *The Days of Queen Mary*. These were intended to combat 'such writers as Hume and Gibbon' who 'have made history the medium of insidiously communicating the poison of infidelity', and to make it instead the medium by which 'the authority of inspired truth' is judiciously introduced into educational works for the young.[12] It is a relatively short step from such an avowed inflection of history to the many historical-cum-sectarian novels which entered the RTS lists in subsequent decades.

Stokes' first children's books, however, were at the opposite end of the spectrum of readership: in 1824 he launched a series of 'Short

Stories for Children' under ten. They were to replace the commercially produced 'halfpenny books' which the society's report for the year inevitably tells us were 'the most puerile and absurd' of old juvenile stories, either uninviting moral tales without religion, or 'of darker description' still. The method, once again, was to model the replacement on the supplanted popular form, and Stokes produced fifty-one little picture books which would be 'useful as Reward Books, for the *youngest* children at Sunday and other Schools' and turn them away from 'poisonous trash'. By 1827 titles included suitably christianised versions of ancient tales like Jack the Giant-Killer and Little Red Riding Hood. When the 1824 report appeared, 928,000 of these stories had already been issued, 2,000 of them as grants in aid to schools in Spitalfields and Westminster. By the time Stokes died in 1847, 5,084,958 of them had gone out from the depositories.

Merely moral tales, and 'trash' like ancient folk stories, were not the only threats the new tracts sought to meet: the under-tens were also provided with some factual, quasi-scientific reading, a *History of Beasts* and a *History of Birds*. These exemplify the anxiety felt by the religious societies about the proselytising ventures of the Society for the Diffusion of Useful Knowledge: publications of a scientific nature, like the *Penny Magazine*, were felt to be weekly threats to the evangelising of the nation, to be fought against by science presented in a context of Christianity.

Stokes and Lloyd were keenly aware not only of the kinds of writing they had to combat which other publishers were offering, and the age ranges and differences of use for which they had to provide, but also of the effect of the presentation of the publications upon both purchasers and readers. New forms of publication were continually sought, to cover all parts of the potential market, but at each price level the children's titles recur, presented in more splendid forms. *Jane, The Young Cottager*, for example, is available according to the 1835 catalogue in 32mo, the Reward Series Tracts, at 6d or 5s per dozen; in marble paper, with leather back, at 8d each; bound in red, at 1s each; in silk, at 1s 6d, or in a fine edition with superior engravings, in boards, at the same price; this same fine edition, in silk and half-calf, with gilt edges, at 2s 6d; or, finally, with Richmond's other narratives, as *The Annals of the Poor*, either bound in calf or with ornamented silk covers, for 5s 6d.

Stokes did seek for new material, however, and the spearhead of his assault on the fiction market for children was a succession of periodicals. The little weekly magazines of the early years of the Sunday school movement were very simple compilations following set formulae, and with very little material beyond a cut, a short exhortation to the scholar, a few verses of the Bible and a hymn. A brief moral tale, like those which appeared in school readers, might or might not be included. As the nineteenth century advanced larger periodicals were begun such as the *Youth's Magazine*, an evangelical undertaking which began in 1819, and the *Children's Friend* which William Carus Wilson began to publish in 1824, carrying an unusually intense concentration of pious infant deaths. Also in 1824, however, Stokes set up the RTS monthly *Child's Companion* simultaneously with the *Tract Magazine*, the latter intended for adults as well as for prizes and rewards. By the time Stokes retired, six million copies of the *Tract Magazine* had been issued. In 1850 William Jones in his history of the RTS noted smugly that the *Child's Companion* had held its own against very severe competition, and had 'been invaluable as a reward book for schools, and also very acceptable in private families'.[13]

It was recognisably descended from the earlier little papers, still in the small 32mo format, beginning with an ornamental title and a cut, and subtitled 'Sunday Scholar's Reward'. The first number, the model for the series, started off with a dialogue between two fictional Sunday scholars, but immediately relapsed into the old exhortatory vein with their teacher's admonition: 'Let every boy ask, "Am I fit to die?"' It followed this up with 'A Minister's address to the children' about the fact that 'You may not live to the end of the year'. It concluded with a prayer and a hymn. Besides these traditional elements, however, it had several new features. It is much longer than the older papers, with more variety of material: several 'anecdotes', which are usually extracts from books, are included in this and the subsequent numbers, and they move away from the oppressive stress upon death, often to stories of quaint infant converts in the mission field, or to snippets of other information about foreign lands, illustrating or explaining Bible stories. In this the influence of the desire to combat periodicals offering 'useful knowledge' can be observed; and indeed the facts proffered by the *Penny Magazine* are really no more 'useful' than these curious bits of lore about the Holy Land. There are even 'Arithmetical Questions' in the *Child's Companion* couched in terms of hundreds of scholars learning thousands of texts, and tract distributors spreading millions of good words. Mingled with these factual articles, and exhortations to scholars to consider their standing with God, and improve their gravity of behaviour and their application to their books, there are several stories in each issue. These are often the first publication, either entire or in parts, of tales which were then brought out as separate tracts in the series of books for the under-tens. This function, of serving as a testing ground for new stories and new writers, was of great importance in later RTS periodical publications. We must take William Jones's enthusiasm about the eagerness of readers with a pinch of salt; but it does seem to be the case, from extracts published in the magazine itself, that there was a feedback about the material published in the periodicals from the schools to the society, and so they became an important trial method of publication, and a point of departure and of growth for the society's writers.[14]

Growth, in the field of fiction, was not rapid after the initial decisive moves by Lloyd and Stokes. The enthusiasm of the first entry into the children's book field and the efforts of the 1820s promoted on the whole new forms of publication rather than of writing, except for the short stories for small children. During the period 1835 to 1855 the drive and forward movement of the whole RTS programme was affected by the vicissitudes of evangelical activity in general. There are clear signs of the settling down of the society into efficient and comfortable business practice. The catalogues suggest that the evangelical thrust had been tempered by other considerations. By 1840 children's books form a catalogue to themselves, 'Catalogue C, Publications for the Young', within which annotations denote morocco bindings, calf bindings, works for children just beginning to read, works on missionary subjects, and even show which of the 32mo tracts are most suitable for families and Boarding schools, and which for Sunday, National, British and common day schools.

This last is the most significant division: the society in settling into a routine of publishing children's books becomes more and more conscious of a need to offer different material to different social groups. The purpose of saving souls gradually ceases to be so overriding an aim of all RTS books that it makes all social distinctions evaporate: not only the bindings, but also the contents of the volumes begin to be changed by the social groups for which they are intended, and the social lessons they therefore carry. The excuse for this in so far as one was felt to be required, was that the books must appeal to all classes, since all want Grace, and the fastidious might reject tracts suggestive of charitable distributions and modelled on popular forms. Nevertheless, the first effect was to introduce social distinctions into the religious message more openly than before. The steps can be traced in the reports and catalogues of successive years. In 1840 a new 32mo series, in coloured covers with gilt edges, was introduced, to penetrate 'circles, where the tract, in its usual form, would have been altogether unacceptable'.[15] By 1845 there were fifteen titles in this form all specially selected or written for this series only. They include five examples of pious infant death, but also *Euphemia, A Tract for Young Ladies*. In 1840, too, a series of large print books with easy words for small children began alongside the old stories for the under-tens; the new books were 'especially for boarding schools and families'.[16] The first title is *Little Charles*. In 1849 story books for older readers appear on the list specifically intended for 'what are commonly termed the respectable classes'.[17] Such a tract as *Katherine*, by Charles B. Tayler, which appeared in the First Series in 1830 and as a work for the young in 1843, is an example. It is a sabbatarian work, showing the difference between the family Sunday well-spent in attending a Confirmation service and one wasted in wordly pursuits. The two parts bring motifs of early and later tract-writing into incongruous juxtaposition, for the first includes the pious death of Katherine's young cousin, while the second is detailed and domestic, concerned with the denunciation of such modern sins as reading the Sunday papers and taking day trips into the country. It is undeniably fiction, however, and describes just such a middle-class family as became the material of fiction for girls in the second half of the century.

In the next few years the RTS lists progressively increase the number of stories available, and the naming of their authors gains ground. In 1851 the report noted that books for the young were of great importance, and consequently 'the pens of writers established in popular favour are engaged in supplying valuable manuscripts for this object'.[18] The authors thus engaged wrote tales for the more lowly levels of the RTS readership, and brought with them attitudes which had developed from utilitarian thought, which at the beginning of the century had stood distinct from the evangelical attitudes and sometimes opposed to them. This rationalist tradition had produced its own children's books, beginning with the famous *Sandford and Merton*, published in three parts from 1783 to 1789, by Thomas Day, in which Rousseau's principles of education were demonstrated in the training of the sturdy farmer's son Harry Sandford and the spoiled rich boy Tommy Merton, by their all-knowing tutor Mr Barlow. Rousseau was one of the foreign infidels roundly condemned by English evangelicals, but his educative system of experiential learning under direct adult supervision had something in common with theirs, and was similarly aimed at reforming society through the children. In the next generation

of writers for the young, Maria Edgeworth worked under the
influence of his ideas. His doctrines of healthy bodily activity and
empirical learning had been intended to restore the joy of living to
the pampered and book-wearied children of the rich. In her work,
however, they are also applied to the poor, and alarmingly transformed:
for them work is made a moral imperative, the only path to happiness
and prosperity, which they are expected to follow practically as soon
as they can walk. The child of nature is thus entrapped in the toils of
utilitarian materialism.

Evangelical commentators did not entirely disapprove such
recommendations, but regarded them as merely moral in their
intention and effect, and therefore too 'cold'. As the fervour of
belief died down and was overtaken by intensity of feeling about
temporal, social concerns, the legacy of rationalism became
acceptably integrated with religious thought, and writings for children
from the 1830s onwards drew upon both. Harriet Martineau was
responding to the suggestion of the political economist Bishop
Richard Whately when she wrote her stories for the poor and their
children, *Illustrations of Political Economy* (1831), demonstrating
the necessity of submission to the iron laws of laissez-faire
economics.[19]

An illustration of the process by which such doctrines were
absorbed into Christian writing for the young is the career of Esther
Copley. In the preface to an early work of hers, *The Young Servant's
Friendly Instructor*, published by Simpkin and Marshall in 1827, the
purchaser is informed that Mrs Copley has 'for several years
devoted herself to the moral and religious instruction of the rising
generation, especially among the humbler classes of society'. While
promising spiritual guidance, however, the book is really concerned
with practical instruction. It propounds the first question 'Are not all
men by nature placed upon an equality?' in order to summarise the
several theoretical bases for an unequal society in a very few pages,
before moving on to the query 'Can you give any rules as to the time
and manner of dressing different meats?' and maintaining that level
of discourse for the rest of the book. Her works included cookery and
other manuals, even a *Comprehensive Knitting Book*, as well as fiction
of a very utilitarian turn.

One of her characters, a 'thoroughly domestic' young lady of whom
she heartily approves, rejects 'works of mere fiction and sentimentality',
and writes in her commonplace book only 'valuable sentiments, and
striking facts'. She appears in *The Poplar Grove* published by Tegg in

1841, where all the lessons are practical and domestic; the story is as concerned as those of Harriet Martineau with work and its rewards. It is framed by the growth of the grove of the title, which is given to little Harry as an acre of ground newly planted with a thousand poplar slips at the outset, and which by the end has 'taught him the use of property' (he has learnt to cut wood as well as to cast his own accounts) and 'set him agoing in Life'. (Because war has inflated prices, he gets a thousand guineas for his trees which is used to set him up in business as an engine-builder.) Once Mrs Copley was brought into the RTS lists as 'established in popular favour', she offered the Sunday school child stories of the utilitarian world of work, with such titles as *Lads of the Factory*, *Young Women of the Factory* and *The Young Servant*, as well as *Mamma and her Child* and *Female Excellence*; in 1828 she had become the editor of an RTS periodical called *The Domestic Visitor*.

In the early 1850s decisive steps were taken in the importation and discovery of new writers of children's fiction in the setting up of the periodicals *The Leisure Hour* (1852), and *Sunday at Home* (1854). In the address to its prospective readers in its first issue *The Leisure Hour* strikes a distinctive new note, both in describing the audience it aims at and in defining the nature of its appeal to them:

> We dedicate our pen to the thoughtful of every class. We aspire to catch the attention of peer and peasant, of master and man . . . Our sympathies are universal; and though they will adapt themselves to the special circumstances of different classes, they will vibrate, we trust, with true love towards all. And why should they not? Are we not one people, one great commonwealth? . . . Have we not the same sires? Are there not thousands of our lower classes who might claim a Norman pedigree, and does not the Crown of Britain grace a Saxon brow? Have we not the same heart-stirring recollections, the same watchwords of patriotism, the same interests in the pregnant future . . . Yes, we are one people, the inheritors of one mother-land and one mother-tongue; we will have therefore one literature: the same voice shall speak in the same accents to all.

The magazine contains, to some extent, the same mixture as before, with a serial, articles on popular science, on places, British history and institutions, and columns of extracts which are shifting from 'anecdote' to the 'tit-bit' in their character; it also addresses columns to servants, and to mothers, and offers recipes and domestic advice. Its tone is not, however, that of condescension nor of the fruitless attempts to rival useful knowledge magazines which are themselves unappealing. There is a stirring, chatty, bustling air which matches the manifesto quoted here; materials are sought which are not simply defined in terms of the wealth or class of the audience, but begin to appeal to sentiments recognisably popular, ideals actually shared. If the result is a lowest rather than a highest common denominator of taste, that is probably an inevitable part of its success. In the year after the Great Exhibition, a thrusting optimistic appeal to Smilesean self-confidence and 'healthy patriotism' would, one may guess, strike the dominant note in British popular feeling. It was certainly the shape of things to come, in terms of the values offered to the young and propagated in their books.

The Leisure Hour did not in fact carry fiction or any other matter specifically for young people. The *Sunday at Home* was the RTS periodical which became the vehicle for conveying these new stirrings to children and growing boys and girls. Its audience, defined in a brief address printed inside the wrappers of its first issue (wrappers, incidentally, which are clearly an imitation of those covering part-issue novels), was supposed to be twofold. It was to be good Sunday reading for those who would not go to Church, but spent their Sundays over unprofitable books, evil newspapers, and in inappropriate pleasures or even untimely work. These were first 'the masses of our population' and secondly those 'among our middle and educated classes', 'especially young people' who were shamed into observing the Sabbath but spent it in 'painful vacuity'. It includes, therefore, a large measure of fiction (of a moral and elevating tendency) having always a serial presented with a picture on the first page, and a 'page for the young' at the back, which also often carried serialised fiction. The leading story was ostensibly 'family reading'; in practice, therefore, adapted to the tastes and supposed sensibilities of the teenager, Dickens's immortal 'young person' who was so carefully considered and catered for. It was in this slot that writers whose metier was to be the RTS novel for the young were given their first major publications.

The first was G.E. Sargent, who began in April 1855 with one of his most enduring stories, *The Story of a Pocket Bible*, and kept up yearly contributions for some time, moving on to stories of adventures in exotic places. Other genres quickly found a place, with historical romances vying with autobiographical novels for pre-eminence in the rest of the decade. Sixty years of experiment and very cautious development of fiction for the young had led to an RTS style, which was about to be swept up into the great development of children's fiction in the 1860s.

The Society for the Propagation of Christian Knowledge

A parallel, though rather slower, development took place in the publications of the SPCK. At the beginning of the century the older society had no sense of urgency about persuading the new readers to buy good books, for they had a captive audience and an assured sale for their children's publications. When the National Society was set up it was as a venture sponsored by the SPCK, and one of the conditions of its foundation was that the SPCK thus relieved of its century-old responsibility for charity schools was instead to supply all the books used. The society accordingly issued huge quantities of Bibles, Testaments and prayer books, and also of primers and catechisms for elementary instruction. Little else was either offered or, it seems, called for in the schools. The primers did, in fact, contain some short moral tales, and as evidence about the reading of the children educated in this way possess the unique advantage that one may be certain that they were read, since they were used as lesson-books; but they are dull and brief, and certainly would not have held the attention of a fluent reader.[20] There was no thought of publishing books which would offer enough variety and interest to tempt the child or adult readers to buy for themselves.

Fiction was first admitted to the catalogues in 1814, in the shape of a series of 'Exemplary Tales, calculated to promote the practice of religion and virtue in the various occupations of humble life', by Mrs Trimmer. The attitude to the education of the poor which this lady shared with the society may be deduced from the title. Stiffly Anglican in her allegiances, evangelical chiefly in the severity with which she looked upon all forms of frivolity, indulgence and departure from the narrowest of paths, she had felt it necessary to preface her most famous children's book, *Fabulous Histories* (1786), with the warning that its fictional nature must be clearly pointed out, lest any child be tempted to believe that the robins of the story could really talk. This was a tale for the upper-class nursery; for the poor, education seemed to her an urgent but dangerous undertaking of the times, and she was anxious that the children of the poor should not be educated in such a manner to set them above the 'occupations of humble life'. Above all, Mrs Trimmer wished to avoid the undermining of the 'very endearing' connection between 'masters and mistresses and servants' by an education which would enable potential servants to make their own assessment of it, leading them to reject not only humble occupations for themselves, but all 'the wise designs of Providence in appointing different ranks'.[21]

The part played by fiction in this grudging process of social control was that of a very lightly sugared pill of instruction, or a highly dramatised warning. There is for example *The Servant's Friend* in the SPCK series, which is the story of the pious Tom Simpkins. It opens with his profiting from his schoolmaster's advice, which is to give thanks for his education to God and the squire, and to obey all rules exactly; installed in a situation, he proves himself by his devotion to work and strict rectitude, which is demonstrated when he throws a bundle of idle ballads, the property of an overdressed cook, into the fire. Eventually he receives a legacy from his master, and sets himself up as a farmer, so avoiding the dangers of taking service in a less pious household and becoming the 'mercenary slave' of some profligate rich man, or buying a public house and associating with his unregenerate equals.

Mrs Trimmer's preoccupation with social morality is matched by that of Hannah More and the other Cheap Repository Tract writers, to whom the SPCK turned for its next cautious venture into fiction, in 1829. The selection they chose to distribute is exemplified by the story of Betty Brown, a little orange-girl with a strong innate honesty but no moral education to keep her from corruption. She is furnished with 5s for stock and much advice about passing bad fruit and bad sixpences by Mrs Sponge, who then extorts 6d interest per day and sells the girl expensive food and lodging, and bad gin. Betty is rescued by a lady who tells her that she is paying interest in excess of £7 a year, and so should free herself from Mrs Sponge. She does so, indeed Mrs Sponge is arrested for her crimes, and Betty falls instead into the hands of the philanthropic lady, who supplies her with a substitute for the gin and high living and for Mrs Sponge's advice about successful selling, in the shapes of a dress to go to church in and a tabulated set of 'rules for retail traders', all of which deal with the rights of the customer. Eventually 'by industry and piety [she] rose in the world, till at length she came to keep a handsome sausage-shop, near Seven Dials, and was married to an honest hackney-coachman'. Betty never undergoes conversion, but is represented as good from the start, oppressed by circumstances rather than original sin; and her industry is conspicuously more important than her piety.

In 1832 the need for advances in the provision of reading for the poor began to impinge upon the society, and in the midst of some controversy a Committee of General Literature and Education was set up, with the intention, once again, of combating the effects of periodicals such as the *Penny Magazine* and acquiring an 'influence over the minds and conduct of the great mass of the population', which was for the first time now 'a reading population'. The standing committee in making their recommendation for a new branch of SPCK publications noted that 'there are many among the working classes willing to expend small sums in the purchase of works of a more general character and of a more attractive appearance'. They also mentioned that this demand 'has been partially met by other Societies by the production of small books suitable for the purpose, liberally illustrated, and tastefully, though cheaply, bound'.[22] Whatever the RTS were doing, however, it seemed that the older society felt some obligations and perceived some opportunities in this field.

By 1840 the society had a fully-developed procedure for providing books for these new readers, including the young. Minutes of the proceedings of the Committee of General Literature show almost weekly consideration of new titles, sometimes submitted in batches of 10 or 20 items at a time by aspiring writers, and the procedure whereby the stories were set up in print, circulated to committee members, considered, and approved for publication was often rapid, needing only a few months from the submission of the manuscript to a book appearing on sale.

An example of the writers drawn to the society was Jane Alice Sargant, who was already known to the committee when in January 1841 she left a manuscript called *Charlie Burton* at the offices. She sent another in February called *The Swearer's End*. Both were referred to a member of the committee to read; *The Swearer's End* was finally adopted on 23 April, and 'corrected' in some unspecified way by 30 April; on 25 June the author was paid £8 for her work, and it was placed in the next catalogue. Meanwhile she had produced another, *How Will It End?*, which was not liked, and on the 16 July it was 'agreed, that this MS be declined' and that moreover Mrs Sargant was to be 'respectfully informed' that nothing she could do in the way of correcting it would change the committee's mind. *Charlie Burton*, still under consideration, was also in trouble, and on 30 July a letter came from Mr Short, reading it for the committee, to tell them that it was insufficiently clear in its statement of religious views. By 29 October Mrs Sargant had revised the text to their satisfaction, and on 5 November it was agreed to print the tale, with illustrations. On 17 December the author was sent, apparently in full settlement, 25 copies of her book. It remained on the catalogue until 1905.[23] She was undeterred, however, and produced other successful titles for the society: *The Broken Arm*, for example, and *Ann Ash, the Foundling*.

Mrs Sargant's style is as forbidding as her Dickensian name. *Charlie Burton*, expressly intended for child readers, begins with the perfectly repellent sentence, '"Father! in vain do you attempt to reconcile me to my loss; in vain you argue . . ."' The speaker, mourning her excellent husband who has just died in his prime, is told to mind that her grief 'does not exceed the bounds of duty'. The bounds, indeed the bonds, of duty are Mrs Sargant's chief preoccupation and their delineation is the point of all her stories. Charlie and his brothers, thus bereft of their father on the first page, are described as they seek out ways of supporting themselves and their mother and grandfather, by market gardening, becoming servants or, in the case of the crippled Charlie, making exquisite toys. Their work might be interesting, but it is incidental to their failings, the least of which may at any time have dreadful consequences: Tom, the brother who takes service as a page boy and is vain of his own beauty and his silver and blue uniform, inadvertently causes little Charlie to go into a fatal decline, when the child notices how inferior to Tom's is his own reflection in a peer glass.

More repellent still, however, are the authorial maxims concerning the restraints and obligations of the poor children and their parents. The dead father is commended because 'from prudential motives, he had cautiously concealed the state of his real feelings' from his beloved, until 'he found himself in a situation to marry'. Brother William goes to his job in the market as usual when Charlie dies, because 'the best cure for unhappiness . . . is activity in our lawful calling': a truth, if it is one, of the utmost convenience to our employers. Similarly, in *Ann Ash*, the heroine is honoured with a funeral sermon in which her life of self-sacrifice is held up as an illustration of the notion that we are bound to make Christian sacrifices and 'that riches are not necessary for the complete fulfilment of the obligation'. Having been abandoned as a child and brought up by a good man whose 'first step was to lay, even in infancy, a foundation of obedience and self-denial' she had devoted herself to being first a good servant and then a nurse, refusing to marry the man she loved in case he should be incommoded by the reappearance of whatever disreputable relative deserted her as a baby.

The austerity of the lives of these characters, the adults who will not without permission open their own letters or step over the threshold of their master's houses to save their relations' lives, and the children who regard eating a single raspberry from their humble parents' gardens as stealing from their well-to-do customers, is incredible; the code which enforces it seems perfectly inhuman. It reaches obsessive proportions in the work of another writer of this period, Charlotte Adams, where, paradoxically, it is even less attractive largely because she concentrates in a detailed and often vivid way upon the lives of young children. Her SPCK stories concern servant maids in their first employment, aged eleven or twelve, and errand boys of only nine or ten. She had previously written stories of children in much higher walks of life: *The Stolen Child*, published by John W. Parker in 1838, tells of a little girl who is vain of her dancing, and who is therefore snatched from her birthday celebrations in her papa's park by a showman who wants her as a tightrope walker; *The Etonian*, published by L. Booth in 1841, concerns a young blade who runs into debt at school and is only cured by his father's masquerading as a money-lender. *Little Servant Maids*, however, which she sent in to the SPCK early in 1847 and which they published a year later, after demanding extensive revisions, is a far less fanciful piece. The episodic — not to say shapeless — story describes in turn each of the girls who comes into the household of Mrs Sewell to be trained by Martha, her servant. The first is also the last, for Jessy the blacksmith's daughter, who is slovenly and rude and rebels, running back home, learns in her subsequent places 'to estimate herself and others more justly, and to be contented in her state when she was free from actual suffering'. This lesson absorbed, she tries twice more to satisfy the standards of Matha, and eventually succeeds, to the encouragement of all those girls who hope to become good servants but have the disadvantage of being clumsy of figure, and heavy-footed.

Between Jessy's periods of employment other girls are tried, including Caroline whom 'Mrs. Sewell, thinking fine names unsuitable for little servant maids living in a tradesman's family, always called . . . Mary', and Esther Price, who eats odd raisins and plums when Martha is cooking and so infallibly puts herself on the road to transportation for burglary. A real Mary succeeds her, who is portrayed as discontented and ungrateful because she had been educated at a charity school and so led to believe that she has rights. There is in fact a continued discussion in the book about the education of servant girls; Martha is inclined to think that right training in household matters at home is essential, and reading and writing undesirable. Mrs Sewell feels book learning is not necessarily a bad thing; but the evidence presented by the author, in her succession of girl characters, rather inclines to Martha's side. Meanwhile all her inventive powers are expended first on showing the faults of the little maids as vividly as possible, and then on impressing the details of proper behaviour and methods for the reader to imitate.

There is a difference of background, and in the degree of graphic individualising of the message, between the Cheap Repository Tract story of the orange-girl's rescue from exploitation to become a useful tradeswoman to the gentry, and the scene, for instance, in which Martha unpacks for little Jessy and finds the smelly grease her mother has given her for chapped hands carelessly spread over her unsuitable undergarments; but there is no real change in the preoccupations and intentions of the writers. The message repeated over and over again in this book and others like *The Errand Boy* is 'remember your time is your employer's': servants exist to serve, and if their souls are their own, Charlotte Adams and other SPCK writers seem to find that their least important dimension, and one with which it is not these educators' aim to interfere.

The effect of these attitudes on their books for children is curiously contradictory. Several writers, including Charlotte Adams, present a circumstantial account of the lives of their prospective readers, in much more concrete detail than do the writers working for the RTS; in some ways mimetic realism is clearly their aim. But the physical substantiality of the fictional worlds they offer is offset by their invalidity in other ways. While it might well be felt that the death-haunted intensity of the RTS conversion story has little direct correspondence with the lives of shopboys and maidservants, it at least offered them some sort of focus of personal feeling, and one which claimed to concern them intimately and exclusively, as souls of equal value with all others in the sight of God. The ideal servant of the SPCK tract leads, by contrast, an entirely relative existence, in subservience which is usually rewarded only by the security of further servitude. If she performed miracles of honesty, loyalty and self-denial, a maid might aspire to the approbation of her betters, and so to further opportunities to exercise her virtues. If a child in an evangelical tract achieved conviction of sin, and lived or died in the knowledge that Jesus saves, she could expect as her reward transfiguration and

everlasting joy. Emotional life thus chanelled may now present itself
as morbid or undesirable; but it is life, not instrumentality in the lives
of others, and its goal is fulfilment, even ecstasy, not subservience and
abnegation.[24]

The SPCK thus continued to work on old assumptions during the
1840s and 1850s, as children's literature developed rapidly; their
authors created stories which were expanded versions of the kind of
tract that concentrated all inventive effort on representing the poor
child's interest as coinciding with what their employers required of
them. The realism of the settings of their books was thus a function
of the message they carried, serving to press home the relevance of
their warnings and advice to the boys and girls who saw lives and
expectations like their own displayed. It did not explore, except for
purposes of admonition, the nature of adolescent feeling and
perception nor seek to foster the development of any but the most
practical, and least attractive, aspects of maturity — reliability,
obedience, and a realistically low self-estimate. SPCK lists of later
decades did include authors, like Mrs Ewing, Austin Clare and F.
Englebach, whose horizons were wider, and who wrote for boys and
girls inhabiting a world not entirely confined to the basement floor.
In the 1850s the first suggestions of their work can be found in
stories dealing with the lives of middle-class girls, like Ellen Taylor
of *Early Discipline* (1852), or historical events and adventures in
colonial islands, like *Stories of the Norsemen* (1855). The prevailing
conservatism of the society in addressing its special audience of the
lower orders in country districts is evident, however, in the periodical
which it began in 1852, presumably as a competitor to the RTS
Leisure Hour and *Sunday at Home. The Home Friend* was nothing
like as progressive, and did not provide a platform for new children's
authors. The avowed intention of its fiction precluded that: it was to
publish 'those narratives which, with fictitious names and incidents,
convey to the mind, in the most pleasing manner, lessons of meekness,
love and charity'. In the first years the primary lesson, of meekness,
largely predominated, but all the fiction tended in any case to be
submerged by extracts from learned tomes about Nineveh, or the
production of cotton, or by articles on such 'Seaside Pleasures' as the
fauna of rockpools or the topography of Ilfracombe. The magazine is
supposed to be useful for giving to poor parishioners; but even
allowing for theories about offering useful knowledge in a harmless
Christian context it seems very imperfectly directed to them or their
supposed interests.

The Commercial Publishers of Religious and Educational Books for the Young

The large societies were by no means the only publishers who found moral and religious works, and especially books for the young, to be an expanding market at the end of the eighteenth century. All shades of opinion, materialist and philanthropic as well as variously religious, sought to influence the newly-discovered audience of children, and parents and teachers at every social level found they had a need for their wares. In such an atmosphere many enterprising publishers made their way into a field previously left to the humblest chapbook printers, or at best to such an eccentric as John Newbery, who used superior cuts, print and paper to dress up his fables and ABCs. The Evangelical movement was sufficiently powerful to maintain a fashionable bookshop devoted to its interests, Hatchards in Piccadilly; and besides the many metropolitan and provincial booksellers who turned to providing similar wares, there were men with no capital or stock in trade except their own enthusiasm who floated substantial businesses upon juvenile publications in the first thirty years of the century.

An instance of London publishers who achieved a modest success in the field that lasted as long as the evangelical readership remained was the venture of T. Hamilton and J. Naylor, who published a solidly respectable juvenile periodical, the *Youth's Magazine or Evangelical Miscellany* from 1805 to 1867, when it merged with *The Bible Class Magazine*. It was well thought of, edited by well-known evangelicals including W.F. Lloyd, and closely allied with the RTS to whose funds the publishers contributed. Fiction regularly appeared in its pages, and it had contributors of note in the early part of the century, including Jane Taylor; but it never led, or broke new ground, or moved on from the circumscriptions of the early formulae of children's writing. More spectacular success came when a firm had the good fortune to discover a best-selling writer for children; one such author was enough to finance a major expansion of business. A case in point is the story of F. Houlston and Son of Wellington in Shropshire. In 1807 they began by printing tracts which were sold in London by Hatchards, then moved to Paternoster Row in London in 1825, and set up a second shop in the Strand in 1835 where they carried on until 1906.[25] In 1814 they began to publish the works of Mrs Sherwood, and their prosperity lasted as long as her books were read. Mrs Sherwood's popularity sprang from the fact that her preoccupation with the saving of infant souls (brought about by her experience in India, where English

children were all too likely to outlive the respite of innocence afforded
to the new-born and then to die before they could arrive at salvation
through the recognition of their sins and of their Saviour) was inspired
not by mere duty, but by a real and intense love of children. Liking
young company, she adopted orphans to add to her own large brood,
and took children seriously, as autonomous beings, who had a right
to their own likes and dislikes, and responsibility for themselves.

Her first book for the young published by Houlston's was the
epoch-making *Little Henry and His Bearer* (1814), and it was one of the
first of the new tracts to mingle fictional appeal effectively with the
lessons it taught. It tells of a white child's rescue, conversion and pious
death in India, and is a good example of the fictionalising of the
progress to salvation which is the basis of popular evangelical theology.
Henry is sunk in ignorance and original sin, a neglected orphan being
brought up by affectionate but Muslim servants; he is rescued from his
corruption by an English girl who teaches him to read, to repent, and
to trust in God's mercy; eventually he converts another, his Indian
bearer, and dies in completing his task. There are clear links with other
moral writers in the pattern of such a story. Henry dies a pious death,
after finding his salvation through reading the Bible, which is the
foundation of all evangelical educational endeavour. His duty to
convert others is bound up with class relationships, for it is his
bearer, a social inferior, who is the proper object of his efforts. But
Mrs Sherwood's story also has elements which take the children's tract
a decisive step onwards. The circumstantial detail of the narrative is
fascinating, and sets the figure of the pretty, neglected child, a soul
in danger, in the midst of picturesque physical peril. The pathos thus
evoked was one of the major weapons of evangelical writing for the
young for the rest of the century.

In addition she had hit upon the incident which was to provide
an heroic dimension to the central childish figure in many subsequent
books: Henry himself, thought he is no older than the readers who
have sympathised with him in his peril, becomes the agent
of conversion for an adult. The reader too, therefore, may participate
in the one noble activity John Wesley urged upon his followers: 'You
have nothing to do but save souls'. In this and many later instances
infant heroism lays down its life for that cause, and its pathos is
plangently dramatised.

The instant and abiding admiration which greeted Mrs Sherwood's
publication of this her first tract, led to her writing a series of little
books for children of various classes, in which charm as disarming as

that of Newbery's chapbooks is brought to the inculcation of social
and religious lessons. The charm stems from the author's real
observation of children: whatever was to be learned from a story,
it was written in a way designed to interest and please them. Writing
for very small children she would couch her message in stories of
kittens and pet dogs, giving tiny domestic detail about such things as
brown worsted mittens or little baskets lined with moss for the
collection of snail shells and primroses; addressing boys she expends
her ingenuity on how to earn sixpence, or the importance of useful
pieces of cord and books with pictures of Red Indians. Her children
may be carefully adjusted to the social group expected to read any
particular story, or they may be drawn in a way which suggests that
their appeal is as exotic as that of Little Henry's Indian surroundings.
In stories like 'The Heron's Plume' there are upper-class children who
are miniatures from a Jane Austen world, preoccupied with balls
and head-dresses and living in mansions full of retainers; their
amusements are shooting and riding, polite evening games of fox-and-
geese, or beautiful wax dolls dressed in pink and silver and seated on
ivory and ebony chairs before their china cups. For the majority of
readers, whether in Sunday school or middle-class nursery, the tales
must have seemed both vividly concrete and fascinatingly remote.

Mrs Sherwood's most famous book was *The History of the Fairchild
Family*, begun in 1818. It was intended 'to shew the importance and
effects of a religious education'. The latter-day religious version of the
educative family in which the general evangelical responsibility for the
saving of the souls of others is focused in the duty of parents to
educate their children so as to lead them to salvation, is here described
and illustrated in all its activities. The dangers of the idea (which was
perhaps pursued more often in literature than in life) include the
tendency to set up parents and guardians as God-substitutes, because
of the inevitable analogies that will be made between the care of God
for man and of a parent for children: from a debased and self-satisfied
version of the evangelical notion of the family arose the rigid and
repressive family structures implied by the notion of the Victorian
father. Mrs Sherwood herself, however, must be exonerated from any
such intention of glorifying parental authority and suggesting that
any human being is infallible. Her adult mentors are clearly as weak
and erring, in their duties to God, as the children are in their more
elementary social obligations; the usual context of instruction in her
families is the scene in which a member of the older generation, who
recognises his or her own faults in a child relative, takes the child aside

and explains how such problems afflicted the speaker in youth, and sometimes still do so. The solution is mutual prayer, for themselves and for each other.

This pattern is part, in effect, of Mrs Sherwood's entirely serious attitude to the child, and an acknowledgement of its individuality and importance. Other aspects of her vision of the unbroken continuum between childish and mature sin, the passions of childhood and the passions of maturity, lead to scenes within *The Fairchild Family* which are apparently grotesquely disproportionate, and it is these incidents which were depreciated by later writers, even those professing evangelical conviction. In the most famous of these episodes the Fairchild children fall out and fight, and their parents are alarmed; they are pulled apart and caned. After they have cooled off, the appropriate text is delivered and expounded, and they express themselves sorry, and admit that they do not really hate each other. They are forgiven and comforted, and their father prays with them. Then, when all is over emotionally, but while they are still receptive to the lesson, he takes them to see a man hung in chains upon a gibbet, for murdering his brother. They are frightened by the sight; he gathers them close to him and tells them the story of the long-standing family quarrel which led to this end. To subsequent generations this has seemed gratuitously horrible. Of course the sight of a gibbet may well have been horrifying; to the child Wordsworth the place 'where in former times a murderer had been hung in iron chains' precipitated an experience of visionary force, even though the gibbet itself had long since gone. But he chose the moment for recounting in *The Prelude* as one of the greatest importance in his moral growth; certainly not something he would have sought to forget or be without.

In her obviously very different framework, Mrs Sherwood took childhood experience as seriously as Wordsworth did, and did not seek to deny the importance of moral acts simply on the grounds of the youth of the participants. Within the unfailingly supportive, and clearly ordered, moral world of their parents, the Fairchild children are taken entirely seriously as moral beings. Such scenes were part of the appeal of the book for children, as many memoirs suggest: even those who most strongly disclaim any influence from or even understanding of the religious implications of the book were conscious of its powerful situations and sensational action. It was only those adult readers who were increasingly solicitous of childish sensibility, or in evangelical terms who were so foolish as to put their children at risk by sentimentally concealing from themselves the inevitability of original sin and infant corruption, that complained of the book.[26] Even so it remained in print until at least 1902, a reminder of the tenacity of educational attitudes, and a support for the essentially one-author firm of Houlston, which never had a comparable success.

A constrasting example is the firm of Nisbet where the energy which fuelled evangelical publishing at the outset was sufficiently powerful to adapt itself to make use of changes in writing for children in the middle of the century. James Nisbet, the son of a Scottish farmer, came to London as a poor clerk in the first years of the nineteenth century, and immediately entered into the Evangelical revival with great enthusiasm; on visits home his family found his fervour positively embarrassing. He started a Sunday school in a carpenter's shed in a court, and in 1803 was one of the founder members of the Sunday School Union; his Sunday school became a day school and then the Fitzroy schools, with buildings in Hertford Place and six hundred children a year being educated, many as ministers or missionaries, so that by 1853 14,000 children had passed through its hands. When Nisbet himself taught in the Sunday school he 'took care to read all the little books' he gave the children, and got up at 4 a.m. to study the lessons he was to teach. This was necessary partly because he was only rather basically educated, but also because he was so enormously busy; his charitable activity began with schools and extended to a huge list of offices and duties, from director of a sailors' home in London docks to secretary of a committee for relief of highland destitution.

In 1809 he set up his own business selling exclusively religious works, and delighted in his immediate success because he was able to buy larger premises and so entertain missionaries and ministers and imperilled young men from the country. He not only published tracts, and sold those of the RTS and others, but he also gave books away to all and sundry, supplying theology to poor ministers and stories to village libraries, and tracts to emigrants and children. He vetted his stock strictly for soundness in principle, doctrine and morality, and, remarkably for publishers with a sense of mission, he forced generous payments upon authors who were happy to take less. He never met with any serious reversal or loss in his business, though his life as a member of his church was stormy and self-willed, and so involved him in repeated disputes and scandals over the schisms which rent the Scottish Church of the time.[27] His energy and enthusiasm kept him in the vanguard in all his activities, whether managing hospitals, disputing doctrines, or teaching a Sunday school

child: it is particularly interesting, therefore, to see the lists of books
which constituted his 'Select Theological Circulating Library', founded
in 1824 'to promote the cause of pure and undefiled religion, so that
Christian Parents may, with safety, allow their Children to select any
Book from the catalogue'. Societies are cautious, and committees are
dilatory; Nisbet's library is an alternative check-list of evangelical
reading, and may be regarded as a gauge of the progress of moral
fiction for the young.

The catalogue for 1832 gives Nisbet's terms as two guineas per
annum for a borrower taking four volumes in town or eight in the
country, which compares very favourably with the famous Mudie's,
also a 'select' library, which opened in 1842 offering one volume for
one guinea to town subscribers, but charging two guineas to
countrymen; for two guineas the town subscriber could have four
volumes. Both libraries sent out books at the expense of the
subscriber. More fashionable libraries than Nisbet's offering the
latest books of all kinds, not simply those selected as moral and
religious, charged much higher rates. Nisbet's charges may well reflect
philanthropic or evangelical intentions rather than the business acumen
which motivated Charles Edward Mudie, but for families where the
parents disapproved of the old circulating libraries and their uncensored
publications, he offered probably the only access to fiction for the
young.

The 1832 lists include, of course, a majority of theological works
of all weights, from the works of the Puritan divines of the seventeenth
century to modern Protestant periodicals and the sermons, anecdotes,
tracts and familiar addresses of Evangelicals from Burder to the Rev.
Carus Wilson. There are also many works of history and travels, of
the kind Mudie was to make the backbone of his non-fictional stock,
some poetry and other literary works, and tractates upon modern
social issues such as education.

Nisbet's fictional stock ranges from the Cheap Repository Tracts
and extensive holdings of the works of Mrs Sherwood, her sister
Mrs Cameron, Hannah More (in 19 volumes), Mrs and Miss Taylor,
Maria Edgeworth (*Early Lessons* in 6 volumes), Mrs Trimmer, 40
volumes of Rewards and children's books, and select tracts by authors
including Richmond, the Swiss divine Lalan, and Mrs Carus Wilson,
to a very few of the three-decker novels which were Mudie's speciality.
Between the slight tracts and books for small children, and the
carefully-selected novels, there are more than a hundred titles which
represent the growing area of fiction for older children and young

persons, including examples of the several varieties of story that were to develop into the genres of the 1860s. There are school stories, adventures set in exotic places, historical tales, especially stories of Judaism and early Christianity, and nearly forty stories which have a girl's name for their title, some of which anticipate the serious novel for young ladies which developed in the following decade. Examples of these new forms of writing do not approach the numbers of the simple tracts which Nisbet held, and which were to remain the basic ingredient of commercial religious publishing for some years; but they indicate the direction it was to take as the tracts were superseded. Appearing in 1832, Nisbet's list shows how far ahead of the religious societies commercial publishers were.

Thomas Nelson is a good example of such commercial enterprise. He was another Scottish evangelical, who had begun more slowly and humbly than Nisbet, as a secondhand bookseller; in 1843 the firm opened its first London office, and before the founder died in 1861 his son had invented the first rotary printing machine, installed in their Scottish factory in 1850, and opened a New York branch of the company in 1854. Their pioneering business and production methods went into the publishing of books for children, which were the foundation of their commercial success. They include cheap papercovered tract stories like *Robert Dawson or the Brave Spirit*, which appeared in 1857 (and is curious for its ambiguities about scenery, manners, schooling and especially currency which occur because the writer was trying to accommodate readers on both sides of the Atlantic) and, by the early 1860s, much more elaborate productions 'for the family library' with gilded bindings and such titles as *The Early Choice, a Book for Daughters* and *Christian Principle in Little Things, a Book for Girls*. In 1869 Nelson's started their own magazine, *The Family Treasury*, in which an enduring piece of historical fiction, *The Chronicles of the Schonburg-Cotta Family*, first appeared. Also in the 1860s they secured the works of two major children's authors, Charlotte Tucker and Robert Ballantyne; they also became specialists in school books, responding quickly to new opportunities by tailoring their Readers to the requirements of the burgeoning state system.

Nisbet, Nelson and Houlston had reputations to maintain in the eyes of a critical clientele; other firms attempting to break into the market throughout the century were less scrupulous, and one finds repeated complaints and warnings like that which prefaced the Sunday School Union Catalogue for 1824, concerning 'very exceptionable

Reward Books' being sold under 'specious and deceptive' titles.

By the 1840s the risk of giving a child a romance disguised as a moral tale was augmented by the possibility that unwary purchasers might fall into the traps of such a publisher as J. Burns, who issued children's books supporting extreme Puseyite views, and attacking Dissent; the Sunday School Union (SSU) duly warned its members in the *Union Magazine* in 1844 about these 'pernicious' works.[28] Even where neither fraud nor subversion were intended, the lucrative Reward trade attracted publishers with nothing of religious or literary value to offer, who relied on the cheapness or convenience of their wares to attract customers. One way of cashing in on the demand for pious fiction and aids to Sunday school teaching was by setting up as a complete service, claiming to provide for all the purchaser's requirements expeditiously, cheaply and safely. Such an entrepreneur was the London bookseller Benjamin L. Green of 62, Paternoster Row, who published a series of Sunday school books, mostly compiled or written by the Rev. Samuel Green, BA. In *The Sunday School Teacher's Pocket Book for 1851* the Greens offered to supply RTS books at the same rate as the depository — a confidence-inspiring idea — or to undertake to stock a Sunday school library, or to supply as many carefully-selected Sunday school Rewards as were required, at rates even more reasonable from other, unspecified, sources. Which of the family of Green would be their author is not made clear.

If a provincial Sunday school superintendant entertained no doubt very justifiable doubts about such metropolitan operators, he could choose instead to go to a local bookseller for his goods; but there he would encounter a different danger, that of the very miscellaneous list, comprising all the sorts of book that a small firm could sell, to which a few Rewards had been added on spec. J.S. Pratt, for instance, of Stokesley in Yorkshire, had a list in 1845 which swings wildly from the irreproachable and puritanical to the dubious and the merely incongruous: in the order he presented it, it reads:

The Spy, by Cooper. The Pioneers. Lionel Lincoln. Baxter's Saint's Rest. Castle of Inchvalley. Letter Writer. Children of the Abbey. Bunyan's Pilgrim's Progress. Watt's World to Come. Buchan's Domestic Medicine. Robinson Crusoe. Life of Rev. John Wesley. Cottagers of Glenburnie. Young Man's Own Book. Young Woman's Companion. St. Clair of the Isles. Modern Cabinet of Arts. Wonders of the World. Domestic Cookery. Buffon's Natural History, 100 Cuts, Cook's Voyages Round The World. Life of Admiral Nelson.

Burn's Poetical Works. Byron's Select Poems. The Casquet of
Literary Gems. Life of Napoleon Bonaparte. Two Years before
the Mast. Arabian Nights Entertainments. Farmer of Inglewood
Forest. Scott's Lady of the Lake. Popular Geography. The Last
of the Mohicans, by Cooper. The Water Witch, by ditto. The Red
Rover by ditto. The Pilot by ditto.

This list appears in the back of what is perhaps the most shocking of
his publications, a sensational French novel called *Matilda*, by
Eugene Sue; but for the naive purchaser the list is full of sudden
pitfalls. Even if he recognised and managed to avoid Byron and the
Arabian Nights, he might still present his scholars with a mixture of
useful manuals, sober lives of national and religious heroes, classics of
Puritan writing, and sensational romances and adventure stories from
America.

Similarly mixed lists were published by many larger firms.
Opportunism might be on the scale of the small firm which added a
few classic reward books to a heap of hack work, as did, for example,
Knight and Son of Clerkenwell Close, London, offering *Little Henry,
The Annals of the Poor, Sandford and Merton*, to leaven such titles
as *A New Reward Book, The Children's Bread from the Master's
Table*, by Thulia S. Henderson. Or it might be the basis of a large
success, as in the case of the notorious Thomas Tegg, who profited by
the bookselling crisis of 1821 to buy up a large number of copyrights,
and so made a great deal of money and published a lot of very cheap
editions of great works, at the expense of their authors. In the 1830s
and 1840s he was following up this *coup* with a thriving children's list
which was founded on many books under the name of 'Peter Parley', to
whose American originator Tegg paid nothing at all. Conversely, he
published many books by Mary Howitt, a respected Quaker children's
writer and the first translator of Andersen, who found him very
honest and satisfactory. His lists were very eclectic indeed, including
the *Arabian Nights, Pilgrim's Progress*, Charlotte Elizabeth, Lord
Chesterfield's *Advice to His Son, Cinderella*, Mrs Copley, Maria
Edgworth, *Evenings at Home*, Hannah More, *Robinson Crusoe,
Rasselas*, Byron, Coleridge, Milton, Pope, Spenser, and divinity from
Josephus to John Todd's *Sunday School Teacher*, as well as large
numbers of school text books at all levels.

It was such a mixture of doctrinal ingredients, as well as publishers
offering poisonous rubbish in speciously pious wrappers, that the
SSU had repeatedly warned against throughout the century, and the

RTS and SPCK had set out to provide against by offering their safe and vetted treats for good children, guaranteed to spell out the right message all the way through. The vitality of the independent publishers, however, is sufficiently clear from their constant growth and proliferation, and their relative flexibility had good as well as bad consequences: fiction for young people developed more quickly in their hands, as the Nisbet Library Catalogue suggests, and they always had the possibility of discovering major new talent and rewarding and exploiting it more effectively than the societies. The newest trends appeared first in their lists; even Mr Pratt of Stokesley had discovered by 1845 that the adventure story as written by J.F. Cooper was to be a best seller of the coming decades. It was the firms of Nisbet and Nelson who were to discover the major English writers in that vein, which with the other new forms of writing and publishing for the young came to dominate the field in the 1860s. These firms stood shoulder to shoulder with the philanthropic societies in meeting the increasingly complex demands of teachers, parents, and even the readers themselves, for new kinds of moral and didactic fiction, and in meeting, too, the challenge of a quite different kind of writing for the young, which began to appear in the wake of *Alice in Wonderland.*

3 THE FLOWERING OF THE EVANGELICAL TRADITION

The authors whose development was fostered by the religious publishing boom of the 1850s and 1860s had to establish the forms of fiction suited to their task, which were to be used by hundreds of their successors for the next forty years. Their potential readership grew every day, as the network of schooling spread ever more efficiently across the country; the point would soon be reached where an author must address one group or another within that readership, but for a few years many writers, aware of the wide variety of children who might be their readers, still tried to produce books to cater for them all. The RTS practice of publication in a variety of formats meant that the possible readers of one text might include the prize-winners from National schools, small private academies, and humble Sunday and ragged schools, aged from about six or seven to fifteen, and differing widely in experience according to whether they were working or still at school, living in the country or an industrial town. A further group catered for by the same writers were the young children, from the age of four or five upwards, who were too well-off to attend Sunday school, but for whom Sunday reading was needed. Books for this readership were what the trade simply called Rewards, and thousands upon thousands of them were produced.

The writers who specialised in Rewards did so, generally, out of a mixture of motives: a majority of them were women, often spinsters, and for them writing children's moral tales offered a respectable, even feminine occupation less tedious and cramping than the limited round of female occupations, and it satisfied the pressing need felt by very many to be of use in the world, in a social and charitable sense; it also brought in a little money, if that were needed. Most of the individuals one can distinguish in this crowd turn out to have some sort of experience of books beyond the average, but few had an education comparable to the schooling which put most educated men of the period in possession of the classical heritage. Their work, therefore, while it is often very reliant upon and imitative of other writers, forms a distinct, demotic tradition outside the high literary culture, founded upon a very few models endlessly perpetuated, which are either contributed by one or other of the popular traditions, or invented or imported by the few strongest writers working within the genre. These

63

leading, influential individuals were often called to their work by deep feeling, partaking of the second wave of the Evangelical movement, which blended a renewed religious conviction with that strong concern for human suffering which was the hallmark of right feeling in the 1840s. An examination of their writing should reveal the dominant patterns of the Reward tale, and show both their sources in traditional, popular and contemporary story-telling traditions, and their power as models for the later generations of such writers.

The Narrative Line: Popular Romance and the Reward Tale

One of the first writers of children's stories whose fiction was given prominence, indeed called into existence, by the founding of periodicals such as *Sunday at Home*, was George E. Sergent. Sergent was an evangelical teacher almost by inheritance: he was the son-in-law of Esther Copley, and felt himself to be taking on her mantle. He began his mission by writing sermons, which he delivered as a lay preacher in Oxfordshire villages, and had published as tracts by the RTS from 1841. Having contributed tracts on the expected subjects, such as Sabbath breaking, for ten years, he was invited, when the new magazines were started, to write serial stories; in 1869 he became RTS tract editor, in charge of the *Tract Magazine*, until he retired in 1880, and spent his time until he died in 1883 in rewriting his stories.

His two most famous and influential tales, of the many which appeared in the RTS magazines, were *The Story of a Pocket Bible* (1855) and *Roland Leigh, the Story of a City Arab* (1857), serialised in *Sunday at Home* and *The Leisure Hour* respectively. In their framing narratives and in the motifs and scenes which they include, these two serials provided the basis of much later writing. They are by nature episodic: the serial novel, whether handled by popular writers like Eugene Sue and Pierce Egan or set up in opposition by the RTS, gets its immediate effects within the single published part or fails to sell next time. In *The Story of a Pocket Bible* Sergent virtually assembled a series of his tracts, dealing with most of the varieties of youthful sin and repentance in turn, in stories set in a school, a shop, offices and a college, leading up to a deathbed scene of time-honoured kind. He then tackled a series of increasingly sensational adult strays from the fold, a Roman Catholic, a formalist, a sceptic, all of whom are converted dramatically by the influence of the Bible after providential disasters have chastened them to a suitably receptive state. The last and longest story is a departure from the tract tale of sin and repentance, for it draws upon contemporary developments in the novel, and has more vigour and verisimilitude than the conventional episodes which precede it. It is the story of a working man and his wife and their search for some meaning in life, a search which has tended to lead him to the gin palace and her into a flirtation with a popular orator, though they have both tried to find help in more earnest ways, by means of all kinds of philosophies and proffered social solutions. They find, eventually, that there is 'peace in believing'.

The circumstantial detail of their lives, and the opposition Sergent presents between the god-fearing, honest and law-abiding worker and the drunken, profane, misled striker, are drawn from the social problem novels of the preceding decade; more specifically, his debt is to Charles Kingsley, and he shows something like a Christian Socialist's sympathy and degree of understanding of the working man. This story, therefore, with its detailed account of modern poverty set in a narrative framework which offers a providentially happy solution, is not the kind of social conditioning presented to children by the writers of the SPCK discussed earlier; it is nearer to the fantasy version of real life found in the domestic melodrama. Whether for this reason or because of the highly-coloured dramas of the earlier chapters, the serial was a great success, helped to establish a readership for the *Sunday at Home*, and went through many editions in volume form. An edition of the early 1860s offers evidence of the value which was placed upon it; inscriptions carefully record that it was bequeathed to a beloved daughter in 1875, who received it in 1884, and left it in turn to her dear daughter. The importance attached to it reflects the quasi-superstitious manner in which power is attributed to the Bible in the story itself.

Roland Leigh also draws freely on both the sensational events of popular fiction and the social attitudes and denunciatory descriptions of the social problem novel. Its indignant exclamation over the riverside hovels of London and the cholera and typhus-infested homes of the poor English and Irish throughout the land is unmistakably inspired by *Alton Locke* and Kingsley's other writings. Sergent also offers some of Kingsley's criticisms of the neglectful Church and the respectable classes, but since the story is set back to the beginning of the century, the critical edge is blunted; modern Sunday schools, he implies, do not alienate children by beating them, as happens to his hero. Roland is also turned away from a church as being too ragged to enter, and this scene, at least, was not felt by later writers to be merely historical; it became an emblem in many stories for the failures of contemporary Christians in their duty to the poor child. The social problem novel did not offer a narrative line which would serve Sergent's purpose — indeed, *Alton Locke* is an inadequate narrative whole from any point of view — and so he wove the lessons of Christian Socialism into a popular tale drawing strength from the underworld adventure story invented by Defoe, and the more ancient pattern of romance. Roland, who tells his own tale, like Defoe's Colonel Jack, is born of a respectable girl and an adventurer, and takes part in high dramas in thieves' strongholds in the rookeries, surviving trepanning and shipwreck. Episode by episode it is a Newgate novel to rival popular successes like *Jack Sheppard*; but overall it is the story of the quest for identity, set in the modern city streets, which was to become a staple of Reward plotting. The city arab Roland sets out alone — the independent child in the fantastic jungle of the city, a powerfully attractive figure for the child reader — and explores both the underworld inhabited by his father, a villain who suffers continually for his evil successes, and the mercenary respectability of his mother's family, which is just as inhospitable to him, before rejecting them both to make his own way to rural and domestic happiness.

The enthusiasm with which Sergent draws from popular models may have been a deliberate utilisation of material he knew rivalled the religious publications for the attention of working-class readers, or it may have been simply the result of receptivity to popular story-pattern unsuppressed by literary sophistication. However surprising the proximity of moral tales to the kind of amoral or downright corrupt material they sought to supplant may be to the student, it is undeniably an argument for supposing that they were attractive and effective to their young readers. Nor is it necessary to assume that the sensational incidents were enjoyed and the morals to which they are made to point were rejected: even contemporary observers who were broad-minded enough to attend, for instance, the performances of the popular melodrama theatres, were forced to admit that the taste for sensation included a very clear determination to uphold the right and see the evil punished.[1] The proximity of the Reward tale to the popular patterns is made very clear in one of the best-loved and most often reprinted examples which dates from this early period, *The Basket of Flowers*.

Originally *Das Blumenkörbchen* by Christopher von Schmid, a Bavarian pastor, this tale was first translated into English via a French version in 1833, by an American clergyman, Gregory Townsend Bedell. It became the archetype of the Sunday school book; Bedell thought 'it would be a very interesting little work for the libraries of Sunday Schools' and generations of publishers and purchasers agreed, or simply fell back upon the old familiar title. The first English edition which has been traced[2] was an early venture of Nelson's, in 1849, and subsequently numerous children's publishers at every level from Blackie down to the chapbook printer J. Johnson of Leeds produced an edition or new translation or version. It was cited by Robert Roberts[3] as one of the most familiar titles on the richly-gilt prize books decorating the sideboards of his youth; it is the only prize my own mother recalls from her school days. Astonishingly, it was still in print, issued by Blackie and apparently very popular in African missions, in 1972. Only deep roots in popular culture, or a deeply satisfying narrative pattern (often, of course, related qualities) can account for such success.

The story is simple. James (or in other versions Jacob) Rode is an elderly gardener and basket-maker who lives in a cottage and garden given him for his services by the Count of Eichbourg. Here be brings up his daughter Mary to love flowers and the God who created them. She becomes friendly with the Count's daughter Amelia, and on her birthday takes her a basket of flowers. When she leaves, a diamond ring is missed, and on the accusation of Juliette, a jealous lady's maid, Mary is chained, dragged off to prison, tried, whipped and condemned to exile. Father and daughter travel sorrowing through the forest, helped only by an old woodman. Eventually they are taken in by a virtuous old couple, and restored to health and activity, cultivating a garden and making baskets. The old father eventually dies a pious death, and Mary puts the basket of flowers on his grave. Then the friendly old couple hand over their farm to their son and wicked daughter-in-law, and they and Mary are persecuted by her. Mary, cast out again and again accused of theft, goes to weep on her father's grave — where she is found by Amelia, who has noticed the basket while in search of Mary to tell her that the ring has been found in a magpie's nest. Juliette is laden with chains as Mary was, and all is restored: Mary is given the cottage, the ring itself, and a set of new clothes; the old couple who befriended her are also rescued by the Count, and the wicked daughter-in-law is punished. Mary lives with the Count's family, and eventually discovers the perfidious Juliette in extremes of want; she forgives and helps her, but she dies unrepentant. Mary flourishes, restored to her garden; the basket of flowers is carved on her father's tomb.

The motif of the magpie's theft and the false accusation which results is immediately recognisable as belonging to the stock of popular story, and occurred in a melodrama, *La Pie Voleuse*, which was a success in Paris shortly before von Schmid wrote his book in 1822; it also did well on the English stage as *The Maid and the Magpie*, in 1815. In the whole tale, moreover, the romance pattern is very clear, the story little displaced in the direction of realism. It is a doubled account of a heroine's descent from Eden, the idyllic garden, to the world of pain and loss, followed by her restoration. She is accused of theft and violently handled, robbed of her identity, and then further isolated by the death of her father and a second expulsion. In each case a jealous and covetous woman, a contrast to herself, is responsible. Her true identity, her innocence, is carried through the story to be rediscovered at the end by two tokens: the ring, symbol of the dark forces that oppose her, and the basket of flowers, symbol of love and duty. By her retention of the basket through all her trials the defence of her threatened virgin innocence is figured forth.

The true romance would have no explicit dimensions beyond this. This story, however, is a 'kidnapped' one; the pattern being used to demonstrate, or at least to accommodate, Christian truths. The garden flowers are moralised in old Rode's preaching about the purity of lilies and modesty of violets. Juliette's jealousy of Mary, in terms of romance simply a part of her role as evildoer, is provoked by Amelia's gift of a dress to her friend, which would have been the maid's perquisite, and so the author can insert warnings on the love of dress. The death is an opportunity for the insertion of 'Evangelical Truth'; more structurally important, Mary's rescue by the rediscovery of the ring and the recognition of the basket is made a direct answer to prayer, and she takes Amelia for an angel when she appears before her. Stories already discussed also draw on some of these Christianising motifs: the training of Ann Ash by her master-gardener stepfather is like Mary's, and the sermons on flowers are to be found in many books; pious deaths are of course widespread. The structure and stereotypes of the romantic story itself, however, also had a strong appeal to other story-tellers, whether they derived from this model or from the pervasively and often unconsciously-present influence of the popular culture in general, in which romance is a basic pattern.

The process by which Sunday school writers came to use such patterns is not difficult to imagine. When, in response to the need to lengthen the work and shed some of the morbidity of the accounts of infant death, fictional biographies began to bypass the deathbed climax, and take their converted child heroes and heroines through other adventures, older fictional patterns reasserted themselves. The distinctive features of popular romance — the episodic story, sensational, obviously patterned by providential forces, moving through darkness to emerge into the light of rescue, identity and prosperity — were easily moulded to the purpose. Romance patterns could be made vehicles for mythic, in this case Christian, significances with little alteration; Providence could be seen to be firmly in control of the fictional universe. Within such a narrative framework, elements of graphically exotic or realistic description, high adventure, useful knowledge, social protest and fantasy both childish and adolescent may be accommodated, all with the avowed intention of exerting a healthy moral influence. Reconciling the writing of popular romance with the writers' own consciences was not necessarily troublesome either, since a degree of awareness they rarely possessed would have been necessary for them even to know that they were reproducing the patterns of dubious trash writing, which they abhorred but did not read. Most no doubt felt that they were picking stories out of the air or their own imaginations in order to embody the truths they sought to convey. Once fiction has been embraced for this purpose, romance naturally came most easily to writers who were often old-fashioned and unsophisticated in their literary tastes because they repudiated the reading of modern novels which would have developed them. Such conscious artistry as each had led to the admixture of allegorical, biographical or novelistic techniques to greater or lesser degrees; but the subconsciously composed narrative line, which the young reader would no doubt perceive as the story for which the book was read, most often came from romance.

Sunday Reading and the Nursery: Allegory and the Fairy Tale

Romance was not the only narrative mode which evangelical writers captured for their own purposes. Some, particularly those of more extensive education, cast their nets widely, making use of the tradition of Puritan literature, and of the writing for children which authors outside the confines of moral and educational camps were producing. The Puritan tradition contributed one special book, Bunyan's *The Pilgrim's Progress*, which became to writers of Reward fiction what *Robinson Crusoe* was to the boys' authors: inspiration, justification, model, and source of perpetually-recurring motifs. The strictest opponent of triviality must needs accept the inspirational value of this fiction; the more advanced and liberal broad churchman or woman could cite it as a justification for venturing to make use of fairy stories and fantasies, which were the fashionable children's reading in literary circles in the 1850s and 1860s. Such self-defence was necessary for the evangelical writer not because all fiction was suspect, for that battle was over by 1850, but because these particular kinds of story embodied the opposing tradition of writing for children. They were the material which Locke called the 'perfectly useless trumpery' which the didactic traditions had risen up to displace; the battle between the improving writers and the purveyors of the unregenerate chapbooks had been fought at the beginning of the century, but it had not been conclusive; and while the traditions of moral, utilitarian and realistic writing had been growing up, the collectors and composers of fairy tales and nonsense had been by no means idle. A steady stream of translation and publication of the wealth of folk tales from Europe and Asia had appeared, and now a burst of fantasy writing was inspired by the publication of the Alice books, in 1865 and 1872. Appreciation of Alice involved knowledge of the moralising tradition, of course, as well as a response to the fantastic: half the fun is the parody of moral tales, rhymes and children's hymns which the books contain. Retaliatory raids on the fantasists' territory were made by the opposing tradition, to the fury of many commentators.[4]

The didactic takeover of the tale of fantasy derived from fairy tales had been, indeed, substantial. Bolstered by the ever-present, justifying memory of Bunyan, the evangelical writers to whom domestic tales seemed unsatisfying, or whose chosen readership was conceived as the child still in the nursery, had produced a stream of allegorical tales, beast fables and other stories using magical transformations by moral fairies. This practice, which began with such stories as Mrs Trimmer's *Fabulous Histories* and the earlier *The Adventures of a Pincushion* by Mary Jane Kilner, had a steady following during the first half of the century, and built up to a concentration of books in the 1840s and 1850s, like Francis Edward Paget's *The Hope of the Katzekopfs* (1844), Richard Hengist Horne's *Memoirs of a London Doll* (1846), Mrs Gatty's *The Fairy Godmother* (1851), and her *Parables from Nature* (1855). Many didactic writers drew on this tradition, as well as directly on Bunyan and on the traditional tales, and from the fertile period of the 1850s and 1860s several books and writers are still remembered: Kingsley's *The Water Babies* was published in 1863 and in 1867 George Macdonald began his series of didactic fantasies for children, which are in some ways the culmination of this tradition. Their forerunner, and in some ways the most thorough-going of the evangelical allegorists, was Charlotte Tucker.

Charlotte Maria Tucker, who always published as ALOE (A Lady of

England) is not a typical evangelical lady, either in background or in the books which she produced. She was born in 1821, a middle daughter in the large family of a wealthy Indian civil servant. The family were well-connected and maintained a lavish establishment in Upper Portland Place, entertaining the best of London society. The girls had a daily governess; their father wrote plays, their brothers distinguished themselves in India, one dying heroically in his post as a judge during the Mutiny. Charlotte was a child of great physical and mental energy and many talents, inclined to be conceited and ambitious. She set out on the customary lady writer's course of producing family magazines, and in her late teens and early twenties wrote and directed her family in several full-length plays, historical dramas and farces. In 1847, her brother Robert's three children came to live in the house, and their care and teaching devolved upon her. Whether this beloved family sobered her, or she simply succumbed to the evangelicalism prevalent in the social atmosphere, some time around 1848 Charlotte underwent a quiet conversion and, like the heroine of a tract, respectfully but firmly excused herself from such of the dissipations of Society as she now felt were at odds with true profession. One imagines this meant balls lasting until after Saturday midnight, and such Sunday entertainments as oratorio, as it does in the letters of the young George Eliot — whose opportunities, however, were far less tempting in this direction than Charlotte Tucker's, who cheerfully gave away tickets for such things as concerts by Jenny Lind. How her father received this, and what part it played in keeping her single, is not recorded.[5]

The next step, for the serious woman of the period, was 'something to do'.— active benevolence. In 1851, after a struggle with her mother, Charlotte became a regular visitor at Marylebone workhouse. She went no further in her parents' lifetimes, except that after the loosening of home ties by the death of her father and the marriage of her closest sister she suddenly expressed her desire to 'add my mite to the Treasury of useful literature' and sent *The Claremont Tales* to W. and R. Chambers to publish. They were stories, she explained, 'originally composed for the young children under my own charge'. Her biographer perceives this as a deliberate decision to make a greater offering than the exchange of attending oratorio for work among the poor — the dedication of strong literary ambitions to useful purposes, glorious only in the sight of God.[6] In fact, though her plays are quite good, one doubts if she would have contemplated seeking public acclaim as a writer of farces — it was not a respectable profession for ladies. She did, however, write verse, and when Gall and Inglis brought out *The Claremont Tales* (passed on to them by Chambers, because it had been submitted without any name or return address) she showed some signs of literary ambition by eagerly sending them her poems. She had a pleasant, rather Rossetti-like gift for chiming and rhyming which she continued to exercise in her stories and in small volumes of verse. The success of *The Claremont Tales* turned her main creative energies into the field of children's stories, which were a double dedication of her gifts, useful themselves, and earning money for her other charities.

This pattern of life continued until the death of her mother and the breaking up of the family home in 1869; she then lived with her brother in the country, and found herself unequal to some of the parish work which she took on, unable to control a class of big boys in the Sunday school. Retreating temporarily to her writing, she gathered her courage for an astonishing decision: at the age of 54, she announced that she was going to India as a missionary. At her own expense, she set out to become a Zenana visitor, carrying the Christian message into the homes of Indian women. In Batala she found an enormously happy and fulfilling role for the last eighteen years of her life, learning four Indian languages and teaching both the women in the Zenanas and her beloved 'brown boys', who proved more amenable than the Berkshire Bible class. She was buried, without a coffin or a single rupee of needless expense, by her loving flock.

Charlotte Tucker is atypical in her upper-middle-class background, and in her Indian venture, which was perhaps a result of her wider horizons; but the pattern, of a talented and strongly individual girl making her stand against the role of society butterfly or child-bearing invalid offered by her position, is recognisable in many evangelical writers. In other circles writing was one of the few means of financial independence for a woman; Miss Tucker had no need of the financial rewards, but the imaginative and creative fulfilment were clearly necessary to her, and her more than usually fervent dedication to the life of evangelical witness may well present itself to us as the instinct for self-preservation of an original mind, too powerful to be repressed into wifely duty though too conditioned by its society to reject repression completely. Dedication to God was perhaps partly a higher ambition for this aspiring mind, than dedication to house-keeping.

The Claremont Tales are obviously experimental, trying out most of the existing modes of writing for children, and attempting a little of the manner that was to be her own speciality. There is little to unify the book, and she is trying to reach a wide audience: writing in the first place for her nephews and nieces, she was anxious that Gall and Inglis should publish the tales 'in a *very cheap* form, for distribution amongst poor children, Ragged Schools etc.'[7] She therefore includes both a middle-class family, the Claremonts, whose mother tells them stories in the furtherance of their moral training, and various 'peasant' Christians linked only by living in the same village as the Claremonts. The adventures of these young persons in pursuit of salvation range from rescuing a dying bully from a blazing building to standing up for right principles in a godless kitchen. The latter story, called 'Mary's First Place', would not be out of place in an SPCK tract for servants, and is hard upon such faults as entertaining guests in the kitchen, though reading novels on Sundays is almost as bad. On the whole the duties of servants are not so much stressed as service to God, and the book contains as much graveyard meditation and deathbed conversion as an old-fashioned RTS story, though it is thoroughly fictionalised, and avoids the horrifically literal description of the pains of little sufferers.

Instead of making a crude attempt to shock, such realism as the stories have is directed towards provoking the readers to identify themselves and their own failings in the stories they are told. To this end the writer repeatedly compares the behaviour of all the classes of children she introduces, often commending the behaviour of the hard-pressed peasants and condemning the idle and selfish rich. In some sections she abandons all indirection in her earnestness, and punctuates the tale with '*Reader, have you ever known this sin?*' In other stories her didactic intention is more deeply submerged: she turns her only real experience of the lives of the poor, her visits to the Marylebone workhouse, not into a direct appeal for charity but into a purely romantic tale. The story is of a poor shopkeeper who tends an orphan boy, exhausting all her savings, until his rich relations come and carry him off, without a word of thanks. The old woman spends years in the workhouse, until she is suddenly claimed as a beloved stepmother by the boy, now come into his own fortune and eager to make all right. Perhaps the author's intention here was to stress that not only the profligate poor are to be found in the workhouse, while seeking to avoid any impression of blaming the social system which put them there.

The most fruitful experiments in the book are two tales which make use of allegory, the mode by which the stories of ALOE were to be distinguished. Here she frames allegories in two ways: in the first she presents a story about a soldier defending a fortress, told by Mrs Claremont to her son to teach him Christian forgiveness; the second is a dream in which her daughter learns, by means of a magic mirror which clouds when she transgresses, of the inherent sinfulness of human nature. It was from these uses of story, which have a strong imaginative appeal and yet offer her opportunities for direct and unmistakable moralising and preaching, that Charlotte Tucker's individual style was to develop. She derived it consciously from two sources – *The Pilgrim's Progress*, and the Bible, which she regarded as the source of both the message and the method Bunyan used, but almost too sacred for her to approach directly for artistic purposes. She did in fact write several volumes of stories based on the scriptures in one way or another: *Precepts in Practice* (1858) are 'stories illustrating the Proverbs' in terms of modern children; she published a volume called simply *Tales Illustrative of the Parables*, treating Christ's teaching in the same way; at her mother's suggestion she tackled the retelling of the stories of the Pentateuch in *Exiles in Babylon* (1864), *Rescued from Egypt* (1871) and *The Triumph over Midian* (1866), but explained in the preface to *Rescued from Egypt* that 'So sacred do I feel the subject to be, that I have a repugnance to mixing anything like fiction in my work,' and accordingly she took the precaution of 'carefully isolating the sacred history from the mere tale, by giving the former in the shape of lectures'. It is to be doubted whether any of her readers have ever heeded her appeal to them 'not to pass over those portions of the volume': skipping the serious parts is seldom made so thoroughly convenient for the reader of Sunday school fiction. Miss Tucker is less tentative in her handling of *The Pilgrim's Progress*, and its pattern and episodes are so thoroughly engrained in her story-telling that they influence many stories besides those like *The Young Pilgrim* (1857), *Places Passed By Pilgrims* (1868) and *The City of Nocross* (1873), which avowedly reproduce or extend the original in modern dress. She was not, however, dependent upon her models, and could create striking allegories of her own, a skill which developed by practice.

Taking up the frameworks for allegory she had used in *The Claremont Tales* she worked out two successful patterns for books primarily intended for nursery reading. In one she tells a double story, a tale about a family, often very like the group of children who were her current responsibility and audience, and the story which their mentor tells them, which is the allegory itself. The first full-length example is *The Giant Killer; or the battle which all must fight* (1856). Here a clergyman's wife tells the story of a knight called Fides who slays a succession of giants called Untruth, Sloth, and so on, culminating in the most difficult battle, with Pride. She addresses herself to her own children, well-behaved and well-brought-up, whose giants take the form of arrogance and self-satisfaction, and two pupils of her husband, whose failings are more obvious, the result of wealth and indulgent treatment. The progress of the children depends wholly on the mother's teaching (in almost all her books Charlotte Tucker makes moral training exclusively the preserve of women); when she is absent neither his family nor even his pupils look to the clergyman for guidance, and he leaves them to fight their battles quite alone. They fall back upon the story they have been told and eventually, taking the lesson of conviction of sin and the saving grace of Christ, which is ALOE's central message, upon prayer. They are lively children, with concerns that ring true, especially the good little girl Bertha, hating the boys for messing about with her neat paintbox and wanting them flogged for hitting her brother; their scenes are largely conducted in dialogue, drawing on the author's quite polished skills as a dramatist. The allegory, too, has its vivid moments, though they are much more graphic in conception than execution. Ingenious and imaginative ideas, like the hot spring of Anger which maddens and weakens those who drink at it, and the palm tree Forgiveness, up which Fides climbs when the rabble pursue him with darts, and from which he pelts them with fruit, are diluted by being made too explicit – the darts are called 'bitter words', the fruit 'benefits' – and narrated in a language which is stilted and archaic.

The pattern is pursued in several later books, such as *Old Friends with New Faces* (1858), where, exceptionally, the teller of tales is male, the eldest brother of the family, who attempts to instruct his siblings by moral versions of old nursery stories. This is exactly the kind of perversion of well-loved stories which Dickens and others found so reprehensible; but Bluebeard as Procrastination, or 'Baron Put-off', killing as his brides a series of maidens from the town of Good Intentions, is still an exciting ogre, for the story is stronger than the bias the author gives it, and in this book she tells the tales with some zest, since their narrator is a schoolboy rather than a matron. And again the family story carries conviction, with attractive infant characters and a successfully realised affection between them.

The alternative pattern for allegory with which she experiments is that suggested by the dream of the magic mirror in *The Claremont Tales* – a story in which no narrator is present, and a fantasy is used alongside a story of domestic life with the links between made or implied by the omniscient authorial voice. The first full-length example of this is *Wings and Stings* (1855), her second book for children. Its inspiration must have been Mrs Trimmer's *History of the Robins*, since it takes an animal fable alongside the story of human children. Sipsyrup is a young bee in a hive, grumbling, when we first meet her, about being 'obliged to look after these wretched little larvae'; Polly is a little girl in a schoolroom, separated from the hive by only a patch of garden, and she is declaring that 'I hate the care of children — mother knows that I do — and I think that baby is always crying on purpose to tease me!' There are moments when the stories overlap, used, as Mrs Trimmer used them, to make points about cruelty to animals; on the whole, however, the two strands are hardly necessary to each other, and the story of the bees illustrates characters and teaches lessons both factual and moral which are not related to the human drama enacted alongside. This story of cottage life, warning against love of dress and neglect of babies put in one's charge, could perfectly well stand as a Sunday school book without the chapters of allegory; Charlotte Tucker's relentlessly metaphorical imagination would not, however, have been satisfied.

In later books she attempts to improve upon the integration of these stories. *The Story of a Needle* (1858), told by the needle in the first person, fails to find an interesting character for its narrator, but *The Rambles of a Rat* (1857) is much more successful. She puts Ratto's story into his own mouth, and avoids anything an intelligent rat could not be supposed to know about: it does not mention the name of God. She enters with imagination into rat character and pleasures, and the book is full of jokes: about pride of ancestry — he is a Norman rat — about vanity — he has a despised piebald brother called Oddity — about foreign rats, whom he visits at the zoo, including two lemmings yearning for a good cold wind in Lapland and a savage German Hamster with a horrifying habit of inflating his face — even about useful information, for which an old rat called Furry has a tiresome taste. Ratto makes friends with a rat hero called Whiskerandos, and together they roam the world, eating in kitchens from London to Russia. The source of this access of sprightly language, which frees her naturally lively imagination, may well be indicated by a clue in the human story which the rat retails to us: it concerns two street urchins, alone in the world, who sleep in Ratto's native warehouse, one of whom is caught picking a pocket, and replies to the question 'Has no one taught you to know right from wrong?' with a quotation from the writer who obviously inspired the whole character — 'Nobody never taught me nothing!' Dickens would not have cured the ills which Jo represents with a ragged school, as Charlotte Tucker does for her waif; she makes no bones, however, about the inevitability of such a child actually being a thief — he is preserved by no heavenly innocence,

he steals before he will starve, and when he is taught different
behaviour and given an opportunity to practice it he becomes an
honest man. He does not hide his past, nor is he banished to the
colonies or to heaven to atone for it. The rats, meanwhile, batten
cheerfully upon the goods of others in warehouse, kitchen and field,
explore the sewers and the ports of the world, and escape from
shipwrecks, exhorting each other to dash bravely into the waves 'like
rats!'

Successful integration of fantasy and allegory and other elements
of her stories can be seen in several books which followed these. *The
Young Pilgrim* (1857) combines close reference to *The Pilgrim's
Progress* with a romance. The modern Christian is a boy who begins his
pilgrimage as the eldest son of a drunken ex-gamekeeper, but is
discovered, after being beaten senseless by his father in the role of
Apollyon, to be the lost heir to a peerage, recognisable by the
strawberry mark of a cross upon his shoulder. This enables him to
encounter Vanity Fair in the shape of high society, and to be
accompanied by his noble brother as Faithful and his tutor Mr Ewart
as Evangelist to the point where he sacrifices his life rescuing the
gamekeeper's real son, an evil and envious lad, from a death for
which he is unprepared. He thus achieves entry into the celestial city,
converts several people by his pious death, and integrates his hidden
and his heroic identities in one compendious incident.

Other combinations with romance followed. In *The Mine, or
Darkness and Light* (1850) Charlotte Tucker used an action-packed
boy's adventure story, and in *The Light in the Robbers' Cave*
(1862) an extraordinary Gothic tale of an Etonian captured
by Italian banditti; in each the notion of light carries allegorical
connotations. For older readers she couched allegories of
the fate of the soul and the dangers of pride and intemperance in
stories of disputed inheritance and Society intrigues, such as in *The
Lost Jewel* and *Pride and His Prisoners*, both published in 1860. Much
younger children were offered the story of an ingenious family game
in *The Parliament in the Playroom* (1861), followed by an eccentric
story called *The Crown of Success*, which is a complete allegory in
which four children are left by Dame Desley their mother under the
guardianship of Learning, a gentleman who eats paper and ink, to
spend their 'time' — it is coined into copper and silver pieces —
furnishing their 'heads', represented by four thatched cottages. The
ingenuity of the details with which the story is worked out is very
pleasing, and the framework of competition between the four to win

the crown for the best-furnished head has sufficient narrative impetus to carry along the moral messages with which it is laden. The idea of playing at house and at shopping has great appeal, and there are incidental delights like the red cockatoo Parade, who screams '"Ain't I fine?"' and the pictorial carpets from the history shop which have to be nailed down with brass-headed dates for tacks.

Charlotte Tucker went on producing improving fiction in great profusion throughout the 1860s and into the 1870s, alternating allegories for infants, like the instructive stories of *Fairy Know-a-bit* (1866) and his sister *Fairy Frisket* (1871), with allegories for adults, like the story of *The City of Nocross*, where the evil doctor Smoothaway (Bunyan's Civility) poisons his clients in a room cooled by a flapping vampire and festooned with fat, spinning spiders. She also produced historical romances, hymns, a verse tragedy, boxes of scripture puzzles, regular New Year's Addresses and many other tales, getting up regularly at 6 a.m. to write before her household duties called her away. When she entered the mission field more actively in India, the children's stories became her holiday task, and her main creative effort went into Christian tracts for the conversion of the Indians, where her allegorical turn of mind was curiously appropriate to the story-telling traditions of her adopted land. Her collections of these stories, published in English under such titles as *Pomegranates from the Punjab* (1878) and *Little Bullets from Batala* (1880), were offered to the English public as an appeal for funds, rather than in their own right, and they demonstrate how completely and naturally she had succeeded in her desire to 'Orientalise' her approach. Despite their obvious Christian bias, they have more than a little about them which is suggestive of Kipling and his intimate love of India.

Assessment of Charlotte Tucker's writing have always stressed its strenuous didacticism. Both her admiring biographer, Agnes Giberne, and also Emma Marshall, perhaps because they were writing as professional children's authors of the 1890s whose main intention was to please and to sell their work, regarded the books of ALOE as old-fashioned and too inclined to preach. Miss Tucker sought to please only in order to instruct — any payment for her work that she accepted was applied to charitable uses. It is undoubtedly true that a strenuous seriousness of intention runs through all her writing, and is often presented in direct and earnest addresses to the reader. Her characters do discuss and brood upon their moral state; her fairies do give detailed explanations of the production of cocoa-beans and the classification of butterflies. I am not convinced, however, that children of the 1860s and even of other periods have not been interested in these things.

Nor is it true to say, as one modern critic has suggested, that the author was wrapped in a 'strange ignorance of the harsh facts of Victorian life', so that 'the roses twine around most of the porches of the poor in her books'.[8] Drunkenness, brutality, wife and child abuse, starvation, rapacious landladies, fevers, harsh employers, swindling and jeering fellow-servants are regular features in many of her stories, though they are of course unswervingly attributed to personal sin rather than a faulty social system. It is also the case that her lovable children, her convincing girl characters and her most realistically-conceived stories are set in middle-class nurseries rather than in cottages, though often the respectable family concerned is struggling with poverty. This is as much as to say that when attempting realism she wrote best from personal experience. Her publishers, especially Thomas Nelson, obviously concurred in her own desire to reach a wide audience, since many of her books were published as packets of penny stories as well as in volume form. Their very availability at a cheap rate no doubt ensured their sale to poor schools and to philanthropic visitors of the poor; whether the gifts were read remains imponderable. It is true to say, however, that the allegorical dimension of the tales and also their frequent recourse to the patterns of romance do extend them beyond the stifling confines of the nursery, offering fantasy and some sort of imaginative richness to an audience used to much drabber fare.

The other evangelical moralists for the young who used allegory were most often men,[9] who were bringing the resources of a wider education and outlook rather exceptionally to bear upon writing for children. The allegories they produced were notable individual contributions to the stream of educative fiction, often famous in their own time and sometimes still remembered, but they were not widely imitated so as to form the basis of a story-telling convention; presumably the difficulties of such writing outweighed the usefulness of the strong lead they gave, for lesser writers in search of a form. The most outstanding example is probably Charles Kingsley's *The Water Babies*, published in 1863 and still too well-known to need to be described. It is worth noticing in this context, however, that in his own contentious and discursive fashion Kingsley is using allegory for exactly the same purpose as Charlotte Tucker. In the course of Tom's adventures the reader is bombarded with miscellaneous information (much of it left out in modern editions), and the outcome of his story is governed by the learning of moral lessons. Kingsley only used allegory on a few occasions, but George Macdonald, who was a most unorthodox congregational minister, had a strong tendency to allegory. It emerged first in fantasies for adult readers which are still reverenced by devotees of such writing, but which interacted with his role as preacher to produce a series of moral fairy tales, beginning with *Dealings with the Fairies* (1867), which might be regarded as children's books. They avoid overt didacticism more or less completely, and their moral dimension, although it is pervasive, is always embodied in traditional motifs and methods of narration; he falls into none of the rhetorical and aggressively informative poses Kingsley allows himself. Indeed the subtlety of his approach makes the tales very sophisticated reading for children, and probably prevented their widespread distribution beyond educated and literary circles; they did not go to the religious publishers.

This limitation did not perhaps apply to *At the Back of the North Wind* (1870), which remains one of the most famous children's books of the period. Its structural model is the popular deathbed tract, and little Diamond's earthly life as the son of a London cabby is vividly realised, despite its grafting upon the curious allegory of the North Wind. Macdonald transforms the usual translation of the dying innocent to a better world into an account of the child's own experience of the process and meaning of death, in symbolic terms. Diamond takes a series of trips with the North Wind, who is death, realised as a cold, awesome but loving preceptress who lifts him out of the commonplace world on to a different plane. He is spiritually educated and guided by this experience, which is presumably a figure for his illness, until he is ready for permanent translation to the land 'at the lady's back'. Both parts of his existence, his homely life and his ultimately more satisfactory death, are vividly realised. But Macdonald, like Kingsley, was an exceptional man of vision and peculiar intensity, and few others were able so to bring their imaginary worlds to life. Dean Farrar, for example, who was a romanticist of some power, produced a leaden book of *Allegories* (1898); and there is a thin stream of books attempting to teach through fantasy which went on for the rest of the century without producing anything outstanding.[10] Some writers for the upper-class nursery and schoolroom made successful use of sparing amounts of fantasy in some of their stories: Mrs Molesworth and Mrs Ewing both did so; but few were able to move from such delicate effects as they sought to stories with sufficient imaginative and moral power to appeal to a wider audience; the results of such attempts were usually very heavy-footed.

The Romance of the Slums: Hesba Stretton and the Discovery of the Perfect Form

The allegorists wrote some powerful tales, but they were not the founders of the school of writing which was to dominate the Reward market; that honour fell to a printer's daughter from Shropshire, who created, in the books of 'Hesba Stretton', a pattern simple and strong enough to fire the imagination of generations of well-meaning writers and soft-hearted children, and to support a great weight of imitation. As these imitations stiffened into convention the earnest, and indeed passionately angry, concern with which she had invested them died away into less worthy feeling and mere sentimentality; but even then the appeal of the story and the motifs she invented had a kind of lingering power.

Sara Smith, who wrote as 'Hesba Stretton', was perhaps the typical lady Sunday school writer. Brought up in a dissenting household that also valued books and learning, she found herself approaching thirty, unmarried, and with diminishing financial prospects as her father neared retirement in the early 1860s. She took to writing magazine stories to improve her status and the family budget, and was well paid, especially by Dickens (as editor of *All The Year Round*) for some very ordinary pieces of romantic fiction and the occasional much more lively transcription of personal and childhood reminiscences. In 1863 family circumstances reached crisis; her closest sister, Lizzie, went out as a governess, and then became a daily governess in Manchester. This meant she had to live independently or in the grim Governesses' Institution. To avoid that fate, Sara went to live with her in lodgings. Her first children's story, *Fern's Hollow* (1864) was written under this immediate pressure, and earned her thirty guineas from the RTS, where she had a cousin, Samuel Manning. Henceforth her books for children, each written in only two or three months, earned her the steady income which supported her in increasing comfort. She aspired to be a novelist, encouraged by the fact that her first published adult fiction, *The Clives of Burcot* (1867), was favourably compared by reviews to *Jane Eyre* and *Felix Holt*; but it was as the author of *Jessica's First Prayer*, in 1867, that she became nationally and even internationally famous.

Before this book, the formula upon which the rest were to be compounded, she tried out four possible mixtures. The early books all show the quality which made the RTS committee exclaim 'Each character delineated is life-like, and the whole is well-written, far above the usual average of such works.' They owe something to Dickens's training of his young journalists, and more to a sharp and observant interest in people and their social life. Her own social position was not clear-cut, and her world was not divided, in any case, into gentry and servants and a remote class of 'peasants', as Charlotte Tucker's was. She wrote of the mobile, intimate social relations of the West Midland industrial districts, where coalmining, shepherding, potteries and small industrial-cum-market towns made a rich and volatile social mixture.

Fern's Hollow presents this situation in the story of a boy, Stephen Fern, who lives in a squatter's hut in a picturesque hollow of the Shropshire hills, but works in a coalpit to support his two sisters, his dying father, and his senile grandfather who is a convict returned from transportation. The setting, described with graphic detail which is much more particular and specific than the literary or Blue Book borrowings of previous authors, is a description of Sara Smith's adolescent home, her Uncle James's colliery and village at Leebotswood near Church Stretton. There is a character, the saintly Miss Anne, who sets up an al fresco Sunday school for Stephen and his mates, whose long-sufferance in the house of her miserly and cruel uncle seems a fantasy upon the author's own youthful aspirations to virtue. So far she was attempting a relatively untried method of writing a book for children, giving an account of the settings and experiences of her own youth. The transcription of social detail is meticulous, and is not dictated by any doctrinaire or socially manipulative intention. It is given shape by an idea which is not unlike Charlotte Tucker's allegorical frameworks: Stephen's story of suffering for his faith and forgiving his persecutors is a modern domesticated version of the martyrdom of his Biblical namesake. The story is thus given a religious dimension in a way which both lends a dignity and importance to the individual child, and offers access to the Bible story for the young Victorian reader.

The success of the first story in financial terms moved her to embark immediately upon another, *Enoch Roden's Training* (1865). The RTS paid thirty-five guineas for it, over which she rejoiced as 'capital pay'; it 'quite stunned' her elder sister.[11] The book shows signs of her haste, repeating the devices which shaped *Fern's Hollow*. The settings, the back alleys of Shrewsbury and a printer's office where business is failing through the neglect of a too-unwordly father, are again taken from her own experience and observation. They are sharply realised, with touches like the use of the Shropshire name Roden to authenticate them. A Biblical name, Enoch, is again used to shape modern events to a mythic pattern, and the boy is an initiate, dedicated to walk with God: that is, he wants to be a missionary, and the book is the story of his struggle to discipline his life to that end. The printer's eldest daughter, who becomes a governess and is soured by the effort to support herself and her sister because their father has failed to provide for them, may well be another, less idealised version of the writer herself.

The only new element of the book is a strongly romantic story upon which she falls back because no narrative line is in this case provided by the Biblical parallel. Enoch has a scapegrace brother, Titus (the name indicates one converted from pollution), who runs away to sea and who is responsible, together with a piece of plate providentially sent from Shrewsbury to Melbourne as a wedding gift, for the discovery of a previously unheard-of rich uncle, who returns to England and rescues all. This piece of mechanism sits rather uncomfortably with the serious examination of Enoch's character, and his struggle to accept the faith which the women in the book all achieve so simply. This growth and attainment of maturity is the serious business of the book.

The next attempt was a return to the more direct transcription of the writer's own family affairs: *The Children of Cloverley* (1865) concerns the characters of *Fern's Hollow* and a new generation, their children. Miss Anne has not only grown up, but grown worldly, married to an artist, and wrapped up in the possession of her uncle's wealth and her own household affairs; her children Dora and Gilbert are in consequence snobbish and selfish. The names and occupations, if not the personalities, are those of Sara Smith's only married sister and her family, who inherited from Uncle James. Stephen Fern is now a methodist patriarch, far more of a support and strength to the colliery village than are the gentry who own it; when Canadian cousins come to Anne's house — they are drawn from Sara's brother Benjamin's family — they are happiest when allowed to live at Fern's Hollow and work energetically in house and farmyard. Once again the setting is drawn in loving detail, though without the nostalgia which made the earlier version more picturesque.

The community suffers because the coal seam has run out, and the men are obliged to tramp for work, while Anne and her children are reduced to misery, and actual deprivation, as their reliance upon worldly success is shown to have been a snare. The Canadian children

are the saviours: first Ben attracts the attention of a rich old lady by
his wildness, and then his sister Annie softens her heart towards her
neighbours, and so she finances a new shaft. To effect the more
important rescue, that of Dora and Gilbert from jealousy and sin, Annie
is given a protracted pious death, ending as the life-giving coal seam is
discovered. The oldest model of Sunday school fiction is thus blended
with the graphic transcription of circumstantial reality from the author's
own experience, as it was in a different way in the original accounts
of dying children, which were designed to impress as true stories. This
book is a fully fictional, and therefore a simply and satisfyingly shaped
version of that kind of story-telling.[12]

In *The Fishers of Derby Haven* (1866), the last of the experimental
books which preceded *Jessica's First Prayer*, Sara Smith repeated the
use of circumstantial detail taken from life, and a plot derived from a
Biblical namesake. Peter is a fisher boy who, under the pressure of the
fear of a harsh master and mockery from evil associates, denies his Lord
three times. The Manx community described is one she knew only from
brief holiday visits, however, and she peoples the story with largely
conventionally-conceived types. Only Peter himself is drawn with vigour,
and as in all these stories the boy's spiritual and emotional problems
are treated with the utmost seriousness. He is an individual struggling
to understand and find his place in the world. The book is the least
impressive of the four, however, partly because he is too articulate
about his search for Christianity, and partly because the intensely
romantic dénouement, in which Peter travels the world with a saintly
sea captain, is shipwrecked to convert some coral islanders, and finally
inherits the captain's position as leader of the fishing community, is at
odds with the psychological realism of the earlier handling of
character. It is the same difficulty as in *Enoch Roden's Training*, but
on a more destructive scale.

The RTS, however, had no misgivings about the tale; they accepted
it with alacrity on the strength of the author's previous sales record,
the readers giving it such a perfunctory perusal that they reported it
as set in Devonshire before hastening on to the fact that 'It is likely to
be an attractive volume to sell at 2/-'.[13] It was published in December
1866. All four books draw from deeper levels of personal experience
than is usual in tract writing, presented with a graphic realism stiffened
by structural reliance upon parable and Bible story. They give a new
immediacy to the RTS story of conversion, with settings and characters
which bring it nearer than ever before to the apprehension of the
childish or adolescent reader.

In 1866 Sara and her sister Lizzie went to live in Northern France, where Lizzie had taken a schoolteaching post. Sara, who saw herself as a novelist, was most concerned about the publication of her first novel, *The Clives of Burcot*, at this time, and did not mention in her diary the delivery of the manuscript of her fifth children's story to the RTS offices. The editors thought it good enough to promote her to serialisation, and *Jessica's First Prayer* appeared in *Sunday at Home* in that year.

It caused something of a sensation. Lord Shaftesbury wrote to the RTS in praise of it, and 'numerous and urgent' other letters demanded its appearance in book form. The little, nearly square, plain blue volume was the first of a long series of editions, which proliferated into penny pamphlets, services of song (a kind of juvenile oratorio favoured by ambitious Sunday school teachers), lantern slides, and even a film, made in 1906. It was also the foundation of a school of writing, the Sunday school story of the street arab, the homeless waif, the pathetic and ill-treated child found in settings of poverty and vice which grew ever more picturesque, and rescued by crusading clergymen or benevolent ladies, to be translated either from a hospital bed to a home in the skies, or via the Liverpool emigrant packet to a Canadian Eden. The genre's appeal is through pathos, and the frisson of a sort of literary slumming. Many readers have testified to its effectiveness in touching the hearts of children better fed and clothed, but also better guarded and controlled, than the picturesque urchins of the fabulous London streets.[14]

It is possible even at this remove to see what is so remarkable about *Jessica's First Prayer*. It was a breakthrough for the author in her conception of writing for children. Previously she had put her best efforts into making her books vivid, and her characters interesting, but often by means of a prose little adapted from her adult-fiction style. The story-patterns were more emblematic, but hardly less complicated, than those of her novels and magazine stories. In *Jessica's First Prayer*, these basic matters are changed. The prose, though it uses a length of sentence which would place it at the very top end of most modern scales of reading difficulty, is much simpler and more straightforward than before; vocabulary is simple, action and dialogue predominates over description. It is very brief; the reader need not be more than barely literate to achieve the reward of understanding the story. The author's serious interest in the central child character, previously a matter of exploring adolescent spiritual sensitivity, is not laid aside, but expressed in narrative terms with little explicit analysis, its complexities implied or understood through action. Personal feeling is not here poured into the loving description of events idealised from personal experience, but is passed through a much more complete transformation. During her stay in Manchester, Sara had felt herself on the brink of social extinction, living in squalid lodgings, with no settled income, and cut off from the protection of her home community. The sisters had regularly attended a chapel for over a year before anyone there condescended to speak to them. All this insecurity is behind the sympathy with which she presents the little outcast Jessica, daughter of a drunken actress, who has grown too ugly even to be a pantomine fairy.

The child is seen in relation to Standing, a professed Christian who is caretaker of a fashionable chapel, where he has only learnt to care for the outward display of religion and respectability. Jessica's precarious innocence and her pathos, of which she remains unconscious herself, are the means by which he is converted. The reader sees the significance of Jessica through Standing, and is spared a display of childish religiosity; it is also made clear in their relationship that the child receiving charity confers benefits far greater than the merely material help she is given. These didactic purposes are served by the story, not added as exhortations to the reader. Even the minister of the chapel, who oversees both conversions, is not allowed to preach to us, and speaks simply, aware of his own shortcomings and appreciative of the child's worth. This is, in fact, one of the first books in which one can imagine the Sunday school reader fully understanding and accepting the moral notions the author has to convey and, moreover, not feeling threatened or diminished by those notions.

In literary terms, the effect is of a sudden clarity and simplicity in the conception and execution of the story; it is a matter, however, of art concealing art, for it is a skilfully constructed narrative whose strength lies in its apparent simplicity. It is not, of course, all newly invented: Sara Smith owes much to her master Dickens in this and in subsequent pictures of street children. Even some specific scenes are not new; that in which the ragged child is turned away from the chapel to which it has been attracted by the music had been used, for example, by Sergent in *Roland Leigh*. But she has achieved the transformation of the available materials, both in terms of current social problems and specific motifs in which they are embodied, into a pattern which was to become archetypal.

The next book, *Pilgrim Street*, was written before the great success of *Jessica*, but she is already repeating the effective patterns. The influence of Dickens is even more evident, both in the vivid opening sequence, in which the Manchester assizes are seen through the eyes of a young and ignorant child, and in the character of Nat Pendelbury the poor bill-sticker, who closely resembles Trotty Veck. She repeats the criticism of self-righteous Christians, this time in the figure of an authoritarian policeman whose vengeful creation of God in his own image brings disaster upon the street-boy he has reluctantly agreed to help. The committee of the RTS thought that this book would 'prove of great service to policemen', and so were prepared to sell it in bulk, at half-price, to anyone who would then give it away to individual constables.[15] The reception they, and their tract about being kind to vagrants, must have invited can only be imagined. The policeman in the story is specifically criticised, but he does at least see the light, and understands his mistake; the father of the boys, who is released from jail in the middle of the story, is presented as a figure of evil, stealing from his children both their material and spiritual gains. Sara Smith repeatedly presents God the father as a substitute for fathers on earth, to be understood as an alternative rather than by analogy. There is no suggestion that the readers should be taught to regard their parents as infallible, or even that it is their duty to obey them, if they are in the wrong.

In *Jessica's Mother*, which is obviously written as a sequel because the first book was so successful, the gin-sodden old actress is presented as disgusting, soiling Standing's neat little house and degrading Jessica by her presence. She is the trial of the new-found Christianity of both adult and child. Jessica goes to her unflinchingly, not out of duty, but from instinctive love, repeating 'She's my mother' as an excuse, pleading for her even after she discovers that she is not to be converted by telling her about Christ. Standing, repelled like the reader by the old woman, makes a more conscious act of charity towards her, and in a highly-coloured scene in the London fog dies trying to save her from drunken suicide. As usual when she writes in a hurry, Sara Smith falls back upon a very sensational story; but the book's unflinching presentation of the mother, and its open attack upon evangelical high society, in the shape of the minister who is struck dumb by a stroke as he gives one of his famous sermons, make it a remarkable production.

The next children's book was *Little Meg's Children*, which completes the pattern of the waif romance, supplying motifs and characters for which there was no room in *Jessica's First Prayer*, and confirming the elements already present. It begins, in a manner which was to become classic, with a description of a slum, which has a name suggestive of its antithesis, in this case Angel Court. In a garret a family of children,

Meg the eldest aged beyond her years by the unnatural life of care and responsibility, watch beside their dying mother. Their sailor father survives at a distance, and will be part of the dénouement of the tale. The death of the mother occasions pathetic childish reflections on Heaven, and sets up the talisman which is to control the events of the story — they promise her that they will preserve forty sovereigns she has in keeping for a friend of their father's. Meg's fierce protection of the other children and the gold (suggestive once again of Dickens, for she is very like Charley Neckett in *Bleak House*) is set against the story of their neighbour in the next-door garret, Kitty, who has disobeyed her mother in the past, and is now a drunken young prostitute. Eventually, after much graphic detail about pawnshops and touching childish faith, the father returns with the news that they could have spent the gold, since it is really his, and Kitty's mother, Mrs Blossom, a Dickensian obsessive who has spent the last decade gazing out of a shop window waiting for Kitty to pass by, is also discovered. Meg has been protected through her ordeal by faithfulness to her promise, and by the memory of a chance-heard text about God seeing all his children; Kitty is redeemed by her contact with Meg's innocence and faith. They are all shipped off to a new life in Canada, except for the baby, who has died of starvation and of being given gin or opium by a friend of Kitty's to keep it quiet. As Nancy Cutt has pointed out,[16] even this rather lachrymose tale has two great strengths: it is far more willing to face and name ugliness and vice than most writing about the slums, even for adults — it is more obvious, for example, what Kitty's profession (and Meg's threatened fate) is, than is the case with Nancy in *Oliver Twist*; and on the other hand it is a perfect romance story of the heroine's quest, trial and reward, her innocence shining forth like a jewel from the city jungle.

Until the success of *Jessica*, Sara Smith had been happy with her treatment by the RTS. They had accepted her work, paid her well for her copyrights, and only once, in the case of *Pilgrim Street*, asked for alterations, to strengthen the religious message. It is not clear what was paid for *Jessica*; but they probably purchased it outright for less than £50. In 1867 they paid the author an extra £5, and £10 in 1868, either *ex gratia* or because they were extending the use of the book, for slides, or perhaps foreign language versions. *Little Meg's Children*, however, was a different matter. Miss Smith knew it to be a very valuable property indeed. When she sent it in in April 1868 the readers reported to the committee that they too thought so, and said it 'is thought even to exceed *Jessica's First Prayer* in pathos and power'. They wanted an addition to its religious teaching, however, and they wanted it cheap. They offered £50 for copyright. Sara rejected this with some asperity, noting that 'they are quite aggrieved that I do not accept it gratefully', and promptly took her MS to Nisbet's, who were delighted. The next day Dr David of the RTS offered her very different terms, a royalty of £25 for the first 1,000 copies and £10 per 1,000 thereafter. 'Utterly amazed', she retrieved the MS from the disappointed editors at Nisbet's, who pleaded for another book to be written for them, and delivered it to the Row. Four days later the society said the offer had been a mistake, and all they could do was £5 per 1,000. 'Excessively indignant', she wrote to Houlston and Wright. Sight unseen, they offered only 4 guineas per 1,000, but the second threat to withdraw gingered up the society's offer to £6 5s. Sara noted with some disappointment, 'I suppose we must take it'.

This was not the end of their sharp practice: in July 1869, W. Tarn, in charge of payments, reported to the author a sales figure a little over one-third of the real number. Seventeen years later his 'stupidity or malice' was still active against her, when he took to sending royalty cheques to her at an old address. By then, however, she was a comparatively wealthy woman. *Little Meg* sold over 10,000 in its first few weeks, and 14,000 in the first six months of 1969; in February she bought her first £200 worth of consols. Her income from royalties and investments was sufficient to keep her without the actual need to write at all during the 1880s, and she and her sister travelled extensively in Europe, often for several months at a time. The instincts of her uncle – the money-making coalowner – were not dead in the fervent author; indeed, if one may judge from characters in her books, the sin of which she was most painfully aware was that of covetousness and devotion to the acquisition of money.[17]

With *Little Meg* a period of success and widening activity began. In the first weeks of 1869 she wrote another waif story, *Alone in London*, which appeared in *Sunday at Home* in August and September. It adds another variation to the pattern, the figure of an old man whose last days are brightened by a little child. *Silas Marner* had been published in 1861; but *The Lamplighter*, with Trueman Flint and Little Gerty, had been in the Sunday school mythology since 1854 (see Ch. 5). More important is the relationship between the small child and the street-boy Tom, whose love for her leads to his redemption: after her death, he escapes, and the old man returns to Shropshire, a more personal Eden for the author than Canada could represent. There is something of the directness and seriousness with which she habitually approached her Sunday school readers in the figure of Tom, and the strength and independence of his affection for the helpless old man and child; the death of the little girl, however, is turned into an appeal for support for the London children's hospitals, and thus betrays the fact that wealthier readers were at least part of her envisaged audience. The appeal, apart from one footnote confirming a particularly horrific fact about child poverty, is dramatically contained within the story; but the danger of perceiving the characters as object lessons is barely avoided.

The blurring of focus is partly, perhaps, caused by the fact that the author still aspired to writing for a wider audience, and for adults. She had her way in her next publication, which she regarded as her third novel. It was called *David Lloyd's Last Will*, and was serialised not in *Sunday at Home*, but the more literary, general RTS periodical, *The Leisure Hour*, from January to June 1869. Again she fell out with the RTS editors, who surpressed parts of the text, to her vexation, because Dr Macaulay thought the character of Lloyd (another of her grasping misers) caricatured religion. She negotiated a separate volume publication with a Mr Tubbs of Manchester. In 1870 she contributed a story called *A Miserable Christmas and a Happy New Year* to the Christmas supplement of *The Leisure Hour*, and in 1871 her tale *Max Krömer*, intended 'for all readers especially the young', appeared from February to April. The RTS demanded alterations to this story, and in May 1871 she recorded what she hoped was a final 'disturbance' with them. One more story actually went to the RTS, again with additions they demanded: *Bede's Charity* appeared in *Sunday at Home* from January to April 1872. After this point, relationships between the author and the society decisively broke down. She wanted to write novels for adults, they wanted to publish children's stories. They altered her material to suit their needs; she presumed on her value to them to ask them to publish the material that she preferred.

Max Krömer and *Bede's Charity* were both interesting experiments in romance writing, vivid with observed detail and full of interesting manifestations of old character and story-patterns; but they were not simple, strong didactic tales, ammunition for the Sunday school worker. She was in fact producing such propaganda material, but selling it elsewhere: in 1870 she had sold two hack-work temperance stories, *A Sin and a Shame* and *Nelly's Dark Days*, to the Scottish Temperance League, and had a dispute with them, in turn, because she had arranged simultaneous publication in the USA. In 1871 she was strengthened in her battles with the RTS by her first remittances from the New York publishers Dodd and Mead. The RTS was perhaps too big, in the end, for her to manipulate as she wished; her next move was to withdraw from them completely for some years, and become instead a star turn, the most respected and cherished contributor, for a small commercial publisher, Henry S. King. Her story 'Michel Lorio's Cross', her own favourite work, appeared in the introductory Christmas issue of King's new magazine *The Day of Rest* in 1872.

Henry S. King had been trading since the late 1860s from offices in Cornhill and White Lion Court, specialising in wholesale stationery and publications for business purposes. The firm had a strong connection with Indian trade, extending from publication of the Overland Mail for India and the Homeward Mail, to acting as East India army and colonial agents and bankers. It was only in 1872, with the setting up of *The Day of Rest*, that they moved into the expanding empire of religious publishing at home. The magazine, edited by Alexander Strahan, carried the usual statement of its intention to provide 'Sunday Reading' for the poor which would compete with the evil publications currently available to them. It survived rather longer than its publishers; Henry S. King disappeared from the trade directories in 1878, while the magazine was taken over by Strahan and Co. Ltd and produced a new series, in 1879-81, and the beginning of a third series, transformed by colour printing and a new, genteel format, in 1882. After that apparently unsuccessful experiment it merged with Strahan and Co.'s successful *Sunday Magazine*, established since 1865. Hesba Stretton never confined her work wholly to one publisher again (though the RTS bought up all the copyrights they could after her retirement), but the bulk of her stories for children as well as some of her adult novels and incidental journalism appeared in these King and Strahan periodicals after 1872.

The children's stories largely repeat the patterns, motifs and messages of her work since *Jessica*, though they also often display a fertility of invention and graphic, even sometimes comic, detail in setting and character. Situations in which prematurely independent children care for helpless old men or toddlers, first tried out in *Fern's Hollow* and polished to their maximum pathetic and didactic effect in *Little Meg's Children* and *Alone in London*, recur in several books; parents are still absent, inadequate, or actively evil. In *A Thorny Path* (1879) a destitute mother gives up in despair, and deserts her old blind father and her little girl in Kensington Gardens; in *Lost Gip* (1873) a boy tries to save successive baby brothers and sisters from his drunken mother's fatal attentions, and, having raised one of them past infancy at last, runs away when his mother contrives to lose the child in a gin palace. He is taken in by a woman who already has to support a crippled dying son and a husband who has delusions of grandeur because he had respectable ancestors, and so will not work. These various situations are of course the occasion for much moralising, but also for protest and indignation on the part of the author; they are not always treated sentimentally, and there is no attempt to represent the social conditions which give rise to them as ideal or wisely ordained.

In, for example, *Cassy* (1874), the life of the wandering people who spend the summers encamped in Epping Forest and the winters in East End workhouses is described. It is wretched and uncomfortable in the tent where Cassy is beaten by her father and stepmother, but it is idyllic in the caravan of the misanthropic dwarf Simon, who lives there to avoid taunts at his misshapen body. The winter in the workhouse is gloomy, and escape to the forest welcome; Cassy has learnt some 'good words' in the Union, but her garbled version of the Lord's Prayer — with a clear, obviously better-taught petition to 'keep my hands from pickin' and stealin'' ironically inserted — is mere magic. Forced to seek a 'little place' — a job as a maid of all work — in the city, Cassy is rejected and moved on until she fetches up in the bizarre household of Mr Tilly, who keeps, or fails to keep, a Celebrated Shaving Saloon. Cassy's is not an easy job:

> Now and then he condescended to make her a butt for his rough jokes, and very often he vented his drunken fury on her in preference to his wife, who sometimes proved stronger than himself; but Cassy did not resent either. All her life long she had known that was the way with men, and that women and girls like herself existed only to submit to their jokes and fury. It was so simple, and so self-evident, that it was not at all a mystery to her.

She also tends a monstrous child called Alfred Fitzgerald Tilly, and Mr Tilly's bedridden father, who loves *The Pilgrim's Progress*, but since he is senile cannot convey a very clear impression of it to the little girl who sleeps in his room and calms his nightmares. Mrs Tilly, her mistress, ignores these harsh realities and lives in a fantasy world, bullying Cassy like a grand lady. Her husband leaves, money runs out, and finally the old man dies; Mrs Tilly stays in bed reading romantic novels while Cassy attempts to keep the remains of the family alive. Finally the confused and 'shallow' mind of her mistress conceives a way out — she too flees, and Cassy is left to deal with the saloon and the corpse. Mr Simon, her forest friend, rescues her, and buys her from her father for 10s. One can hardly conceive of a picture of a young girl in service less like those drawn by Mrs Adams and company of the SPCK, nor a poor girl less likely to grow up to know her place than Cassy. In fact she does not grow up, but dies a long-drawn-out death, very fruitful of conversions, including her own and Simon's, in the caravan amidst the forest glades. One might see the tale as a fricasseed version of *The Old Curiosity Shop*; Cassy, however, despite her eventual death, and details such as an unexplained Lancashire accent, is more vividly childlike, more robust, and much more entertaining than Little Nell.

Sara Smith's attitudes to her characters and the messages she uses them to convey are clearly conditioned by her own social position, coming of working stock and an industrial society, as much as by her religious convictions. She is not, of course, free of many of the assumptions of her tract-writing predecessors which seem to us strangely short-sighted: her children, for example, are naturally expected to work for a living from a very young age. She is not, however, bound by divisive class attitudes to that work; for her not only are children fully human and responsible, but servants are people, autonomous individuals. Religious conviction of the importance of each human soul is reinforced by direct experience of and sympathy with the kinds of life she portrays. Conviction of universal sinfulness and the existence of evil seems to have been more truly levelling, for her, than for any writer for children at least since Mrs Sherwood; all sorts of people in her books may be evil, and human institutions are as fallible as their creators and operators. Not only are most free hospitals too small, which is a mere defect in the money supply, but some employers are brutal, some policemen harsh, some magistrates unjust because of prejudice and overwork, and some institutions, notably the workhouses and prison system, are cruel, unjust, and the cause of many of the evils they are supposed to suppress. Living with an atheist dwarf in a caravan is not necessarily morally disastrous, while being jailed for begging, on false police evidence of a previous conviction, at the age of 13, is.

The seriousness, and the sheer anger, with which Sara Smith wrote about the conditions of the poor child increased as her familiarity with London life grew. She became very tired of London evangelical circles, and contemptuous of much of their parade of piety; RTS editors who took their children to see pantomines in which child actors were cruelly driven and exploited, infuriated her. By the early

1880s her active involvement in philanthropic work for children dominated her writing: in 1884 she helped Baroness Burdett-Coutts and others to found the London Society for the Prevention of Cruelty to Children (LSPCC). From that point, cruelty to children, rather than their neglect, lack of education or abandonment to solitary lives in the jungle of the city, seemed to her the most important abuse, and it prompted a series of articles and stories which have a new tone of anger, and in which the graphic detail, previously often picturesque, has a quite unprecedented grimness. The intention to reach Sunday school children by a description of lives which romanticised their own gives way, in these works, to a concentration on evoking horror, with the avowed purpose of supporting her society's campaign to suppress cruelty, but an obvious further dimension in expressing, and perhaps trying to exorcise, her own feelings about the suffering she had seen.

After writing to *The Times* and attending meetings to get the LSPCC set up, she made her contribution as a committeewoman and by appeals in the periodicals describing the work of the society and some of the spine-chilling cases that made it necessary. Others were also writing accounts of their observations and their work amongst poor children, and making appeals for help. Dr Barnado, for example, wrote an account of his work in *Children Reclaimed for Life* (1875), to which Sara Smith wrote a foreword. Lord Shaftesbury had of course repeatedly raised the matter in the House of Commons, and some legislation had been pushed through to deal with specific problems untouched by the education acts that still troubled philanthropists, like the 1877 Canal Boats Act, providing for boat children's schooling, the 1879 Children's Dangerous Performances Act, and the various laws about begging. These first steps in legislation were not, of course, anything like an adequate answer to many complex problems which are still unresolved; the emotive issue of parental rights and reluctance to interfere in families, however, was one in particular in which popular writers and journalists pleading the cause of unnaturally treated children could hope to have an effect. George Smith, 'The Boatman's Friend', with *Our Canal Population* (1875); Mr Weyland, describing his observations as a visitor in East End homes in *The Man With the Book*; and E. Barlee, pleading for the children she had sought out in *Pantomine Waifs* (1884), were some of the many philanthropic journalists of this sort. Their work was used as the basis of fiction by many of Hesba Stretton's imitators and descendants; few of these, however, combined her personal knowledge, her journalist's eye for graphic details, with her sense of effective story-telling; nor had they all the burning earnestness, springing from imaginative sympathy with the children she describes, which renders her use of horrific detail artistically and morally acceptable.

Hesba Stretton's choice of the areas of child abuse on which to concentrate illustrates her seriousness of intention, and her avoidance of the cheap exploitation of romantic and sensational material. Most writers picked on picturesque areas such as the theatrical children as most suitable for fiction. Here horrific details of cruelty in their training, gleaned from published sources, could be used to give an effective contrast with their apparent glamour, which could be covertly enjoyed and then turned into a moral lesson. Children on the stage, or employed on canals or in hop-gardens, were also firmly located in a world separate from that of the nursery reader, and conscience about them could be assuaged by a relatively easy act of philanthropy. Picturesque pathos and self-righteous thrills of horror were not, however, the emotions Hesba Stretton sought to evoke; she wrote one short story about the theatre, 'An Acrobat's Girlhood' (1889), in which the physical horror of acrobatic training is doubly distanced, presented by the child's sister from her own letters home. The stressed emotions are the sister's sense of loss, and her fear and impotent unhappiness about the evil her father has done in letting plausibly rich foreigners carry the girl off. Hesba Stretton's longer efforts are focused upon the much less pleasant, quite unpicturesque problem of begging by means of children, and the ineffectual and indeed unjustly applied laws designed to prevent it. Here the guilt attaches to just the uninvolved, sentimental acts of philanthropy, costing the giver little, that less responsible books encourage; the only answers involve radical reassessment of assumptions about the law and social relationships.

In 1879 she published *In Prison and Out*, in the *Sunday Magazine*. It is the story of two contrasted boys; David, the bright, promising son of a poor widow unable to support her family by taking in washing who lives on 4s 8d a week from the parish, until she gets cancer, and Roger, the weak and cowardly son of a professional thief. David is taken up for begging to feed himself and his family, when no one will employ him, and sent to jail. Thereafter his record ensures that he keeps going back there, slowly sinking into hopeless brutalisation. He learns a trade in jail, although not the one he had always wanted, but in any case no one will employ him in it; he is bored and stupefied inside, and suspected and rejected outside. Roger, for robbing an old man of his life savings, is sent to a training ship, and freed of a family intent on perverting him becomes an honest and prosperous merchant seaman. The last words of the book accuse the reader of rocking the jail cradle in which the infant criminal is bred. Earlier, a more aggressive attempt to bring home common humanity to the perpetrators of inhuman laws is made by comparing children jailed for stealing food or doing petty damage to property to the rich boys whose escapades are described in *Tom Brown's Schooldays:* 'Had the same measure been meted out to them that every day was meted out to these desolate, degraded, uncared-for street lads, how many a brave and worthy English gentleman — ay! and magistrate — of the present day must now have been a greyhaired convict in penal servitude.'

So much for the law's attempts to deal with begging as the first step of the youthful criminal. In *The Lord's Pursebearers*, published in *The Day of Rest* (1882), Sara Smith described the systematic exploitation of begging children which she had been shown by philanthropists like the Rev. R.C. Billing, rector of Spitalfields. The figure of the crossing-sweeper, previously a romantic hero in her books bravely earning his own bread and supporting his helpless brother or mother or adopted grandfather, is transformed by her contact with the ugly reality into a five-year-old slave with three 'fathers', who fleeces passers-by and is in turn relieved of his gains by a minder lounging always within sight outside a pub. His gains, by dancing conspicuously about his crossing, amounted to 'only a half-penny less than a shilling; collected in sixteen minutes from the well-fed and well-clad citizens of the richest Christian city in the world, who thus did what they could to perpetuate the sin and shame of having almost naked children to sweep their crossings'.

The garret where Little Meg nursed her charges is similarly consigned to the realms of forgotten fantasy, and replaced by the vision of Mrs Moss, who deals in old clothes and starved children, whom she keeps in a cupboard:

> There was no furniture of any kind in it; and the old plaster of the walls reeked with dirt and damp. At the farthest end was a heap of filthy rags; and lying on it, in the dismal darkness of this den, were two children, whose age it was impossible to guess at . . . The child who showed some sign of life had a small, white face, with scanty fair hair upon its little head, and shrewd eyes looking keenly about her. 'That's little Lucky, as always draws silver sooner or later,' said Mrs Moss, 'but for my part, I'd as soon take

Fidge.' Fidge moaned a little as she spoke. His bare little legs and arms were so thin that it seemed impossible they could belong to a living child. The yellow skin was drawn tight over the small head and face, and his eyes were starting from their sockets. The baby seemed scarcely human.

He is described, the preface tells us, from personal observation; the owner's chief anxiety is that no hirer should be so soft as to feed one of the children while employing it. It is a very grim tale; the author wrote no more romances of street arabs.

The street arab formula, however, was a winning one, not lightly given up by either the publishers and purchasers who knew a good line and stuck to it, nor by writers who found it easy to follow and effective. There were many of these whose motives were perfectly genuine, but who had not Hesba Stretton's acute feeling for the children they wrote about and for, and who saw no harm in reproducing sentimental effects and conventional pathos without much thought beyond their immediate appeal. Some of these writers became very well-known, and their books eagerly sought, but none achieved the balance which Hesba Stretton's best stories had maintained. Two in particular, Mrs O. Walton and Mrs Castle Smith, illustrate the disproportion which even the most popular of writers tended to introduce.

Mrs Walton's bias was religious. In her books the narrative hinges upon sermons, always given in full, and climaxes in conversions, always described at length; character and event are mere excuses for the overriding intention of setting out the Christian message. Her books, more than any others of this kind, are directly descended from the deathbed tracts of earlier generations; the circumstance of their being fiction rather than records of real events means only that they can be more rigidly schematised and directed to the point than were the old accounts of children actually observed. Thus *Little Dot* (1873), for example, is set in a churchyard for the convenience of gravestone meditation, and the child is a distilled essence of Richmond's Little Jane. Mrs Walton is content to use the motifs already to hand, arranged in providential patterns: her concern in each story is for its effectiveness in conveying her message about the need to be washed in the blood of the Lamb. She has little leisure to consider the aesthetic or imaginative effect of the reiteration of this, her favourite cliché, or of any aspect of her tale, and any picturesque or realistic embellishment is unashamedly and sometimes, it seems, unthinkingly laid on for the sake of holding attention for her message.

Religious conviction is, of course, a driving force in Hesba Stretton's writing, and the wish to carry the message to others is openly expressed; but it is inseparable from her humanitarian mission, and indeed perceived to some extent in social terms. In all her books she graphically illustrates her reason for stressing the need to believe in an everlasting life: 'What a poor, miserable, wretched thing this [life] was, at any rate for poor folks, if this world were all!' Mrs Walton, though, habitually presented belief not only as an urgent remedy for the despair otherwise liable to engulf this harsh world, but as a purpose and justification of all action and experience. It is in her books, more often than those of any other English writer in this mode, that the child protagonist is put through lengthy searchings of the soul, and agonies of conscience, leading to conversion; and after that stage, especially in her smallest children, they are inclined to enquire earnestly about the state of grace of all they meet. Despite these blatancies, however, she produced two of the longest-lived stories of poor children, *A Peep Behind the Scenes* (1877) and *Christie's Old Organ* (1882).

These both deal with poor entertainers. *A Peep Behind the Scenes* is the story of Rosalie, the child of a lady who ran away with an actor and is dying, throughout the first third of the book, in the living van of the travelling theatre to which they are reduced. Rosalie dances in the show, but is totally innocent — she has never crossed the fairground alone in her life — and she is converted by a picture of the Good Shepherd in the first chapter. Thereafter she converts all those she meets by enquiring whether the Shepherd has found them yet. Her mother's downfall, we are told, began with the reading of romantic novels, but the story is itself a romance, of the child's journey through a very picturesque hell to the discovery of her rightful heritage and establishment in 'The Green Pasture' of her uncle's country vicarage. In the last chapter she sallies forth from this haven to take comforts and treats to the dwarfs, giants, trainers of dogs and pigeons, and other fair-folk to whom she previously brought the vital message of the picture. She is beautiful and winning, they are quaint; little sense of harsh reality interrupts the tale, for we are always sure some picturesque, near-magical assistant will appear to deliver her from the perils she encounters. One of the most popular and longest-lived tract tales ever written, it is, as Nancy Cutt has said,[18] an evangelical fairy tale, perfect and unique.

Christie's Old Organ, written in 1882 but ignoring all such realistic inconveniences as school boards and mendicity legislation, concerns a waif who takes to an old organ-grinder, nurses him in his last illness, and brings him to conversion before he dies. It is remarkable for being a sermon about the proximity of death and the urgency of conversion that could have appeared in the first issue of the *Child's Companion*, nearly sixty years earlier. The overriding importance of the author's message sweeps aside for her not only all artistic considerations which might have led her to question the conventions which she uses in so undiluted a form, but all the complexities that could arise from attempting to reflect social realities. The fairground, the lodging house, the old hand organ with its outdated tunes, are narrative conveniences whose significance, if any, is emblematic, not graphic, and with which she would willingly dispense if fiction were not a necessary medium for her message. In some of ther books, indeed, she abandons fiction, and bases her sermons directly on biblical exposition, showing that any consideration of the responses or demands of her audience was as secondary to her purpose as any artistic self-consciousness.

An acute if not very carefully considered awareness of her audience is one of the main impressions the reader has of Mrs Castle Smith, who wrote as 'Brenda', and produced the other book which was long-remembered amongst the multitude of street arab tales. She published *Froggy's Little Brother* in 1875. For her, the balance between religious concern for the soul to be saved and sympathy for the suffering child tilts decisively in the humanitarian direction, with two artistically deleterious consequences. The more obvious is sentimentality. Froggy and little Benny, orphaned children in a garret, pull with such determination at the reader's heart-strings that they lose all artistic decorum. The scene of Little Meg and her charges trying to understand their mother's death and to comfort each other is at least touched with some human observation, such as the little boy's inclination to give himself tragic airs to show off to his friends in the court; Froggy, assured by his father that his mother has just departed to a Better Land, returns '"Then that's good! . . . Goodnight, Fader, dear! I'm going back to my little bed again"'. When the father is also removed, the two children struggle on, melting all who meet them with their pathos; Benny's climatic death is not made the occasion for a sermon or a conversion, since both are entirely good and scarcely even tempted throughout, but for buckets of sympathy for Froggy in his loss. He is carried off to an orphanage where his comforts are so fully attended to that a policeman brings him a substitute baby brother, conveniently orphaned at the door. The whipped-up emotion is then, at the end of the book, turned into fuel for a homily to the reader — but not about the need to turn to God. She exclaims:

How many a beautiful lesson can we learn from the poor — for sufferings nobly endured and heavy burdens bravely borne, where can we look better than to them; but what *generosity* they teach us! They show us how to be truly and greatly generous in their willingness to share the last crumb of comfort, whatever that may be, with a neighbour, kindly and ungrudgingly, without hope of return or reward. Theirs is not a generosity which costs them nothing — it often entails going without a meal or sitting by a fireless grate, but a self-sacrifice of some sort, *always* . . . We are not called upon to lay down our lives, but we *are* called upon to make very great sacrifices, not only once, but daily and hourly, for one another . . .

These passages highlight the other artistic pitfall of her work. Their assumption is that the reader is well-off, comfortable, completely insulated from the story; Froggy and his brother, therefore, and all the detail of their lives, are a display put on to prove our tears and our generosity, to each other and especially to them. The book concludes with an appeal to 'Parents and little children, you especially who are rich, remember it is the Froggys and Bennys of London for whom your clergyman is pleading, when he asks you to send money and relief to the poor East End!' There is some attempt to assert common humanity — 'they may be street arabs, but they have immortal souls, and they are our brothers and sisters, though we may not own them' — but no mention of common sinfulness (compare Brenda's exhortations with ALOE's 'Reader, have you ever known this sin?', and no suggestion of any source, whether spiritual or social, of the evil which is displayed. It is a very long way indeed from *Jessica's First Prayer*; but the book was still sold and offered as a Reward, and bought as a Sunday school prize as well as for Sunday reading in the nursery. It is difficult to imagine a ragged school child finding Froggy anything but a sham, indeed an insult; but the ironic fact is that the poor did indeed feel the generosity which Mrs Smith ascribes to them, and children of working-class families, who did not identify themselves with starving waifs, were often deeply moved with sympathy for their plight, though they were without the means to do anything about it.[19]

Mrs Castle Smith in fact writes well when she takes the nursery child as her subject, as well as for her expected reader; presumably such children had some reality for her, while the waifs are ciphers. She describes beautiful, well-cared-for children with animation and humour.

Her mistake, and that of many lesser writers in this genre, was to confuse and confound her aims, to write a book that tried to appeal to the poor child and also to appeal for him, with the effect of falsification, sentimentality and condescension. The prize book system, perhaps, should take some of the blame, in that the publishers' categories lagged behind developments in social stratification, still offering only one kind of book to a group that was fragmenting and becoming more complex as its numbers hugely increased. In the author's consciousness, and in the system for which she was working, the overriding religious impulse that had brought and held disparate groups together had ebbed, and the connections between classes which remained stressed social obligations, and so social inequalities. What had previously been for the Sunday School movement a matter of conscience, the rescuing of souls from damnation, had become by the 1870s and 1880s a question of social duty, state education for the poorer classes. The waif romances became, therefore, in the last quarter of the century, exercises in a convention whose original life had departed, within which a new message was artificially implanted. Didactic fiction is an art form very limited by its conditional nature, and though the convention was in this case strong enough to seem to survive autonomously, tempting many writers to perpetuate it under the impression that they were still writing tales like Hesba Stretton's, and for the same reasons, they produced only vitiated, and in some cases positively vicious, imitations. Some of these will be discussed later, as part of the general decline and rebirth of moral fiction for children that was a consequence of the shift from religious to other values at the end of the century.

By that period the evangelical children's books had largely had their day. The long survival of their conventions, however, is an indication of the success with which the writers of the mid-century whom I have been discussing set about their task of discovering methods, story-patterns and fictional modes when the demand for moral fiction for the newly literate arose. The fantasies and allegorical tales of ALOE and the romances of humble life of Hesba Stretton are archetypal; in them, especially in Hesba Stretton's case, the message was embodied in fictional forms which grew out of the various traditions of popular writing, which were therefore appealing and satisfying to the new readers, and which the multitudes of writers for the many presses producing their books could themselves respond to and adopt.

4 BOOKS FOR BOYS

The proliferation of readers for moral and educative fiction for the young, for whom the old style of Sunday school tract was an inadequate provision, was dealt with in the 1860s and 1870s by the development of kinds of fiction for specific sections of the juvenile market. The outlets for such books were multiplying, and the expectations of the purchasers were much more various than those of earlier generations of Sunday school superintendants and philanthropic gentry. Publishers and writers found a way of supplying them all by catering for readers not by religious or social categories, for these were becoming too numerous, but by the simpler criterion of sex. The change was of course not complete, for old-fashioned tracts remained, often thought of as one of several kinds of girls' books, and in publications for boys class distinctions remained in, for example, the range of provision of non-fiction; but the boy's story, from the 1860s onwards, was a genre which commanded a readership from ragged school to country house.

As early as 1830 a magazine appeared called *The Excitement: or a book to induce boys to read*, 'containing remarkable appearances in nature, signal preservations, and such incidents as are particularly fitted to arrest the youthful mind', and the need to capture interest came to dominate other considerations in prizes for boys, transforming the plain tract into an elaborately-cased and illustrated book of action and adventure, appealing at all market levels. By 1865 boys' books 'combining instruction and entertainment . . . whilst gratifying their liking for wonder and adventure', and also inculcating 'wise and practical lessons in a most attractive manner', were being recommended for gifts and prizes even by Sunday school journals,[1] and a long list of publishers, from highly respected houses like Macmillan's to cut-price opportunists such as Partridge and King, were competing to supply uniformly cheap, bright, unexceptionable tales of adventure. Their potential market was huge, but highly selective, including busy committees, cautious aunts, and the boys themselves, who were as conservative as any institutional buyer, and as likely to choose exactly what they had had before. Under such conditions fortunate individuals became massive best sellers, and all such books developed a high degree of uniformity.

At the beginning of this boom, in the 1850s, readers in the category previously known as 'youth' were being catered for by the specialist publishers in one or two limited ways. The obvious next step from the childish tract for the new reader was assumed to be to non-fictional material. The undeniable boyish taste for facts and figures was recognised by the religious publishers as harmless, even wholesome, and also as a possible vehicle for religious instruction and moral suasion. The SPCK, specialising in any case in books of instruction for schoolroom use, had an extensive list of non-fiction for the young which could be used, in appropriate bindings, for presents and prizes: volumes such as the *Natural History of Quadrupeds*, the *Life of Nelson* and *Mungo Park's Travels* were established on their educational lists, at prices of around 2s. The RTS, too, published factual material, though not in the quantity warranted by the SPCK school connection. In 1860 the youngest readers had a series of 3d 16mos to inform them about everything from 'The Animalcule' or 'The Ant' to 'The Tongue' and The Valley'. Older readers, in families or schools, could find in the Monthly Volume Series information on the Court of Persia, or British Fish, at 6d in fancy covers.

At some periods commercial publishers found facts paid them as well as stories, or better; in the first years of the century the thrust of rationalist educational theory had brought into being countless dismal titles like *The Little Conchologist* by Samuel Clark, and Lady Fenn's *The Rational Dame*. Miscellaneous information had its appeal, however dryly presented, especially to boys; history and geography, in the form, for example, of the many Peter Parley books of travel, remained popular and saleable even when a strictly factual education had ceased to be the fashion, and such books were often used as a means of introducing homilies upon moral and spiritual matters.

In the 1840s, however, a new, exciting style of factual narrative dealing with adventures and travels began to appear, in which cultural and moral attitudes were conveyed as an element in the story. The best-known example is probably Richard Dana's *Two Years Before the Mast*, first published in America in 1840. Its appeal is simple: it is a true story of adventures theoretically available to any able-bodied youth, of any class — Dana was an undergraduate at Harvard before he went to sea for his health. It is not a collection of anecdotes got together for the sake of fragments of dry information, but a consecutive, though very artlessly shaped, account of an obviously real voyage. The reader learns about the winds of the Pacific, Californian hide-trading, the routine and structure of the merchant service of America, and many other matters just as fascinating in their remote usefulness, but it is never a lesson; rather the abstruse, detailed information about working a ship presents itself as a language to be learnt which is the key to mysterious excitement and romance. The journal's movement is straightforward and rapid, going from sea-sickness to sharks and tropical gales, and on to Cape Horn and icebergs in quick succession, varying the periods of action with physically minute detail about shipboard life which is scarcely less strange, whether it concerns the prosaic tarring of rigging or dramatic incidents in which men fall overboard or are capriciously flogged. There are moments of intimate feeling, when Dana describes the solitude of night on the Californian beach, or the beauty of the ship seen from far aloft; but he makes no comment on this sensibility, stressing rather the need for a hard outside and the ability to joke about everything from potentially deadly falls from the masts to letters from home. It is not a childish narrative, and the difficulty of following it may seem considerable; its power over the imagination, especially the adolescent imagination, lies in this toughness, and the contrasting dream-like exoticism of the life that is so prosaically and vividly described.

Such accounts became very popular in the 1840s, and old travel books such as *Anson's Voyages* were frequently reprinted, along with sober journals of more recent expeditions. Any apparently true adventure story could find readers, however poorly written it was: thinly fictionalised collections of miscellaneous information passed muster under such titles as *Uncle Ned's Stories of the Tropics* or *The Boy's Book About Indians*; shapeless and crudely-written voyages, such as *Life in a Whaler* by 'Sailor Charley', were the more eagerly accepted because their very lack of polish seemed to guarantee their veracity, and freedom from didactic ulterior motives. There was, however, more demand for such books than could be supplied by real adventures; and shapeless strings of anecdotes or journals of shipboard life are only acceptable if they are 'true'. Some structure, however rudimentary, is needed on which to hang a tale. The boys' writers of the 1860s turned to certain fictional models, therefore, for the structures of stories which they fleshed out with the vocabulary and information taken from traveller's tales. There was a handful of adult novels which by the 1860s had come to be regarded as good books for boys, and from them the juvenile writers drew their patterns and methods, establishing a convention strong enough to support many thousands of stories written in the next fifty or sixty years.

The Fictional Models

Pre-eminent among these books, occupying a special place in the ancestry of the boys' story, was *Robinson Crusoe*. Just as the strictest Evangelical ban upon fiction for the young made an exception of *The Pilgrim's Progress*, so *Crusoe* was the one fiction which all followers of a rationalist, Rousseauian theory of education gave to their pupils, on the authority of *Emile* itself. Its continued popularity after the strictly doctrinaire period had gone by was founded on its fictional appeal. In shape hardly removed from true accounts of adventure at sea, it had the vital fictional addition of a hero in whose character and fortunes the reader was interested, and moreover included an episode, Crusoe's life on the desert island, so powerful and compendious as story and as symbol that it was capable of holding interest through infinite numbers of imitations, repetitions and adaptations.

A few other books had comparable status at the mid-century: Marryat's *Midshipman Easy*, with a more general approval extending to his other stories of the sea, particularly *Poor Jack* and *Peter Simple*; Michael Scott's *Tom Cringle's Log* and *The Cruise of the Midge*; the works of Sir Walter Scott in general; and the works of James Fenimore Cooper, especially the leather-stocking tales. These were often the books remembered by fathers from their own boyhood, or recognised vaguely as classics, rather than carefully chosen as suitable; probably few purchasers bothered to re-read them, or reflect that they had been thought childhood reading in a period which had far less choice in such matters, and moreover a less fastidious discrimination of what might be too coarse or rough for young eyes. Consequently boys were cheerfully allowed to form literary tastes on novels which derived from the eighteenth-century tradition of Fielding and Smollett, and on romances which dealt largely and freely in adventures social and sexual as well as heroic. The justification for allowing such books to be read was primarily that they dealt with factual material which boys should be encouraged to master: Scott was full of historical facts, of major and minor importance, Marryat spoke as a practical seaman — often, indeed, he aired his views on the navy and its masters in roundly authoritative tones; and Michael Scott and Cooper described the New World and extolled the self-reliant, nautical or pioneering life in ways which might inspire those with their way to make in the world. Thus the factual content of such books was reinforced by their teaching of qualities of mind and character which were also good for boys to imbibe: practical self-reliance leading to self-confidence, and thence to confidence in the superiority, potential or realised, of one's larger self — the Service, or the nation.

As a literary experience, these books cannot have been demanding, as long as the reader had plenty of time in hand; and they have strong attractions for the adolescent boy. Marryat's *Midshipman Easy* is a good example and, after *Robinson Crusoe*, perhaps the most famous. Though virtually unread today, it became a 'standard' novel almost as soon as it appeared. First published in three volumes in 1836, it immediately went into a second edition, was one of Bentley's Standard Novels in 1838, appeared in the USA by 1840, and has been reprinted regularly from then onwards: the British Library has four editions of the 1850s, four of the 1870s, six of the 1880s, 17 of the 1890s (presumably when copyright expired), 15 of the 1900s, and so on; it remained a favourite well into this century.

The book's first attraction is that although it begins with the hero's birth and childhood, and centres upon his life at the ages of 16 and 17, it is clearly not a children's book. There are reminiscences of the grotesque descriptive style of Smollett, and even of Sterne, in the opening, when the Easy parents are introduced in a flurry of puns on their name. Punning, one of the recurrent comic effects of the novel, was by no means only juvenile humour at the time, but rather suggests the objective, Fielding-like relationship with the reader and the tale to which Marryat often has recourse. Jack Easy is a spoiled child, a veritable Tommy Merton, because of his father's belief in the equality of man and his mother's stupid partiality; but his selfish escapades are chastised not by a rationalist tutor's demonstrations — since they actually arise from half-baked philosophy — but by a hearty caning. Jack begins to get his own back on authority, however, as soon as he goes to sea as a midshipman, where his status as a very wealthy young gentleman enables him to defy the crude discipline of the old naval hierarchy, which places uneducated, lower-class bullies in charge of him.

Marryat has an axe to grind in this matter, being engaged in the protracted struggle to rid the navy of its eighteenth-century brutality, and the accompanying independence which it had enjoyed from the restraints of a society increasingly concerned with propriety and a new code of gentlemanly breeding and behaviour. The naval hierarchy conflicted with the social one, which was now beginning to acquire, by associating duty, responsibility and polite behaviour with the status of gentlemen, a sort of sanctity which brooked no rival arrangements of rank. The old naval system gave power to men whose only breeding was its own hard discipline, accustomed to the endurance and the exercise of despotic authority with little regard for rank, feeling or education not connected with sea-service. It was scarcely, however, an equitable system, for though it did allow men to rise to minor positions of power without advantages of birth, they were always led by others whose only qualifications for the absolute power they enjoyed were wealth and influence. Marryat was concerned with the establishment of naval officership as a profession, in modern terms, whose status depended both on the technical, educational qualifications of its members and the exclusion of those unable to pass its other test, of professional, that is gentlemanly, behaviour. In this he uses the example of Jack Easy, who can defy his officers if he finds them arbitrary because he can grandly pay his own way and confidently brave himself out of the scrapes he gets into; he is justified in each instance because he behaves with perfect good manners, and Marryat maintains that, however mistaken Jack's personal philosophy, he is a gentleman, and the navy is at fault if its rules conflict with those of polite society.

From the boy reader's point of view, however, this useful piece of Victorian social dogma is imbibed by means of a series of comic and often violent escapades in which fantasies of triumph over old and ugly superiors and despicable petty restraints can be gratified. In one sequence Briggs the boatswain, who is Jack's superior, though he is not on the quarterdeck, bullies a ship's boy for failing to come on deck instantly when ordered although he was half-dressed. When, later, Briggs is drunk ashore, he loses Jack's trousers, which had been hung out of a window to dry, by opening it to be sick. Jack pays him back for both misdeeds by taking the boatswain's trousers and obliging him to run the gauntlet of port and ship in his shirt-tails. In retaliation Briggs eggs on a cockney pickpocket (who is the purser's steward and bears Jack a grudge for having spurned his pretensions to equality) to challenge our hero to a duel. The gunner of the ship arranges a preposterous three-cornered fight, in which Jack is to fire at Briggs, Briggs at the steward, and he, a coward, and no hand with a pistol, at Jack. This piece of slapstick results in Jack sending a ball through Briggs's cheeks, depriving him of some teeth and the capacity to blow his boatswain's whistle, and the steward taking Briggs's shot ignominiously in the backside.

Jack escapes, of course, unharmed, and takes off on a protracted spree, pretending to be frightened of punishment for the duel. His 'cruise' only ends when he is discovered, being feted for his bravery, wealth and breeding by the best Sicilian society, by a Captain Tartar, who has none of these gifts, though he admires Jack's money excessively, until he discovers his naval rank. He then gives way to despotic temper, and not only claps Jack in irons for being AWOL from his own ship — a proceeding Marryat allows is just, within the terms of the Service — but also gives free rein to his abusive tongue. This crime Marryat regards as the outward sign of the unprofessional power structure which does not respect juniors as potential equals, and no punishment for it is too harsh: Tartar is shot dead in a duel with one of Jack's noble Sicilian friends. Jack comes off unscathed, having chastened everyone who fails to know his proper place and its duties, from the over-familiar pickpocket who pretended to be a gentleman to the captain who allowed himself to abuse his superior position.

Jack's own behaviour, like that of Tom Jones, is scandalous, but he is forgiven by the writer and the reader because those whom he abuses are so much further in the wrong, and all his own misdemeanours spring from qualities we are asked to admire; in this case, dare-devil bravery, gallantry, high spirits, good humour and an unshakable, instinctive knowledge of the proper respect due to and behaviour worthy of a gentleman. Occasionally Marryat invites us to laugh at the impeccable good manners with which Easy creates mayhem; but they are the outward sign of his inward grace.

Many of Jack's adventures are as exciting and exotic as these are comic: in lieu of Sandford and Merton's Mr Barlow, Jack has for his tutor an Ashantee prince, Mesty, who has been a slave and is now the servant in the midshipmen's berth. In this alliance Jack's adherence to the equality of man stands him in good stead, for Mesty is well versed in the vices of ships and sailors, and the bloodier tricks of a warrior's trade, and protects Jack from certain disaster on his first cruise of adventure. As Jack gains experience himself, Mesty has other roles, able to help his friend by doing necessary murders which a gentleman might hesitate to commit, becoming a trusty servant, and even a parody of the heathen converts whom Little Henry and his like made by their Christian example, when he feels compassion at the death of an enemy because he has observed Jack show feelings above the level of savage revenge. Jack sets up this example of fair play and honourable dealing soon after he comes aboard, by fighting the bully of the berth in defence of a younger boy, who had been picked on for his weakness and stupidity, but is still a gentleman.

This episode of the defeat of the bully in the defence of the weak was to become archetypal in boys' books, as were some of Jack's later adventures, such as his twice-repeated rescue of a beautiful girl, a Sicilian noblewoman whom he eventually marries; but many of his escapades go beyond what were to become the bounds of boys' fiction. He becomes involved, for example, in the feuds of the Sicilian nobility, which are finally resolved in favour of his beloved's family by Mesty poisoning and knifing several people, including a corrupt friar; Easy himself plays a complicated practical joke in which he dresses a British proconsul in skirts and baulks a merchant captain of his lady love in order to rescue his best friend, Gascoigne, from an intrigue with a Moorish girl.

The sexual morality of the book includes both near-bawdy humour worthy of Fielding or Byron (Jack's wet-nurse excuses her bastard child on the grounds of its being 'only a very little one', and Jack and his beloved are so young — aged only 15 and 17 — that their passion does not interrupt their other appetites, and they are never back late for their dinners), and the beginnings of Victorian niceness, so that Gascoigne's designs on the Moorish girl are strictly honourable, and also socially unthinkable, so that he is eventually grateful to Jack for tricking him out of her. Jack is a fantasy hero, and leaves the Service at the end cured of his doctrines of equality by the adventures he has had pursuing them and by the grotesque death of his father, a victim of a craze for corrective phrenology, which was to bring about greater equality, but actually results in his hanging himself by machine.

On coming into his estate Jack buys himself a ship and takes a final cruise, collecting his friends to be his officers, lining his pockets with cleverly-won prizes, inflicting defeat on yet another set of ungentlemanly naval officers who insult him and try to press-gang his men, and collects his bride in triumph from her grateful family in Palermo. He ends as a model of the (Victorian) old English gentleman:

> Becoming a great favourite, [he] kept a pack of hounds, rode with the foremost, received a deputation to stand for the county, on the Conservative interest . . . Jack had no occasion to argue the point with Agnes; she conformed at once to the religion of her husband, proved an excellent and affectionate wife, and eventually the mother of four children.

His allies are disposed of equally succinctly, Mesty proving himself trustworthy and holding his post (of majordomo) with dignity, and Gascoigne, who by his association with Easy had been nearly unfitted for the naval discipline which his modest circumstances made essential, 'soon obtained the rank of post-captain . . . by the interest of the Conservative member', that is, of Easy himself.

Marryat's novels remained standard prize and gift books, and by 1895, when *Japhet, in Search of a Father* was reprinted by Macmillan in a very handsome gold-blocked jacket, with Brock illustrations, David Hannay was prefacing his introduction with the complaint that if, as he hears, 'the boys of this generation do not enjoy Marryat . . . Scott, Dumas and *Robinson Crusoe* . . . it is so much the worse for them', and for their future prospects as men. He went on to acknowledge that if taste had changed in this way, nothing could be done about it; but in fact over the 50 years of steady reprinting which had passed, Marryat had become an anachronism supported by tradition, and while much had been learnt from him both by readers and writers of boys' books, there had developed a style and a message which did not square with his. Both in narrative method and the values which the stories conveyed, the writers of succeeding generations had honed down the romantic, old-fashioned novel style they had inherited through Scott and Marryat to match their narrower purposes more comfortably.

Much was lost in the transition: Scott's novels have a seriousness and subtlety in their handling of the human implications of political matters which was quite lost in the transformation to historical romance; and the establishment of the boy hero as the central figure in confrontation with the natural world cut out almost entirely the internal psychological and religious elements of Defoe's study of Crusoe. Cooper's heroes also needed to be amended, for if their stupendous physical power and its accompanying simplicity and innocence was suitable for a boys' hero, their American and sometimes anti-British bias was not what was required. Adaptation by the narrowing of the scope and interests of the adult novel and the engrafting of clearer statement of the lessons to be learnt from the action of the tale was felt to be necessary, for the instruction of the young.

The Invention of the Victorian Boy

The consciousness of the demands of this new readership marks a further stage in the recognition of the separateness of various age groups discussed with reference to the child in Chapter 1. 'The child' distinguished for special treatment as a reader was often assumed to be the child of the poor; 'the boy' who now became the focus of attention was primarily, but not exclusively, thought of as belonging to some level of the middle classes. Education above the elementary level now commanded the attention of reformers like William Rogers, who felt that the sons of 'clerks, for instance, and tradesmen with moderate resources'[2] were urgently in need of moral and social guidance, if they were to acquit themselves like gentlemen. The greatly expanded ranks of the industrial and administrative middle classes needed all recruits who could be persuaded to make the effort to rise into them; messages, therefore, concerning the privilege of education and the values which it opposed began to be addressed to this group, both formally, through the reformation of middle-class schools, and by means of wider and more subtle persuasion in prize books given in schools of all levels and kinds.

Concern for the boy and his moral and social state can be traced very clearly as it enters the early Victorian consciousness. The most outstanding signpost is that of the career, beliefs and influence of Arnold of Rugby, and the transformation that his ideas underwent as they were turned into a code of practice for mid- and late Victorian schooling. Arnold was concerned, as David Newsome has pointed out, with producing a breed of Christian scholars, distinguished by their godliness and good learning.[3] His sermons to the boys about their sinfulness and shortcomings were the apex of an educational structure which contained many innovations, all aimed at cultivating Christian ideals in a group whom Arnold perceived as primitive, morally weak and especially at risk — the immature male. To follow his path was to learn to recognise, confront and overcome evil, both internally and in the world around. To achieve this he set up a system which took control of the freedom which boys had been allowed before their parlous state had been noticed. Tribalism and independence, which had led to public school riots serious enough to require control by the troops, were firmly chanelled into competition between groups for scholastic success, and controlled by the revised prefect system which captured the boys' fierce sense of loyalty and honour. Privacy, which had sheltered vices of a less public kind, was watched over by the actual supervision of these elders of the tribe or the emotional guardianship of the teacher, whose status in the life of the boys was changed from that of servant to social equal and wise personal friend. It was primarily a moral and intellectual training, aimed at producing a learned moral elite, for the betterment of a Christian society.

The popularisation of Arnold's ideal was partly the work of a hugely successful boy's book, *Tom Brown's Schooldays* by Thomas Hughes, published by Macmillan in 1857. Hughes shows the development of his hero in the special environment of Rugby: the book is an exposition of Arnold's method in its effect upon an average boy, using Hughes's personal memories of what it was like to be trained to think and read earnestly, eschew childish vices in preparation for facing adult temptations, and become if not godly and learned, then at least responsible, honourable and a public-spirited Christian gentleman.[4] Popularising an ideal almost necessarily robs it of subtlety, however, and may transform it completely; *Tom Brown's Schooldays* was read as a glorification of boyish simplicity and the world of school. In becoming the basis of the Victorian public school system, Arnold's ideal of the leading of boys towards maturity and moral responsibility was debased into the instilling of a rigid behavioural code by means of powerful emotional and physical sanctions. Hughes's emblematic use of school games to indicate his hero's progress was unintentionally prophetic: incidental in Arnold's day, team games first became organised in the 1860s, then compulsory in the 1870s and 1880s, and thereafter a cult dominating school life, for they provided exactly the level and kind of training the schools sought to provide.[5]

The reason for this mid-Victorian transformation of Arnold's attitude to boys is indicated in another Macmillan's boys' book of the 1850s, *Westward Ho!* by Charles Kingsley. Appearing in 1855, his contribution to the current debate about education was coloured by Kingsley's excited reaction to the Crimean war.[6] It is an amalgam of romantic, fanciful, blood-thirsty, religious and patriotic sentiments thrust all ways up into the story of an Elizabethan sea-farer. He is simultaneously the average Englishman, and a perfect hero. A diatribe in the first chapter about the moral training of the young indicates Kingsley's purpose, and the flavour of his constant button-holing of the readers:

> Now this young gentleman, Amyas Leigh, though come of as good blood as any in Devon . . . was not, saving for his good looks, by any means what would be called now-a-days an 'interesting' youth, still less a 'highly-educated' one; for, with the exception of a little Latin, which had been driven into him by repeated blows, as if it had been a nail, he knew no books whatsoever, save his Bible, his Prayer-book, the old 'Mort d'Arthur' of Caxton's edition, which lay in the great bay window in the hall, and the translation of 'Las Casas' History of the West Indies', which lay beside it, lately done into English under the title of 'The Cruelties of the Spaniards'.

He devoutly believed in fairies . . . and was in many other respects
so very ignorant a youth, that any pert monitor in a national school
might have had a hearty laugh at him. Nevertheless, this ignorant
young savage, 'vacant of the glorious gains' of the nineteenth century,
children's literature and science made easy . . . had learnt certain
things which he would hardly have been taught just now in any
school in England; for his training had been that of the old
Persians, 'to speak the truth and to draw the bow', both of which
savage virtues he had acquired to perfection, as well as the equally
savage ones of enduring pain cheerfully, and of believing it to be
the finest thing in the world to be a gentleman . . . and though he
had never had a single 'object lesson', or been taught to 'use his
intellectual powers', he knew the names and ways of every bird, and
fish, and fly, and could read, as cunningly as the oldest sailor, the
meaning of every drift of cloud which crossed the heavens. Lastly,
he had been for some time past, on account of his extraordinary
size and strength, undisputed cock of the school, and the most
terrible fighter among all Bideford boys; in which brutal habit he
took much delight, and contrived, strange as it may seem, to
extract from it good, not only for himself but for others, doing
justice among his school-fellows with a heavy hand, and succouring
the oppressed and afflicted; so that he was the terror of all the
sailor-lads, and the pride and stay of all the town's boys and girls,
and hardly considered that he had done his duty in his calling if
he went home without beating a big lad for bullying a little one.
For the rest, he never thought about thinking, or felt about feeling . . .
Neither was he what would be now-a-days called by many a pious
child . . . (the age of children's religious books not having yet dawned
on the world) he knew nothing more of theology, or of his own soul,
than is contained in the Church Catechism. It is a question, however,
on the whole, whether, though grossly ignorant (according to our
modern notions) in science and religion, he was altogether untrained
in manhood, virtue, and godliness; and whether the barbaric
narrowness of his Information was not somewhat counterbalanced
both in him and in the rest of his generation by the depth, and
breadth, and healthiness of his Education.

Here the revolution of thought about children's books and moral
education which led away from Hesba Stretton towards Henty and
George Manville Fenn is taking its first violent turns. The new ideal
is to be a lad like Amyas, who is tongue-tied and thoughtless, but

strong, brave, and simple in his faith in God, England and himself, and in his right to rule not only his social inferiors at home, but all the world abroad: 'as he stands there with beating heart and kindling eye, the cool breeze whistling through his long fair curls, he is a symbol, though he knows it not, of brave young England longing to wing its way out of its island prison, to discover and to traffic, to colonise and civilise, until no wind can sweep the earth which does not bear the echoes of an English voice'. The reader is invited to follow him on these adventures, and the simultaneous inner voyage of discovery of himself. Kingsley disapproves of the religious tract, but his own handling of the story is unashamedly didactic and dogmatic; Amyas is at the mercy of his every whim.

The opinions for which the tale is made a vehicle initiated trends in moral and emotional training of the young which were to be carried on and enforced by the books for boys which came after. He harangues us, for example, about Nature, and about man's failure to respond adequately to its wonders, castigating the various writers who are his sources for the description of exotic places, and impatiently telling us to use our own imaginations in lieu of description by him. He immediately goes on, though, to point to his own moral about the response of his heroes to the sights they saw: because they were 'high-hearted', they were inspired by natural wonders to 'a lofty, heroical, reverent frame of mind'; but their only articulate responses were severely practical. They found out the uses of the plants and creatures they encountered, but 'they knew as little about the trees and animals in an "artistic" or "critical" point of view, as in a scientific one'. Kingsley seems to think that heroism is totally un- or anti-intellectual, a matter of blood and instinct trained by physical discipline issuing in moral conviction. It is a doctrine related to Arnold's belief in the primitiveness of boys, but instead of seeking means to advance them to maturity and self-knowledge through learning and analysis, Kingsley and his successors glorify the boyish character, having the hero arrive at maturity with instinctive responses trained by physical experience until they are a reflex substitute for reflection and a guide to action in any circumstances, from the school close to the blood-soaked desert sands.[7] The loose mixture of a sensational romance, a great deal of interspersed information (whether intensely opinionated, painstakingly researched or merely dutiful), and the binding ingredient of the boy who grows to be a man with 'his English heart full of the divine instinct of duty and public spirit', one of 'the heroes who from that time forth sailed out to colonise another

and vaster England, to the heaven-prospered cry of Westward Ho!', is
the model of the boy's books that were to follow.

Evangelical into Imperialist: W. H. G. Kingston's Books for Boys

The Victorian modulation from evangelical Christianity to the work
ethic and expansionism, eventually leading to a quasi-religious belief in
the British Empire, has been explored from many points of view.[8] Its
progress can be clearly seen in boys' books by individuals who made
use of modest talents to further beliefs which were neither controversial
nor unique, but which flowed with the stream of current opinion. One
such man was William Henry Giles Kingston, who wrote over a hundred
books for boys between 1850 and 1880. When 2,000 schoolchildren
were asked to name their favourite authors in 1888, Kingston ranked
second only to Dickens in the choices of the boys, with 179 votes
out of 790.[9] The judgement of posterity has been dismissive, the
Dictionary of National Biography mentioning merely that 'his tales
were quite innocuous, but most of them have proved emphemeral'. He
was, as this would imply, a man of his times.

Kingston was born in London in 1814, one of eleven children of a
solid family of English gentry: Fellows of the Royal Society, members
of parliament, justices of the peace, dons and admirals were his
ancestors, and the only exotic touch to his background was the family
firm, which was one of the hereditary English wine trading concerns
in Oporto. He spent his childhood, therefore, in Regent's Park, by
the sea at Lymington, and in Portugal. His school was Eagle House in
Hammersmith, where he was a contemporary of the egregious Martin
Tupper, who was later to acquire a sort of fame as a popular writer,
producing reams of verse in praise of progress, industry, homely
virtue and other values of the age of Samuel Smiles and *Self-Help*.[10]
Whether Kingston imbibed a regard for hard work and a confidence in
the Englishman's capacity to conquer all by its means at the same time
as Tupper did may only be conjectured; he represented in his breeding,
however, the union of gentle birth, gentlemanly public service,
earnest evangelical Christianity, and wealth drawn from overseas trade
which constituted the ideal Englishman as envisaged by his generation
when they came to educate the young. From this same school, owned
by the Rev. Edward Wickham, six of the most prominent public
school headmasters of the period during which Kingston wrote his boys'
books also emerged, to set their marks on Winchester, Harrow,

Haileybury, King's School Canterbury, Wellington and Eton.[11] After school Kingston went out to Portugal to live, in 1833, and saw some action during the siege of Oporto; this, and a short cruise on board His Majesty's sloop of war *Orestes*, in 1834, was all the experience of the active life that he had on which to base his stories, except for travelling about as a private gentleman. He began to write romances with a strong Gothic vein, for adult readers, while he was still living in Portugal.[12]

On returning to live in England in 1844, presumably still supported by the income of the family firm, Kingston became interested in the question of emigration, and became a member and later the honorary secretary of the Colonization Society, for whom he wrote manuals and publicity pamphlets, and edited from 1849-52 the *Colonial Magazine*. There are large and obvious differences between the mood and motives of the enthusiasts of colonial emigration in the 1840s, and later Imperialism. The first inducement to settlement overseas was poverty at home, rather than pioneering spirit, but in the 1840s philanthropic concern coupled a wish to assist the starving poor with a growing desire to see the colonies themselves, as centres of English cultural and religious values, grow and thrive. The aim was to see evangelical Christianity and the efficacy of hard work link all settlers, from all social levels, into an extended England which was not to conquer, but to convert and make fruitful, the rest of the world. Those left at home would also benefit, in terms of trade and work: by 1850 trade with the Empire accounted for 30 per cent of British exports and 23 per cent of imports.[13]

Kingston's interest in this was balanced between practical and spiritual considerations. He saw the colonies as fields of endeavour for working men of the lower and middle classes, and the men themselves, and their wives and families, as being in urgent need of cultivation by Christian missionaries. As secretary of the Colonization Society, he sought out emigrants everywhere, from the Marylebone workhouse to the Shetland Isles, and urged on the missionaries who were beginning to organise ministration at the dockside and on the voyage, helping to equip them with SPCK tracts, books, prayer books and Bibles, which were supplied to ships from 1846.[14] He assisted the SPCK in this task with a practical manual on how to emigrate, which they published as nos 14-17 of their Emigrant Tracts in 1851. Kingston's philanthropic activity took this form for ten years, until in 1856 he shifted his interest to the Mission to Seamen, once again becoming honorary secretary. This was a related activity, in that he came to it through work on the emigrant ships, where he observed the degraded and godless state of the men who manned the vessels; even more than the Colonization Society, this was evidence of evangelical commitment, and all the first committee were, like him, 'emphatically men of evangelical sympathies'.[15]

Kingston began to publish boys' books in 1851, the year his emigrants' manual appeared. *Peter the Whaler* relies heavily upon current models. The hero is the son of an Irish clergyman, who is sent to sea for poaching on the neighbouring lord's estate in evil company. Thus far he is derived from Marryat's scapegrace young men, and in the course of his adventures he also emulates them in that he is rescued by, and then rescues in his turn, a beautiful girl of highly respectable family and fortune, with whom he has every prospect of uniting himself in the last chapter. Unlike Marryat's old-fashioned heroes, however, he comes home having acquired no material wealth, but 'infinitely richer' having 'learned to fear God, to worship Him in his works, and to trust to His infinite mercy'. Kingston lays claim, in fact, to the presentation of a developing hero, who progresses to maturity by means of the adventures he passes through, becoming a responsible Christian gentleman. The story is to some extent matched to such an intention, presenting a very simply linked series of adventures, but with some attempt to show Peter in each one responding with growing understanding. He accepts his humble and slighted position on his first ship, unjust as it is, by following the advice of a dry American, Silas Flint, who tells him it is sensible to grin and bear matters until he can improve them. He progresses another step by rejecting Flint's offer of a place on a raft, when their ship catches fire, in order to stick to his duty aboard. Flint's pragmatism is essentially selfish, and Peter's moral awareness is not very strong, so when they reach America Flint is able to persuade him to succumb to his old temptation, to go hunting, and he misses his safe passage home.

Seeking to catch up with the ship, which carries the girl he is falling in love with, Mary, and is commanded by her father, he treks south through America, and becomes involved in a series of fantastic adventures. He antagonises a pirate captain, and by a series of coincidences, as is appropriate in a romance, he is first put in a position to prove his personal courage by defying the pirate, and then shows moral courage by choosing to take (and therefore to be bound by honour to keep) an oath to join him, in order to be able to rescue Mary and her father from his clutches. The moral pattern has thus moved into the realm of fantasy; Peter is finally retrieved from his position by showing great bravery and resource, not to say trickery and moral sleight of hand, in delivering up the pirates to justice. He escapes condemnation as one of them by the timely appearance of Mary and her father in the court.

Shipped in the US navy, he finds himself a cheerful Irish comrade, an English lad whom he can protect from bullies, and a mentor, Andrew Thompson, a seaman who is to teach him his trade and also lead him to a true Christian morality. Their adventures begin with a shipwreck on an iceberg, then take in a lengthy whaling cruise in the ship which rescues them, and a protracted period ashore in the Arctic. Marryat and Cooper supplied the earlier events; these adventures are derived from a factual account of whaling, recently reprinted by the RTS,[16] and from *Robinson Crusoe*, which had already perhaps given something to the conception of Peter's bad behaviour to his parents when he began his adventures. The notion of having one's shipwrecked survivors in Arctic conditions was not Kingston's exclusive idea, and became rather a favourite as tropical islands palled.[17] The author's main interest is in the opportunities it gives for Peter to learn from Andrew's wise and Christian manner of managing the rest of the men.

Throughout the story Peter learns by precept and example. At the beginning he has no proper sense of even his first duty, to his parents, but he learns by the contrasting examples of good and bad officers on his first ship, during the fire, and by doing his duty is saved not only from that predicament, but from his later involvement with the pirates. This is enforced for the reader by a brief paragraph of Peter's reflections on having 'acted rightly, according to the best of my belief . . . I have thus invariably found it in all the affairs of my life. When I have conscientiously done my duty, though inconveniences and annoyances may have apparently happened in consequence, the end has always been fortunate when I have been able to arrive at the result.' This is the moral of Peter's story; other messages in the early part of the book are addressed by Kingston directly to the reader, asking in one aside that those who grow up to positions of power should assist the poor seamen, and in another that they should look into the state of the emigrants.

Like Marryat, the author had his own favourite good causes in mind in portraying scenes of shipboard disorder, cruelty and violence, but his is a philanthropic rather than a professional cause. His evangelical intention becomes more personally directed in the second half of the book, when through Andrew he can deliver lectures about the evils of drink, trust in God and all sorts of prudent behaviour. Andrew's practical knowledge and advice is shown to be based on Christian principle, and he repeatedly saves the shipwrecked crew from its own follies. These admonitions, and the passages of information scattered throughout the book about seamanship, whaling, eskimos and other matters, are brief, pointed and fairly convincingly integrated with the action. Though unmistakably derived from the quasi-fictional manner of offering instruction to the young by means of an all-wise mentor, Kingston's tone is far less offensive than that would suggest. Peter and Andrew both speak with simplicity, not bogus humility, and there is no sense that the author is writing down to us; his heroes have an authority in their advice which derives from their bravery and active leadership in the tale itself.

Peter the Whaler was well received,[18] and Kingston found himself greeted not simply as an author but as the veritable Peter by children whom he encountered. Hastening to follow up his success he published three books in that year and the next, and fell back, as others had done, on basic romance patterns of story-telling; he produced in *Mark Seaworth* (1852) a foundling romance in which the hero is discovered as an infant adrift on the ocean in an open boat, and subsequently spends his youth searching the globe for his lost sister. He encounters fiendish pirates and friendly traders and settlers, and finally finds her when he is enslaved in Borneo; on the last page he regains family and fortune, in spite of all villainy at home and abroad. This reversion to a primitive pattern (the hero's journey through peril to the restoration of identity and birthright, and the heroine's preservation of innocence to stand at his side at the end, with all events however unlikely organised to fit into this chain) gives the book a unity which Peter's various adventures did not achieve. Instead of the development of the hero which Kingston was attempting to demonstrate in *Peter the Whaler*, the major lesson to be learnt from Mark Seaworth's adventures, stated in the first chapter and confirmed by all events, to be affirmed at the end, is simply a belief in an all-wise Providence: 'I must now wish my readers farewell. I hope that they will ever firmly believe, as I have been taught to do by the occurrences of my life, that in whatever peril we may be placed, God is at hand to protect us; and that whatever apparent misfortune may occur to us, He orders them for our ultimate and permanent benefit.' Kingston, in other words, handles a romance story as a captured myth, as other evangelical writers do, to reinforce Christian belief.

Kingston's tale is full of action and exotic adventure, with tigers shot or pirate cutters burned on every page, and hair's-breadth escapes the normal outcome of most chapters, but the providential message is, if anything, more insistantly stressed by these means, than it is in a

Sunday school tale of humble domestic life. He is also less careful, in this book, to integrate the useful information and the moral homilies with the tale; where Peter's development allowed the hero and the reader to learn together, the romance story offers only pretexts for the inclusion of informative or exhortatory asides. The opening chapters are particularly self-consciously written with the role of responsible writer, who captures the attention of the young in order to teach them, in mind. Nautical snippets, descriptions of India, Java, coral islands, native villages and racial types crop up at every turn, mixed with exhortations on the need for earnest prayer and the demands of Christian duty.

As the story gets under way, however, a more coherent direction of the reader's responses and reflections does emerge. The author's mind runs on certain topics, which affect the organisation of the story on more than one level. In the matter of education, for example, he is concerned with the changing role of the schoolmaster, and the growing importance of the school as an institution. Perhaps without being conscious of it, he makes this a part of the guiding Providence of the story. in the course of his search for pirates who have carried off his sister, Seaworth's ship rescues a man adrift on a hencoop off the coast of New Guinea, who turns out to be an old schoolfellow, who not only encourages Mark to trust in God's help, but actually proves that it is at work by bringing news that will assist him in his quest. The romance patterning of events, which dictates that all events are meaningful rather than random, is thus made to convey both a Christian and a social message. At the climax of the tale, Mark at last finds his sister, in great danger, and 'holding her light form in my left arm, with my sword I kept them at bay, as I saw the infuriated savages, with brandished weapons, close round us'. In these dire straits he is astonished to see another savage, in fantastic dress, who steps up to him and waves the attackers back, remarking '"Mark Seaworth! . . . I am delighted to find you old fellow . . . you remember Blount at old Liston's. I am the same."'

The adventurous spirit which scatters these young men so opportunely in his path is not produced by the school they actually attended, which is old-fashioned, but it will be fostered, the narrator proposes, by the new education which he recommends. He deprecates private tutors,

who think they have done their duty when they have taught their pupils the sufficient knowledge of Latin and Greek, and mathematics to enable them to enter the universities, without a

thought beyond — without pointing out to them clearly and
unmistakably, whatever may be their station in life, that they must
have responsibilities, and that they should so act in everything
they do here, that they may be ever prepared for entering the
life which is to endure for ever! . . . What I wish you to remember
is this, that every one of you — the poorest and humblest as well
as the richest — may do a great deal of good to your fellow-
creatures, if you will but try to find out the way; and also that
you cannot devote yourself to amusement, as so many do, without
committing a very grave fault.

Seaworth, coming from the wider world, observes that at his English
school the boys were

not sufficiently instructed in their future duties and responsibilities
in life. It was not sufficiently impressed on those destined to
become landed proprietors, that they should consider themselves
in the light of stewards over their estates, and guardians and advisers
of their tenantry . . . little attention was paid to the moral cultivation
of the boys, and still less to their physical development.

Although games and bodily discipline were neglected for Latin and
Greek, he made the friends there who do him such sterling service later:
they are young Englishmen, and the world is their oyster.
  This conviction of the Englishman's potential and his consequent
responsibilities is the other preoccupation which shapes Kingston's tale
and tends to dominate his reflections, in the form of questions of
exploration, conquest, missions and colonial rule. The various
southern and eastern peoples whom Seaworth encounters in his search
for his sister are carefully differentiated, not only by way of useful
information about their huts and headdresses, but in moral terms.
Papuan cannibals, we learn, attack brave but unwarlike Malays, and
the people of Borneo and their fertile land provoke in Seaworth an
interesting chain of reflections, moving from factual jottings to
economic observations, and on to loftier justifications for interference:

I observed extensive groves of bamboo at the back of some of the
houses, and pine-apple plantations luxuriating in the dark damp
shady nooks. Then there are large fields of the most magnificent
maize . . . The cultivation of these various productions of the earth
was certainly very rude; but wherever I went I observed a greater

approach to the arts of civilisation than I expected, but more
especially I was struck with the immense resources of the
country — the extreme fertility which Providence has so bountifully
bestowed on it, and the great reciprocal advantages which the
inhabitants would reap by a free commercial intercourse with
civilised countries.

When I became better acquainted with the people, I felt
convinced that, notwithstanding their many barbarous and cruel
customs, they possessed dispositions which, if properly cultivated
by the introduction of the true spirit and tenets of Christianity,
and a firm and judicious government, would form them into
prosperous and happy communities.

The mixture of the missionary, leadership and economic motives which
led on from an interest in emigration and in foreign trade, to the
development of British imperialism, is clearly present here, in 1852.[19]
An earlier passage in the same book shows very clearly how the
movement from evangelical to imperialist feeling, and specifically the
sense of the Englishman's special duty in this, was felt to derive in
some way from the teaching of Arnold. Fairburn, a pious seaman, asks
Seaworth:

'I wonder how it is God allows cannibals and suchlike savages to
exist. Does he punish them as he would us if we committed the like
acts, do you think?'

'I have been taught to think that we ought not to attempt to
account for many of the Divine ordinances, otherwise than by
believing that they are a part of one great and beneficent system.
As God is just, we cannot suppose that He would consider ignorant
savages equally guilty with educated men, who know and disobey
his laws. I have an idea, that savages exist to employ the energies of
Christian men in converting them to the truth, and civilising them.
I may be wrong; but the great law of nature would make me suppose
I am right. We have to toil to make the earth yield us produce, thus
to strengthen our physical qualities; and I believe we have many
moral duties to perform, in order to draw forth and strengthen our
moral qualities. We have the poor to feed and clothe, the ignorant
to educate, the turbulent to discipline; why should we not believe
that, situated as Great Britain is, with more extensive influence than
any other nation on the earth, she has the duty committed to her of
civilising the numberless savage tribes with whom her commerce brings

her in contact?'

'There is much truth in what you say, though the idea is new to me; where did you get it?' he asked. I told him, from my school-fellow, Prior, who had a particular friend studying under the excellent and justly celebrated Dr. Arnold, then not so well known to the world as he has since become.

When Kingston revised this book for later editions sometime in the 1870s he cut the reference to Arnold; perhaps he thought the idea, which he offers here only tentatively, covering himself by attributing it to an authority, had become a generally accepted truth.

A similar modification, of the evangelical aspects of the novel in favour of more positive statement of imperialist ideas, can be seen in later revisions of other books Kingston wrote in the 1850s. In *Manco the Peruvian Chief*, for example, written like *Mark Seaworth* in 1852, the officer father of the young hero originally delivered weighty warnings against the glorification of his own calling, stressing the inevitable evil of war and pointing out that its only justification was self-defence; this has disappeared in the editions of the end of the century, throwing quite a different light on other passages of the novel, which meditate on the physical and moral superiority of the English.

The book is modelled upon *Waverley*, with David, the English boy hero, making his way through the outbreak of a war in which he is not directly involved, but which serves to educate him both in warfare and in the complexities of political and natural justice. The setting is Peru, and the rebel leader Manco is represented throughout as an Inca nobleman, a rightful ruler whose simple civilisation is superior to that of his decadent Spanish conquerors. David's father predicts 'a day of bitter retribution' for Spanish tyranny, the result of Spain's failure 'to reap any benefit from her apparently glorious conquest of the new world'. Her misgovernment has brought on her a curse, 'and the colonies she planted', the authorial voice adds, 'have been far outstripped in civilisation by those peopled by the Anglo-Saxon race'. As the conflict breaks out, David is wholeheartedly on the side of the rebels, and recounts with approval the execution of a villainous *corregidor*, taken in the luxurious pride of his farewell party, when he is about to return to Spain with the wealth he has extorted from the Indians under his rule.

David's own parents disappear, however, in a further massacre of whites, and while his faith in Manco's rectitude is unshaken, he soon sees enough to modify his first ardent view. He voices Kingston's attitude to colonial rule — that its justification and also its openness to abuse spring from what he assumes to be innate characteristics of the races involved. This god-given differentiation should lead to the acceptance of responsibility by superior races, and where it does not, all will suffer, for the inferiors can only destroy the order which oppresses them, not correct it. David observes:

> From the time that the Christian and the civilised Europeans first landed in Peru, they treated the ignorant and heathen natives with the greatest cruelty; and thus taught by their task-masters, they, on the first opportunity showed that they had not forgotten the lessons they had received, but treated them as they themselves had been treated. Had the Spaniards taught the Peruvians mercy, justice and piety, by their own example, this terrible outbreak would never have occurred, and the weaker race would have become willing servants to the stronger. We ought always to bear in mind that it is by the just administration of good laws, and by the conduct of the rich, the educated, and the powerful, that the lower orders are educated, as much, or even more, than by the lessons given them by their nominal instructors.

Thenceforth David attempts to pursue his own ends, to escape from the country, without committing himself either to the Indians, who were wrong in their revolt, or the Spaniards, who were wrong in their oppression. Dealing with a Spanish officer who wishes him to betray the Indian stronghold, he appeals to 'the old chivalrous spirit of the Castilians', and riding by the side of Manco into battle he assures his readers that 'my great object was, if possible, to mitigate the horrors which I dreaded would take place should my Indian friends prove successful'. Still emotionally committed to the cause of the underdogs, he is quite clear about their inevitable subjection, which is caused by their own weaknesses.

The ambiguities of David's position and his responses are resolved for him by a comic *deus ex machina* who seems to come straight from the melodrama stage of the 1850s — a British tar, simple, intrepid, invulnerably strong and cheerful, and untroubled by any mental or moral complexities. He rescues David from prison, fights without scruple against 'the dons', and convoys both his countryman and Manco out of the lost battle, Manco to exile with a savage tribe, there to await in vain the call to the restoration of his dynasty, and David to a ship to England, on which, of course, he also finds his parents.

Manco shows how Kingston's interest in emigration was broadening out into an ideal of English domination which, through trade, scientific and administrative expertise, and Christian zeal, might embrace the whole undeveloped world. His enthusiasm for emigration as an escape for the underprivileged was further modified until in *The Emigrant's Home*, published in 1856, he was restraining the unfit from emigrating rather than urging it as a universal panacea.

In that year, too, he transferred his main philanthropic efforts to the Mission to Seamen. The new assertive, outward-looking emphasis of his message crystallised into the philosophy of *Kingston's Magazine for Boys*, published from March 1859. The editorial address spells out its orientation to colonial and pioneering ideas: addressing himself to 'the boys of Great Britain, Ireland, the British colonies, and the United States' he says he hopes to give them a periodical 'which you will value and look over years hence as an old familiar friend, when you are battling with the realities of life under the suns of India, in the backwoods of Canada or the States, on the grassy downs of Australia, over the wide ocean, among the isles of the Pacific, or on the distant shore of Columbia'. The relationship is to be reciprocal: he wishes to publish 'the letters and journals of many of those who read the following pages when they commence their own travels in foreign lands'. Kingston's biographer calls the magazine 'a gigantic effort in which he deliberately set himself the task to educate an Empire, and in actual fact he became a great imperial schoolmaster'.[20] The contents illustrate the editor's idea of the interests of future empire-builders. Games and athletic feats are described, the idealisation of England is fostered in descriptions of homes and their presiding mothers, and reports of travels, biographies and direct addresses enforce the message that 'the lot of all people, high and low, rich and poor, is to labour. You were not born into this world for the purpose of amusing yourselves.'

The main attraction of each issue was its fiction. The stories, *The Three Midshipmen* by Kingston under his own name and *Dick Onslow*, a western adventure printed under a *non de plume*, were used to boost the monthly sales, and then published in volume form at Christmas to make good the magazine's finances. It was in these protracted, episodic tales, especially *The Three Midshipmen* and its naval successors, that Kingston's ideal sons of the British Empire were exhibited in action. Kingston had used nautical settings from the time of *Peter the Whaler*, and he had no need to change much of his narrative technique for the naval tales. He still relied upon the impact of set-piece descriptions in a series of loosely-linked scenes depicting battles, escapes, ships sinking or set on fire, which he tended to distinguish by a shift to the historic present or to isolate as frozen, heightened tableaux which he explored detail by detail, each additional stroke suggesting a moral to be drawn. For the purposes of magazine serialisation this method was ideal, and enabled Kingston to extend the story at will, and to provide each episode with a dramatic climax, often a cliffhanger as shameless as those used by the hack writers of penny publications which his magazine sought to supplant. He converted their methods to wholesome purposes by the addition of historical information, detailed accounts of real campaigns, with the full lists of ships and men engaged, which added weight to the adventures of his heroes and took from them a colouring of excitement, suffusing history with patriotism.

The persons presented in these settings were still the array of types and relationships he had used in earlier books, but their functions were shifting to a new imperialist emphasis. Marryat remained his model; his Midshipman Merry, in the book of the same name, for example, is simply a puerile Jack Easy; but the scapegrace hero had become a Christian convert in *Peter the Whaler*, and was now transformed into an example of the salutary effects of good schooling on the upper classes. Dicky Sharpe, the heir to a baronetcy in *Salt Water* (1857), declares himself cured of his puppyish faults by naval discipline; he is not the central character of the story, but is represented as in every way inferior to Neil D'Arcy, who is the equivalent of Easy's friend Gascoigne, the career officer, who here emerges as the model of the serious young man of the professional classes, and is the hero of the tale. The glorification of the working professional is carried into the portrayal of the older officers; Marryat's hard-bitten, hard-swearing old drunks are represented only by the mate Hanks, who is ashamed of his own ignorance and weakness, and seeks to protect the hero from falling into such faults. Most officers presented are exemplary figures, role models for the young men in their charge and repositories of wisdom in whom the seaman may put unquestioning faith.

Kingston's ideal man was the senior naval officer, whom he imagined commanding ships in the heroic days of the 'great war' with France sixty years before. The living exemplar had been his great-uncle, Admiral Sir Harry Burrard Neale, of whom he spoke in the dedication of *Peter the Whaler*, recommending him as a model to his young cousin, then joining the navy. Neale, Kingston affirmed, was a friend and father to his men, never swore, and his crew alone remained faithful at the Mutiny of the Nore. His objective in depicting his simple boy heroes is to show his reader how to become such a paragon. They start with no natural advantages beyond the inestimable virtue of their nationality, and have only to live up to it, and act and develop as required of them by the service of their country, to arrive at its highest rewards.

The nature of the reward had also changed since Kingston had Peter undergo conversion and return home empty-handed but infinitely richer in spirit. The natural consequence of working hard, doing one's duty and taking up the Englishman's destined tasks is earthly success and prosperity: the three midshipmen are promoted in the natural course of a series of sequels until they become the three admirals. What happens is not a return to Marryat's happy ending in a display of personal wealth, but the replacement of the spiritual inspiration of the Celestial City with that of an idealised England. The sailor's ultimate reward, his promised land, is decisively relocated in this world, in an idyllic pastoral vision of the country he has left. Marmaduke Merry, like Tom Brown and many subsequent boyish heroes, is born in the Shires, of a family of unpretentious squires stretching comfortably back to the Conquest; Jack (in *Old Jack*, 1871) is a life-long sailor, born in Ireland, but sustained in the far regions where he serves among savages by one glimpse of 'rich meadows, waving cornfields . . . roses and honeysuckles . . . the sequestered village with its open green and neat cottages . . . the unpretending parsonage . . . rosy, noisy children . . . men in long white smocks . . . and . . . contentment visible everywhere' which represent his English heritage.

Secular, nationalist idealism creates certain problems Kingston cannot satisfactorily solve in these books. In a Christian formulation of duty the reward of good behaviour is alike for all in the next world; but with secularisation of the message comes the difficulty of the manifest inequality of rewards for people of different ranks, and thence of worldly ambition, which the moralist may seem to foster. His insistence upon effort being bound to bring its own reward logically encourages notions of rising and possible prosperity and promotion for all, which is not practical or desirable for the state of society which he wishes to recommend to his reader. When, therefore, he takes a naval hero who is a seaman rather than an officer, in *True Blue*, tensions arise which overshadow the simple heroic message, and the story turns rather upon whether or not Billy will allow himself to be raised to the quarterdeck, and thus leave the humble station in life to which he was born. To justify the inevitable decision in favour of the *status quo*, Kingston turns Billy's humble birth and aspirations into a description of simple, pure-hearted boyhood, represented as superior to the temptations of wealth and sophistication, in much the same way as Kingsley glorified the primitive virtues of Amyas Leigh; and he makes the final scene, in which Billy's choice of his adult role is confirmed, into a fantasy of popular acclaim. Married to a village girl and promoted to warrant-officer, as befits his father's son, he arrives at Portsmouth harbour attended by all his friends, both wealthy and humble, and embarks to rejoin his ship:

> As the boats hove into sight, up went to each masthead, from spanker to flying jibboom ends, lines of gay-coloured flags; a band on board struck up 'See the Conquering Hero comes! . . . Up and down the harbour pulled the bridal squadron, and the crews of every ship, as they passed, took up the cheer and welcomed the bridegroom, for True Blue and his deeds were now well known throughout the British fleet. He had not aimed high, in one sense of the word, and yet he had in another sense always aimed high and nobly – *to do his duty*.

With the departure of the evangelical stress upon the equality of all sinners, the function of the mentor figure in these stories changes: Andrew Thompson was able to guide Peter both spiritually and practically, though he was socially his inferior; their relationship was unaffected by their differences of birth, and Peter was unequivocally the one who benefited from the association. Thompson was a kind of personification of the chastening, converting effect which experience at sea had on the boy; his status and power were considerable. But the mentors dwindle. Billy in *True Blue* has a collection of seamen for his godfathers, and, since he is only a seaman himself, he is allowed to retain them throughout the book, and follows their advice; but they teach him much more about his duty as a sailor than about God. In *Salt Water*, the hero's teacher is an old retainer in his family who primes the boy with the ambition to go to sea and enough elementary seamanship to keep his end up when he first enters; after the opening scenes he ceases to be important, except as a homely comic figure, and Neil's visits to him serve only to show how their difference in rank progressively separates them as he grows up. In *Saved From the Sea* (1875) the mentor who starts the hero on his way with books and advice is not even a seaman, but an eccentric tailor, who is therefore left behind, ashore, after the first chapter.

In a similar way, the role assigned to foreigners in the naval stories is determined by the focus upon nationalist heroics. In sea battles the British tars regularly win because by discipline and simple physical superiority they can work their guns twice as fast as any other seamen; the defeated enemy, usually French, is always treated by them with the greatest courtesy and tenderness. Such an adversary is polite and gentlemanly, and a patriot himself; real villains are bastardised riff-raff with no proper race or allegiance, and so without any motivation other than personal gain, which makes them easy to overcome as they man their grubby pirate vessels. Black characters in these stories, as in the tales of colonial rule, are treated as raw material, like the poor of England, to be moulded by their officers into a loyal and loving servant class: the black ship's boy who is devoted to the service of a kindly midshipman in *Washed Ashore* is no different from Toby in *Midshipman Merry*, who is a peasant from Merry's father's estate who has followed the young master to sea.

Visionary colonialism and naval heroics were not Kingston's final message to the young. The magazine did not succeed. Whether the young men of England were not yet ready for such a strident summons to work out their imperial destiny, or whether the purchasers of annuals were still chiefly adults seeking a primarily Christian message to pass on, while boy purchasers of magazines chose cheaper and less didactic prints, Kingston's venture did not command a sufficiently large sale. He repeatedly explained that he was writing for all ages and all classes, urging readers 'to get it into naval and military libraries, both for officers and men, at home and abroad — into institutes and village libraries', but he lost money on every issue, and the annual volume did not make up the deficit.

After this disheartening failure Kingston lost confidence, to some degree, in himself and his message: feeling that financial failure meant rejection by the boys whom he sought to benefit, and perhaps even touched by the quasi-superstitious notion that the failure of an enterprise must mean that God did not intend it to succeed, he was deeply disturbed, especially when he was almost made bankrupt in 1868. He followed his own often-repeated advice to keep on trying and doing one's duty to the last, and turned out many more books and stories, working at some time for most of the juvenile publishers, sponsored and commercial: when the magazine folded, some unquantifiable mixture of dutiful humility, loss of confidence in his particular Christian-cum-imperialist message and sheer lack of money drove him to return to the SPCK; not as an expert contributor to a specialist tract series, as he had been in 1850, but offering his children's stories for consideration by the General Literature Committee like any unknown lady writer.

The first titles he offered to the society show a clear intention to return to a colonial emphasis, but this time he paints a less sanguine picture of life as a missionary for Christ and England. In 1864 he sent in manuscripts of *The Log House by the Lake*, *Rob Nixon the Old White Trapper*, *The Gilpins and Their Fortunes* (set in Australia) and *Philip Mavor* (set in Africa). The society was not overawed: *The Log House*, *Rob Nixon* and *The Gilpins* were all sent back to Kingston with the remarks of the committee, to be revised in accordance with instructions before they would be reconsidered. Some later efforts were even less eagerly received: in 1870 the committee had readers report their response to *Sunshine Bill* as 'fairly favourable' three times before setting it up in print for final consideration, and then they demanded revisions. In 1877 Kingston wrote to the committee about a book he wanted to write on Admiral Benbow: he 'wished to know if the committee would allow him £50 therefore'. Their cool reply was that they 'saw no difficulty in the way of paying Mr. Kingston this sum for his book provided it commended itself to them, and was the same size as his last'.[21] Fifty pounds was not much more than a basic fee.

Some of the sea stories not published by the SPCK also show Kingston modifying his concentration upon the heroic virtues of the English officer. *Old Jack* includes a rise from absolute beggary to wealth and position which reflects the less class-conscious, more primitive values of *Self-Help*, and a gentleman-born who has fallen to the level of ordinary seaman, and then achieves a shady affluence in the pay of a foreign power, before ending his days as the victim of a sordid sexual intrigue. In the same book criticisms of the abuse of colonial power are levelled at Anglo-Saxons, the slave-holders of Jamaica, and racial superiority is denied in the description of the leader of the Maroons (the revolted slaves), who is allowed to make an impassioned plea for his people, in standard English, and is offered as proof that if blacks had the 'advantages of the whites, I believe as many buds in the one case as in the other would bear rich fruit'. The chauvinism of some of the stories of the 1860s is also tempered. In *From Powder Monkey to Admiral* (1879), Kingston weakens the stress upon the glories of conquest by suggesting that the common people on both sides of the Channel regard the war between England and France as an interruption of trade, and has his shipwrecked heroes rescued and virtually adopted as sons by a French fisherman and his family.

In fact in all the books of his last years, as his biographer noted disapprovingly,[22] the tone was increasingly religious, suggesting the collapse of certainties and worldly optimism, and retreat to the safety of evangelical Christianity from his outward-looking, idealistic imperialism; he focuses increasingly on the need for salvation for the sinful individual. He becomes concerned, too, with definitions of heroism that go beyond the life of action, and preclude the violent. Even in the stories of the navy and its glories he had always been inclined to defuse aggression, and usually portrayed little violence that could be avoided: Jack, the English boy in *The Three Midshipman*, was made to show great compunction about shooting men, even though he had been practising to become expert with his gun, and was only called upon to use it on evil slave-traders. In *The Gilpins* this reluctance to shoot is very marked, even when his heroes must defend themselves or die, and especially when their attackers are not wholly responsible, blacks or ignorant poor men suborned by evil whites. In *The Ferryman of Brill* he republished fugitive stories which originally appeared in *The Quiver*, which show, in the words of the heroine of 'Frank Cotton', that 'it is not necessary for a man to go and fight, and kill his fellow-creatures, to be a hero'. Rescue rather than conquest is the theme of these tales: rescue of the young or weak by the strong, of whole ships' crews by an intrepid individual who trusts in God, of one simple fisherboy by another who has learnt to stick to his duty, of the ignorant in general by the Missions to Seamen and, finally, universal rescue by 'the Good Captain' — Neale, ruling his crew by kindness and preserving them from sin during the mutinies, used like a sermon text as a type of God's rule and rescue of mankind.

In *A True Hero* (1872), published by the Sunday School Union, Kingston explored, to some extent, the contradictions of his Christian and imperialist beliefs and arrived at a synthesis, in his version of the story of William Penn and the founding of Pennsylvania. He opens by showing Penn heroic and saintly in the context of the corruption of Restoration England, rejecting his father the Admiral's way of life for the sake of Protestant freedom, and turning away from warfare which was only a means of worldly advancement and profit. Kingston gives him a young follower, Wenlock Christison, who is temporarily ensnared by the glitter of the court and martial life, unable to bring himself to be a pacifist and a mere shopman. Through this Everyman, adventures, sea battles and conventional heroics are admitted to the story, but its dénouement is the gathering of all good men into the new

colony, formed by friendly treaty between the noble Indian chiefs and
Penn, 'the English governor, the handsomest and most graceful
present', who told them in their own language, 'that they had a common
Father, who reigns above'. 'Thus was Pennsylvania happily founded
without injustice, without bloodshed, without crime; and, blessed by
Heaven, continued to flourish, the most happy and prosperous colony
ever formed by Britons.' True heroism, then, is entering only into the
good fight – the surrender of the world and the endurance of
persecution – like William Penn, and all who do so are assured that
they will find, as he did, 'firm faith even in this life . . . rewarded'.

A *True Hero* is interesting not only for its idealistic reconciliation of
the potentially discordant aspects of Kingston's own doctrine, but for
the form which makes that projection possible, that of historical
romance. It crosses an adventure-story version of the romances of
Scott with that form of protestant hagiography which set up as
models for the young events and figures from the political and military
history of England, bathed in the light of their authors' fervent beliefs.
G. A. Henty's works are only the full development of this long and
highly productive tradition, and despite Kingsley's desire to provoke
a decisive break with the moral writing for children which preceded
his own times, Kingston's books are a point of transition within
the tradition, rather than a new beginning.

Kingston's output viewed as a whole underlines this very clearly,
in its variety, and shifts of emphasis and direction. His many historical
tales include some which are primarily sectarian, some which are naval,
and others which concentrate on the early history of the Empire.
Besides the sorts of book which have been discussed here, he published
versions of earlier children's books, like Agnes Strickland's *The Rival
Crusoes*, and translations, actually made by his wife, of the books
by Jules Verne. He also published quasi-factual accounts of his own
travels, such as *Western Wanderings* (1856) about his visit to Canada,
which merge with books like *My First Voyage to the Southern Seas*
(1860), which are the travels of a briefly-realised fictional narrator; non-
fictional biographies and accounts of *Blue Jackets* (1854) and *Our
Soldiers* (1863) which shade into his military, naval and colonial
fictions; historical tales reaching as far back as *Jovinian* (1877); other
varieties of boys' story, such as the public school tale based on *Tom
Brown*, in *Digby Heathcote* (1860); and books specific to groups
beyond his usual mixed audience of boys, such as *Infant Amusements*
and *Taking Tales for Cottage Homes*,[23] both published in 1867.

If his output was prodigious, it was also very varied in length and in density: there is some careful, planned plotting and character-drawing which represent an effort to substantiate the symbolic or stereotypical figures with realistic detail and even pyschological complexity, and there are also many books which are only a routine rearrangement of threadbare motifs. Even these are a consequence of the seriousness of his intentions as a writer, rather than catchpenny or careless composition; the whole fabric of his stories is coloured by his particular vision of the capacities, potentialities and duties of the boy reader, and the tendency of his work was to abandon the relative density and complexity with which he began in *Peter the Whaler* for urgent iteration of his message through the fictional stereotypes which he established. Much repetition, and only a small gift for lively language, makes the reader whose appetite for shipwreck, sea battle, providential escape and the endless triumphs of the maturing male is limited feel the profusion of Kingston's work a burden; but its intention is wholly serious, and its moral effect, on readers to whom these things did make a strong appeal, cannot have been negligible.

Kingston set out as a pioneer on the path that boys' fiction was to take to the end of the century, leaving his conventional Christian contemporaries behind; but his personal loss of confidence, his adherence, after all, to strict evangelical ideals, caused him to turn back while imitators and later comers forged ahead. His contemporaries in writing for boys were perhaps less serious, less intent upon the complexity and importance of their message to the young, or perhaps just simpler men, whose faith, whether of the old kind or the new, was less self-questioning. They were certainly very numerous and prolific: the ever-growing number of publishers and purchasers of books for children ensured that anyone could have his say in the fictional guidance of the newly-discovered boy.

Other Versions of Boyish Heroism: the Trivialising of an Ideal

The spearhead of commercial publication of boys' stories in the 1860s was the boys' magazine. Kingston's own venture did not succeed, but others, sponsored by publishers with experience of popular markets, began in this period and flourished for many years. Beeton's *Boy's Own Magazine* was begun in 1855, and absorbed *Kingston's Magazine* as it went on; it published extracts from *Tom Brown's Schooldays* in 1858, and its story-tellers included J. G. Edgar, whose speciality was the historical romance, and Captain Mayne Reid. Beeton increased the price of the magazine from 2d to 6d in 1863, but promised readers another magazine at 1d if they could not manage 6d; *Chatterbox*, founded in 1866 by the Rev. J. Erskine Clark, was only ½d, to undercut the penny-dreadful market. Also in 1866, Edwin J. Brett's *The Boys of England*, one of the most popular and long-lived of these periodicals, began, and introduced the hero Jack Harkaway to an eager public. These successful publications precipitated a rush into the field, and many rivals appeared and disappeared in the following decades; they serialised great numbers of stories, of varying degrees of literary and moral worthiness, which formed, on the whole, the lightest end of the scale of acceptable reading for the young. Many famous late Victorian and Edwardian men recorded their adolescent addiction to these magazines, usually concluding that, though by later standards they were strong meat in their violence and fantastic disregard of real life, there was 'no harm in them'.[24]

Authors who earned their bread and butter contributing to the boys' periodicals might add to their income and their prestige and respectability by republishing in volume form, or writing other, perhaps weightier, stories, for the prize book trade. Commercial publishers of children's books in the late 1860s and 1870s were gathering in as many 'tales of incident and adventure' for boys as they could find. In 1873, for example, Routledge, who published a magazine for boys, also had a lengthy juvenile list. It was very eclectic and mixed fairy tales and old-fashioned tract and educational writers — Mrs Barbauld, for example, Mrs Trimmer, the Howitts, Harriet Martineau, and even Legh Richmond — with its books of history and science and a piecemeal collection of boys' stories drawn in twos and threes from most of the available modern authors: Marryat, the Rev. H. C. Adams, Anne Bowman, J. G. Edgar, Mayne Reid, R. M. Ballantyne and G. Manville Fenn. In the same year Warne could only muster for its '2/- Incident and Adventure Library' one book by J. T. Trowbridge, two by Kingston and one by Ballantyne, before sinking to a couple of dubiously appropriate classics, *Evenings at Home* and *Sandford and Merton*, and three Crusoe books. The lucky ones were the publishers with a substantial list of books by the new stars. By 1874 Nelson had their children's books neatly classified, and besides 'stories with a purpose', 'illustrated books for nursery reading', manuals of popular information and standard favourites, their list included categories called 'present and prize books', which were chiefly non-fictional accounts of exploration, history, and the lives of great men, by one M. Jones, 'books of useful knowledge', covering inventions, maritime geography, the history of commerce, and plant and animal life, 'books of example and encouragement for boys', which were real and fictional biographies of men who have risen, and, in pride of place, 'books of travel and adventure for boys' — five by Kingston, seven by R. M. Ballantyne. Even the religious societies began to cultivate and advertise their writers for boys: the SPCK had not only its books by Kingston, which it did not treat as very different from its other general fiction, but historical tales by A. H. Englebach and Hope Moncrieff, which were distinguished by their authors' names in the lists. The RTS relied on G. E. Sargent and Kingston, until the *Boy's Own Paper*, launched in 1879, marked a decisive change in interpretation of their brief, and enabled them to draw on the next generation of boys' writers, headed by Gordon Stables, Talbot Baines Reed, Jules Verne and G. A. Henty.

Of the older generation, Captain Mayne Reid and Robert Ballantyne stand beside Kingston; Ballantyne, indeed, so outlived him in popularity that he has attracted modern critical attention, chiefly because of his Crusoe story, *Coral Island*. The range of emphasis in modulation of the didactic message acceptable in the mid-century can be judged by a comparison between the three writers. All have a common core of subjects, but Mayne Reid specialised in colourful pioneering adventures in the Americas, while Ballantyne, in producing his six-monthly volumes steadily for several decades, ranged over every possible setting and tried all the permutations of plot and character convention. Both differ from Kingston in the matter of fundamental moral seriousness, and in the degree of their didactic intention. They shared with each other an attitude to their writing and the experience upon which it was based with which Kingston would not have been entirely in sympathy; Kingston's biographer, in his analysis of his subject's work, did not mention Mayne Reid, and felt that Ballantyne stood outside the tradition of writing for boys that passed from Marryat through Kingston to Henty.[25] He was perhaps influenced in this judgement by resentment of Ballantyne's popularity, but it represents a true observation: indeed Ballantyne may have been the more popular writer with later generations of readers largely because his didacticism is less marked and his morality easier. He shared with Captain Mayne Reid a confidence in himself and his stories which suggests their limitations of horizons: they write for boys, or for the boy in men, and to a large extent they write as boys themselves.

Captain Mayne Reid might have been invented by Captain Marryat. Irish by birth, the eldest son of a presbyterian minister, he rebelled against entering the church and went off to make his fortune in the

USA. A series of adventures and occupations, including slave-trading and being a strolling player, a schoolkeeper and a poet, engaged him until he had a chance to fight in the US Army in the war with Mexico. He was wounded, indeed reported to be dead, and effectively invalided for the rest of his life; in 1846 he therefore began to write his romances, beginning with one intended for adult readers, *The Rifle Rangers*, first published in London in 1850. Back in Britain, he wrote out all his adventures in a series of such stories; the first intended for boys was *The Desert Home or the English Family Robinson* (1851).

Byronic, swashbuckling, a dandy who was politically not only radical but republican, and without Kingston's patrician family, Reid wrote romances which were such good fodder for the popular stage that he was moved to issue warnings and threats to other writers not to use his story *The Headless Huntsman* while it was in part-publication. Its success was the zenith of his fame and fortune, and he began in 1866 to build himself a folly, a setting for his fantasy life: a Mexican-style hacienda in Gerrards Cross. Like Sir Walter Scott's Abbotsford, it bankrupted him. He returned to the USA in 1867 and started a boys' magazine called *Onward*, which was chiefly a platform for his various campaigns and causes. It was even less successful than Kingston's venture, and rapidly drained him of all remaining financial resources. His health collapsed, the old wound flared up, Harriet Beecher Stowe attacked him for lecturing on Byron, and he retreated to England, where he tried to regenerate 'the drama à la Boucicault' by writing plays based on all his novels, and to retrieve his very scattered copyrights and establish a complete edition; he died in 1883.[26]

His life, then, was as romantic as his fiction, and as dependent upon the willingness of others to participate in his fantasies. He inspired besotted devotion in inexperienced women – his wife was captivated at the age of 13, and married him as soon as was legally possible, when he was already in his forties – and in boys, who followed him in person into absurd adventures and in his books through others more fantastic still. Like Marryat he wrote romances for adults which boys adopted, and they were just as unsuitable for the Victorian young. *The Rifle Rangers*, for example, opens with an irreproachable chapter of rhetorical description with overtones of nature-worship, such as a cross between Kingston and W. H. Hudson might have produced. However it then introduces a Byronic hero, Reid's fantasy self, who casually shoots strangers between the eyes in street brawls, defeats his rivals in fencing matches, leads a mongrel troupe of volunteer horsemen in guerilla warfare, and falls passionately in love – the phrase is wholly applicable – with a ferocious dark-eyed beauty whom he first beholds bathing. She has much in common with Amyas Leigh's wild Indian love in *Westward Ho!*, but she is, and remains, a Spanish Catholic, and the hero still marries her. The object of his own worship is a vaguely mystic sense of God in the wild beauty of nature; there is neither a Christian nor an Imperial lesson to be learnt from the book.

When Reid turned to writing deliberately for boys, the lessons he offered were more or less exclusively practical, or, at most, moral precepts enforced by reason rather than religion. *The Desert Home* (1851) is a story of emigration, giving information about settling in America; it engrafts his personal experience, and the figures of his romance writing (the hunter Lincoln, for example, drawn from Cooper's leather-stocking heroes, appears both here and in *The Rifle Rangers*) upon the fictional model of *The Swiss Family Robinson* (1814). The main story, framed by a first-person narrative, is of an Englishman who is brought up unwisely as a gentleman by his merchant father and squanders his substance before he marries and goes to the USA with his wife, who saves him from himself. He is fleeced by land speculators, sold a plot in an imaginary town, like Dickens's Eden, before being cast away, as it were, in a wagon-train disaster in the desert. He finds a secluded fertile valley, and makes his home there, and the rest of his story concerns the seriatim discovery of handy ways of supplying all the family's needs. Instruction is imparted to the reader in a manner not significantly removed from that of the 1814 model. A salt spring, for instance, not only yields the family the means to preserve meat, but yields the reader comprehensive information on Epsom salts, Glauber's salts, rock salt, bay salt, sea salt, salt mining, manufactured salt, salt panning both industrial and small-scale, and the relative salinity of the sea in various parts, all elicited by the questions of Frank and Harry to their encyclopaedic Papa.

The excitements of the journey to the valley, which involves for example the rescue of one of the babies from the howling wolves which devour the rest of the wagon train, give way to a series of instructive scenes where even fights between various wild animals lead inexorably to lectures about their various characteristics; the convenience with which all necessities turn up taxes the credulity of the reader almost as much as Wyss's island did. The book, however, is far less pious than its model. Some small lip service is paid to Christianity, but the spiritual contentment of the family comes not from resting on God's providential purpose in sending them there, nor

resignation to their present provision, but from the discovery that
valuable beavers have made their home in the valley, and in course of
time may be killed: they thus provide the possibility of 'exercising
our industry, so that *our time should not be wasted'*; and moreover
'we might yet make our *fortune in the desert!*' For all its momentary
excitements and physical crises, as men and boys confront the
hostility of nature, the action of the book lacks tension; the fortunate
outcome of each episode is a foregone conclusion, and the comic,
exciting or 'curious' events of their lives in the valley have no
compelling connection with each other. The framing story supplies a
romance interest, in that one of the narrator's companions turns out
to be the father of one of the children in the valley; but even that
discovery is made in the first quarter of the book, rather than being
saved to form a climax.

These literary shortcomings did not put off the first readers,
however: the desert island story has never needed any excitement
but the basic fascination of the details of survival. In other books
Mayne Reid's undigested mixture of information and adventure seems
to have been equally acceptable; prize and Reward purchasers were
often confused enough by the similarities of titles and style to give his
adult romances to the young, who found in them much the same
mixture, but held together by a story of full-blooded passions instead
of the ancient didactic formulae of question and answer. This chance
error may have added to his popularity with the young readers, for they
were probably able to share most of Captain Mayne Reid's dreams,
which are all very like the fantasies of male adolescence.

R. M. Ballantyne was perhaps a more orthodox figure than Mayne
Reid, with less of the popular charlatan and hack about him, and a
conventional evangelical cast of thought − he underwent a conversion
at the age of 23. They had much in common, however, and their
writing of books for boys seems to spring from common pyschological
sources, as part of a character which never outgrew, and indeed sought
to act out, its fantasy life of daring action, triumph and adventure.
Ballantyne, too, began his career by launching out into the wilds of
America, not in defiance of parental decisions, but as a 16-year-old
apprentice to the Hudson Bay Company, in 1841. His first writing was
done to alleviate the boredom of the snowed-up bunkhouse, and sent
back as letters to his mother; he drew repeatedly upon these six years
for his adventure stories, though much of his time in Canada had
actually been spent idling at office desks. He wrote an unsuccessful book
of travel anecdotes for adults and a revision of a learned work on Canada

before the expedient of popularising the experience, through a boys' adventure story and by lecturing, came to him. It was a truthful reflection of his imaginative relationship with the events of that period of his life. He took to the role of drawing-room adventurer whole-heartedly: growing a beard, and affecting picturesque trapper's costume, he strode about lecture halls telling lurid stories of Indians, singing boating songs and firing off a blank-loaded long-barrelled gun at a stuffed eagle.

He set the first two of his successful adventure stories, *The Young Fur Traders* (1856) and *Ungava* (1857), in the far north; the third was *Coral Island*, also published in 1857 and perhaps the most famous of the nineteenth-century desert island tales. Like Kingston and Mayne Reid, Ballantyne thought he could launch a magazine on the success of his first stories as a vehicle for his ideas and prestige; he could not convince any publisher that it would succeed, however, and so he was spared the financial losses which they both sustained. He was neither as rash in his dealings with publishers nor as reckless in building upon the popular appeal of his fantasy life as Mayne Reid was, and for the best of reasons – the previous generation of his family were the Ballantynes whose publishing business had shared the ruin of Sir Walter Scott's fall. He did continue to allow himself theatrical lecturing appearances, however, based on his subsequent adventure stories; and a critic who pointed out errors in the factual details of *Coral Island* gave him an excuse to involve himself physically in the settings for each new tale: he was collecting realistic detail, he claimed, of the fire service, deep-sea diving, the lifeboats, the Cornish mines, or whatever scene for action he could dream up. He was even able to persuade James Nisbet and Co., who became his publishers after he quarrelled with the terms Nelson gave to their children's writers, to pay him expenses for these excursions. The lectures were modestly remunerative in themselves, clearing £5-£9 a time;[27] he soon had no real need of such sums, and his persistence in the physically and emotionally taxing living-out of his fantasies before an adoring audience reminds one irresistably of Charles Dickens.

Dickens, of course, greatly modified the complexity of his novels by the selection process involved in creating his readings; popular writers whose primary audience was the crowd attending recitations or penny readings are probably more nearly comparable with Ballantyne in artistic terms. George Sims, whose recitation ballads were not written for his own performance, but who still felt it part of his role to conduct himself flamboyantly as a 'great writer', driving out from his house in Regent's Park attended by dalmations, springs to mind. Both Mayne Reid and Ballantyne were more fully part of the demotic sub-culture than Kingston, and their personal popularity and the tone of their books reflect that difference.

Ballantyne, much more than Mayne Reid, retains the didactically moral and overtly religious bias of the earlier writers for children, but his motives were not as simply altruistic as Kingston's appear to have been. His shrewd dealings with publishers enabled him to support a large middle-class family in comfort upon his profits; his conviction that his writings were good for the boys for whom he wrote added to his personal comfort, for the status of children's writer was perhaps rather demeaning for a man of substance unless supported by a sense of religious duty.[28] He was no more than a man of his times in thus eliding evangelical duty and solid success. The publishers with whom he dealt on such a mutually profitable basis had made a similar shift, and the inexhaustible spring of fervent hard work and total personal dedication that had founded James Nisbet's publishing house as a mere part of his offering to the Lord and His people flowed more calmly into commercial channels for his heirs and successors. This is not to say that the bias of firms like Nisbet and Nelson was not still firmly Christian, sober, didactic and wholesome; but that they too felt the changes of emphasis to which evangelical feeling was subject, and found objects worthy of their attention in teaching other things besides the central message of the New Testament to their young readers. By the late 1870s this was even the case with the RTS.

Ballantyne's boys' books demonstrate this movement. Committing himself to writing for boys after his first success, he began ostensibly under the evangelical flag, but even at this early stage, with *Coral Island* and *Martin Rattler* (1858), there is a distinct difference between the moral shaping of his stories and those of his rivals and predecessors. The dilution of the moral and didactic intention is not as much of an artistic improvement as a modern reader repelled by the insistence of earlier writers might expect. If Ballantyne's prevailing tone of jocularity and dash is less heavy, it is also shallower, more suggestive of mechanism and emptier of commitment: ultimately, it is more insulting in its pandering to the reader and its patronising assumption of superiority to him.

The moral admonitions which Ballantyne offers are perfectly sincere of course and tend to concern themselves with popular philanthropic objectives of the day. He urges his readers to support the lifeboat service (*The Lifeboat*, 1864), the campaign against slavery

in Africa (*Black Ivory*, 1873), emigration schemes for London orphans
(*Dusty Diamonds*, 1884) or half-a-dozen other good causes, shading off
in one direction into large praises and claims for foreign missions,
repeatedly expressed in his stories of far-off places, and in the other
into fact-ridden panegyrics about the wonders of modern British society
as exemplified by such matters as the railways (*The Iron Horse*, 1871)
or the fire service (*Fighting the Flames*, 1867). These appeals, like
Kingston's similar urgings on behalf of the Mission to Seamen and other
evangelical writers' messages about city missions and children's
hospitals, are detachable, addressed directly to the reader at some
juncture of the story which seems to admit of the change of focus.

Ballantyne sometimes intended to illustrate the message in the story,
and was often very successful in whipping up support, as in the case of
his appeal for the Lifeboat Institution; but there is always a gap between
the message, and the reader's response to it in terms of action in the
real world, and the story itself, and the reader's response to the
situations and characters portrayed. It is not the magic of art, but the
inserted direct appeal, which is effective. In *Martin Rattler*, for
example, the contrast between English imperial ideals and the state of
the Southern American colonies of the old Spanish and Portugese
empires, which formed the substance of Kingsley's *Westward Ho!* (1855)
and Kingston's *Manco the Peruvian Chief* (1852), is given as a single
chapter, 'The Hermit's Story', which covers the history of Brazil from
1500 to the present in eighteen small pages, the last of which asserts
that 'Brazil . . . has only one want – it wants the Bible!' This need
impinges little upon the hero and his friend as they hear the tale, and
not at all on the course of the action. The chapter could easily be
skipped, and the informative, imperial and missionary lessons
painlessly sidestepped. In a later book, *The Lifeboat*, Ballantyne
actually asks his reader not to skip as he delivers his direct appeal; he
was always conscious of a need to avoid alienating rebellious attention.

In *Martin Rattler* the weight of useful information incident to the
progress of the narrative is also much attenuated, by comparison with
Mayne Reid. The effect is enlivening – the adventure progresses
smartly, and most of Ballantyne's stories have a pace and a brevity
of effect which distinguishes them from the mass of contemporary
writing in the mode. The writer was perhaps unconscious of,
or did not even wish to avoid, a certain consequent impoverishment:
his deftly conventional stories and characters seem empty of any
guiding purpose or *raison d'être*. When he has powerful motifs in hand,
especially in the outstanding example of *Coral Island*, this can mean

that the romance story-pattern which evangelical writers sought to capture for Christian purposes could regain its own power, reverting to its own primitive justifications and meaning. When there is no such pull in the stories he chooses or invents they remain hobbled by values which have become mere assumptions, expressed in conventions which have become cliché and device.

Ballantyne was not an effective writer of romance. When he attempted a structuring use of the patterns of the quest, or of the hero's proving ordeal, he had no sense of the rules of the device, and failed to signal its meaning to the reader, who is therefore more surprised than satisfied by the turns of the story or its providential solution. This is even the case in *Coral Island*, where the narrator is snatched from the island paradise and goes through a series of adventures amongst pirates, cannibals and missionaries before returning with a ship to rescue his friends. The movement ought to be effective but is not, perhaps because of the nature of the appeal which the Crusoe motif has — it should be the proving ordeal, but it is here treated quite unexpectedly as the static condition of perfection from which the hero must go forth. His departure is unprepared for, and his return leads only to the departure of all three boys from the island, snatching away the sensed ending of the quest, and replacing them meaninglessly in the ordinary world.[29]

In *Martin Rattler* the quest or journey does not impinge at all upon the rest of life, which exists as a framing story of Martin as a little boy, before he goes away, and as a Christian convert, when he comes back, the transformation being effected not by his adventure but at the deathbed of his aunt. The same unimportance may be felt in relation to the adventure in *The Gorilla Hunters* (1861), where the heroes of *Coral Island* foregather for a hunting trip to Africa and return to England at the end of it with enough 'boxes of specimens' to furnish a magnificent exhibition, but personally unchanged by all they have gone through. They did not go to seek their fortunes, and their adventures, however thrilling and however influential upon the lives of the natives, missionaries and gorillas whom they met, are unimportant in their own lives except as an amusing interlude. It is not even a formative adventure, for they are presented as fully-developed and in no need of conversion or growth.

Ballantyne was no more interested in the developing mind of a hero than he was aware of the possible reverberation of a story in timeless patterns; many of his tales have a fully-adult main character or group of characters offered as perfect specimens of Englishmen, but

with no invitation to the reader to take them seriously as role models
or points of departure for self-examination. They are strong, silent
types of great physical strength and delicate manners, often described
as being 'fierce as a lion and gentle as a woman': not like Kingsley's
'bear's son' Amyas, fallible and struggling and gloriously sympathetic
for all his power, but gruffly and remotely perfect — the boy's idea
of a man, rather than the man's idea of a boy.

Where such paragons appear in most moral tales for children the
author provides another figure who is less than perfect, whose
aspirations to be like the hero both humanise his perfection and
engage it with the reader's interest in the story. This role in Ballantyne's
work is often given to a very much younger boy, who admires the
hero but whose chief function is as a vehicle for the childish humour
of the book, like the punster and practical joker Peterkin in *Coral
Island*. One of the successful touches of originality in that book is the
mild astringency which creeps in on occasions when Peterkin actually
mocks the learning or solemnity of his elders, though the bookish
Ralph, the narrator, is more often its target than the all-powerful
athlete, Jack. The qualities Jack represents are normally treated here
and elsewhere in Ballantyne's work with automatic reverence and
approval.

In *The Lifeboat* the younger boy Tommy Bogey is presented to
us as

> a little chip of humanity [who] under the training of a modest,
> lion-hearted British sailor . . . [the hero, Bax] . . . was beginning
> to display, in unusual vigour, those daring, enthusiastic, self-
> sacrificing qualities which, although mingled with much that
> is evil, are marked characteristics of our seamen; qualities which
> have gone far to raise our little island to her present high position
> of commercial prosperity and political importance, and which,
> with God's blessing, will continue to carry our flag, our
> merchandise, and our Bibles, to the ends of the earth, and guard
> our shores, as in days of old, from the foot of every foreign foe.

Tommy impinges upon the reader, however, chiefly in his comic
aspect, and is held firmly in his place by his caricatured lower-class
accent and vocabulary. Many examples of the role, like the young
Martin Rattler, Bobby Frog in *Dusty Diamonds*, Puggy in *The Gorilla
Hunters*, or Obo in *Black Ivory*, are further distanced into the
grotesque — they are very young, or very low-class, or black, and

therefore are inarticulate and amusingly physical in their expression of their adoration for their heroes. There is considerable affection in Ballantyne's portrayal of some of these children; one suspects he is sentimentally describing his own offspring and his little admirers, and their adoration of himself; but there is no possibility of participation in their lives by the adolescent reader.

The writer's model for his handling of character and situation is transparently neither didactic romance nor the juvenile *Bildungsroman*: it is the early novels of Dickens. The complication of his plots, his conception of character, the style of his description and the persistent attempts at a sort of unremitting jocularity of tone all bespeak a disciple of that master; and Ballantyne's appeals for good causes and social responsibility fit comfortably enough into a style vulgarised from the Dickensian. One book, *The Lifeboat*, will furnish more than enough examples to prove the point. It opens with an attempt at a Dickensian description of London, using his characteristic method of animating the inanimate:

> There existed not many years ago, a certain street near the banks of old Father Thames which may be described as being one of the most modest and retiring little streets in London.
>
> The neighbourhood around that street was emphatically dirty and noisy. There were powerful smells of tallow and tar in the atmosphere, suggestive of shipping and commerce. Narrow lanes opened off the main street affording access to wharves and warehouses, and presenting at their termini segmentary views of ships' hulls, bowsprits, and booms, with a background of muddy water and smoke. There were courts with unglazed windows resembling doors, and massive cranes clinging to the walls. There were yards full of casks and barrels, and great anchors and chains which invaded the mud of the river as far as was consistent with safety; and adventurous little warehouses, which stood on piles, up to the knees, as it were, in water, totally regardless of appearances, and utterly indifferent as to catching cold. As regards the population of this locality, rats were, perhaps, in excess of human beings; and it might have been observed that the former were particularly frolicsome and fearless.
>
> Farther back, on the landward side of our unobtrusive street, commercial and nautical elements were more mingled with things appertaining to domestic life. Elephantine horses, addicted to good living, drew through the narrow streets wagons and vans so

ponderous and gigantic that they seemed to crush the very stones
over which they rolled, and ran terrible risk of sweeping little
children out of the upper windows of the houses. In unfavourable
contrast with these, donkeys, of the most meagre and starved
aspect, staggered along with cart-loads of fusty vegetables and dirty-
looking fish, while the vendors thereof howled the nature and
value of their wares with deliberate ferocity.

This conflation of descriptions of Todgers' (*Martin Chuzzlewit*) and
Mayfair (*Little Dorrit*) is the setting for the offices of Mr Denham
(cf. Mr Dombey), a cold and selfish merchant, and exploiter of poor
seamen. His good-hearted, comic counterpart (cf. Captain Cuttle) is
Captain Bluenose, an old seadog who shares a 'hovel' — an upturned
boat — on the beach at Deal (cf. *David Copperfield*) with a sentimental
repentant pirate. The aspiring Tommy Bogey is his nephew. Such
borrowings can be as easily traced in most of the books which
Ballantyne sets in England. His young readers may well have enjoyed
the style of humour for which the quasi-Dickensian caricature is an
excuse; Dickens himself was a favourite author with the young[30] and
Ballantyne's version of his wordplay and his grotesque physical
humour, with the horror and the insights into black depths of human
nature all removed and replaced by unremitting jollity laced with
bloodcurdling violence, exaggerates qualities to which the unformed
taste might well respond.

Eric Quayle has argued[31] that *The Gorilla Hunters* (a most
distasteful book to the conservation-minded modern reader, in that it
rests upon the Victorian lust for the hunt) was so popular with its
readers because it enacted for them the conquest of subconscious fears,
embodied as evil monsters hideously like and unlike man. This notion
of the resolution of nightmares of pursuit by the turning of the tables
on the fierce animals is borne out in the story by the number of
occasions on which the young hunters are said to go over the day's
battles in their dreams, Peterkin especially being prone to wake up
shouting and struggling. The whole adventure is dreamlike, detached,
a fantasy taking place in another world, as are so many of Ballantyne's
stories.

The fantasy element of all the adventures under consideration in
this chapter, and indeed all the stories with which this book deals, is
very important, a vital part of their function for the young reader.
Ballantyne's work might be said to represent an extreme in this
direction, however, not because other writers' stories are any less

unlikely or more realistic, but because Ballantyne cuts off his tales more completely from relation to an everyday world. His social messages are firmly encapsulated and quite separate from the story; his characters are perfect or grotesque beings, remote from the reader's self; his stories do not partake of the meaningful patterns. They might be said to be purely escapist. They are free, or as free as possible, both from the overtly Christian or moral didacticism others address to the young, and from the pressure towards loftily-conceived, difficult modes of behaviour and ideals of self that many also build intimately into the fabric of their stories. The reader Ballantyne addresses is asked to be philanthropic, which he is probably willing enough to do as far as his means allow, and he is occasionally urged to take cold baths, or to learn to swim and avoid being a 'muff' at games, which injunctions he is probably either keen to obey, or able to avoid by reading about the hearty life instead of acting it out.

The advice is of a different order altogether from other authors' demands to die for Christ, to kneel and pray in the midst of howling ruffians, or to serve God gratefully in your place as a kitchen-maid. The effort required of the reader is much less: he has only to go on being himself, in the assurance that a good-hearted English boy is the summit of creation. The young men in Ballantyne's stories are too old — usually turned twenty — and too perfect to need the mentors other writers provide for their heroes; instead they have followers who admire their boyish excellencies. Neither introspection nor development is required of them, and certainly no recognition of sin and inadequacy; they are their own justification, and the saviours of the rest of the world. Even that corollary is taken as a matter of course: compare the cut and dried description of the universal role of 'our flag, our merchandise, and our Bibles', quoted above in reference to Tommy Bogey, with Kingsley and Kingston on the same subject. It is suggested, in tales of hunting and exploration, and in stories of home adventures on lifeboats and railways, that physical bravery is an end in itself, nominally justified by a doctrine of love for one's fellow-men, which is best shown by saving them physically from peril. Even the missionaries whose praises are regularly sung in the books about the South Seas do most good not by eloquence or fervour but by their intrepidity, and their work is praised because it saves men's bodies from slavery and cannibalism, as much as for saving their souls.

There is a crude magic in the automatic way in which the advent of a Christian Englishman is assumed to transform the lives of all he comes across: a hero has only to be present, and his superiority works wonders, without his needing to do more than assert himself physically. No responsibility beyond 'having adventures' is therefore upon him. It is the last stage in the development which begins with Kingsley's adaptation of Arnold's ideals: Arnold's concept of manliness, meaning moral and intellectual maturity and full human responsibility, has been inverted and fossilised into a simple code of conformity glorifying physical power, simplicity of speech and mind, softness of feeling, and self-satisfaction with the state not of manliness, but of being forever a boy.

5 BOOKS FOR GIRLS

Just as the ethic of work and endeavour epitomised by Samuel Smiles's philosophy acted upon earlier educational imperatives stemming from evangelical Christianity and utilitarianism to produce the boy's adventure story, the moral fiction of the Empire, so new currents of thought in the mid-century also acted upon writing intended for girls. Here, too, the developments in fiction aimed at the moulding of aspirations and expectations to fit readers for a social role which was being newly defined. The wave of self-consciousness amongst the middle classes which the social, political, religious and economic changes of the century combined to generate had as one of its forms in the 1850s and 1860s a surge of questioning and redefining of female roles.[1]

The paradoxes of the situation in which many middle-class women found themselves were often cruelly painful. Furnished with financial and marital expectations which were not necessarily to be fulfilled, they were expected to continue to regard an unattainable motherhood as their proper sphere, while supporting and occupying themselves in roles in which it was not desirable or even regarded as possible that they should excel. At the same time even those women who attained marriage and motherhood were increasingly relieved of the labours of their envied position, and taught to feel dissatisfied with their contribution to society at large unless their sphere of influence, especially philanthropic influence, extended beyond the home. A quickening of interest in the education of girls coincided with the extension of the public school system to accommodate middle-class boys in the 1860s; for the girls, however, no defined objectives existed to parallel the explicit and implicit purposes of the public schools, and the uncertainties and conflicts of the debate served to create a very different sort of book when they were expressed in moral fiction for the young.

In 1869 Charlotte Yonge wrote of 'the class of literature now termed "books for the young", standing between the child's story and the full-grown novel',[2] as an established genre to which she contributed, and which had been given new impetus by Harriett Mozley's *The Fairy Bower* and *The Lost Brooch*, published respectively in 1841 and 1842. She acknowledged that the class was not a new invention; it is now usual to trace it back as a tradition of writing for girls to Sarah Fielding's

148

The Governess (1749), and writers throughout the first half of the
nineteenth century contributed to the stock of proper stories for the
daughters of gentlefolk. In most cases their work was not profoundly
touched by evangelical feeling, though it could hardly have existed
without cognisance of it; Mrs Sherwood, indefatigable in her
determination to bring enlightenment to the whole of society, saw fit
to revise *The Governess* to stress the evangelical essentials and to cut
out the fairy tales. Her less enthusiastic contemporaries, like Barbara
Hofland and Elizabeth Sandham, contented themselves with the
composition of stories which did meet the evangelical canons of
strictness, but differed little in the way in which they conveyed their
moral lessons from older moral tales.

Barbara Hofland, a prolific writer who by no means concentrated
on an expected readership of girls alone, tended to produce stories in
which virtue and hard work are straightforwardly met with material
reward. In an account of a family which has fallen upon hard times,
The History of an Officer's Widow and her Young Family (1809), she
set up a group of young persons of the type whose characters would
be minutely explored by a later writer such as Charlotte Yonge, and
furnished them with appropriate trials upon the collapse of the
family fortune. The bookish eldest son is obliged to accept a
commission and his adventurous younger brother to work in a shop.
After a sharp intake of breath, or at most a few days of brooding
silence, however, their conduct is perfect, and their progress back to
prosperity is therefore aided by authorial providence in the concrete
form of fires and robbers from which the adventurous brother may
rescue his employers, and a legacy from a penitent comrade admonished
by the pious officer; their final destination is a family house in
comfortable Clapham Common, whence they issue in turn to their
successful marriages. Adversity is not entirely external, in that duty
demands sacrifices, but rewards and solutions are unstintingly
provided when those demands are met. Injustice and evil are sometimes
within the family: in *Ellen, the Teacher* (1815), the exemplary Ellen
is exposed to physical ill-treatment by the keeper of a school because
her father is unreliable over money and her grandmother has cut her
mother off for making an imprudent marriage; her own unshakable
goodness, however, eventually wins all hearts, and she and her brother
inherit their proper share of the family wealth. She opens a school for
poor children.

Elizabeth Sandham was not content with quite so cut and dried a
moral equation, though she too could make use of very Georgian story-

telling devices. In her *Summer Rambles or Conversations, instructive and entertaining for the use of children* (1801), which was dedicated to the Princess of Wales, the pattern, the telling of stories within a framework of pedagogic or parental interaction with a few children, is that of *The Governess* and many other eighteenth-century books for the young. Within it an apparently immutable rural social order is displayed, as little Harry and Anna observe on the one hand the industrious cottagers and on the other their father's provision for his people; they are to learn that all should be grateful to God for this dispensation, and that they must practice industry and virtue themselves, according to their place within it, learning 'how you may be able to be most useful to your fellow-creatures, and how to conduct yourself, in order to gain the love and esteem of your friends and neighbours'. Moral imperatives are easily perceived and enforced: disobedient children are always punished . . . they are very wicked, and . . . God never loves them', while rewards are not only equally certain but also instant, as when Anna gives up a selfish wish to have her breakfast out in the sun to go and keep her sick brother company, and finds that he has a treat of gingerbread to share with her.

Writing for older girls, however, Elizabeth Sandham goes beyond this simple old-fashioned moral and social code. *The Twin Sisters*, for example, is said to be a story which attempts to warn the young of the 'strange contrarieties, perceivable in human nature' which they will encounter in their lives, as an antidote to the too-perfect picture of humanity which books for children often draw. This appeal to realism (comparable with the less theoretically presented but very decided bias to graphic presentation of servant life which mid-century SPCK writers offered their lower-class readers) is made by each successive writer for girls, and underlines their tendency to the integration of religious and social teaching. In their way, they were as concerned with the justification and inculcation of an unpalatable social role as were the writers for the servant classes. But their appeal to realism, together with their consciousness of the kind of reading their particular audience was likely to prefer, led to changes in the medium as well as the message of the girls' story, and brought about a form of fiction for the young which may properly be called a novel.

The Twin Sisters, sufficiently evangelical to have received the approbation of the writers of *The Guardian of Education* (founded by Mrs Trimmer in 1802), already shows the preoccupations and uses the motifs that were to prevail during the germination period of this new form. Its moving force is a moral conflict, crudely and obviously expressed in external forms, but essentially the same struggle which forms the character of later heroines for girls. The twins, Anna and Ellen, have parents who are 'votaries of dissipation', and care so little for their daughters that they not only go off to make their fortune in the East Indies, but on committing the children to their aunt's care cannot tell the two apart. They are wisely educated at home, in a round of Mrs Barbauld's *Evenings at Home* cottage visiting and the catechism, while their aunt 'made every incident productive of instruction of her nieces, and they were soon taught to consider even the most trifling events as under the direction of PROVIDENCE'. The influences of Calvinism and Maria Edgeworth seem nicely balanced. The twins are contrasted with a pair of cousins, educated in frivolity and conceit at a boarding school, and with two poor girls, one of them blind, who are models of contentment with the help of the benevolent.

Anna succumbs to consumption, the scourge of these young girls, and is given an extended, though not very evangelical, deathbed: she trusts in the Redeemer, but little stress is laid upon the conviction of sin or on the Atonement. The real battle is Ellen's, for her parents return, and sweep her into the whirl of fashionable society, where she has to contend with the conflicting demands of religious conviction and filial obedience. The conflict between the earnest and converted young and the worldly older generation must reflect real experience in many early-nineteenth-century households; it is a situation repeated in very many books of the period, and not only became a literary convention in itself, but was the source, along with sentimental belief in the child's power of conversion, which stemmed perhaps from *Little Henry and his Bearer*, of the good little girl who is a persecuted heroine of mid-century evangelical romance.

In *The Twin Sisters* Ellen's resistance to theatre-going, with the excuse of ill-health brought on by initial obedience to parental demands, is not enough, and she finally makes her stand, by refusing to play at a Sunday evening private concert. She is rewarded: dissipation carries her mother off, and her aunt rescues her father; she herself marries an exemplary gentleman. The presentation of universal and therefore of parental fallibility, used as a means of conveying Calvinist truths to the young by Mrs Sherwood, takes an extreme form in these stories, as it does in tales of the poor child and his drunken mother and violent father discussed in Chapter 4. In the stories for girls it was to become a divisive issue, causing the generation of writers who were inspired by the religious and social upheavals of the 1840s to take diverging paths according to their beliefs about the family, as well as the complexion of their religious convictions.

There were other ghosts to be laid before progress could be made in the novel for the young. The evangelical distrust of fiction held back several writers who were on the verge of breaking through into this mode: Charlotte Elizabeth Tonna, for example, produced in *Conformity* (1841), a promising story of two related families and their different characters which is swamped by many pages of argument, set out with texts, quotation, chapter and verse, which is attributed to the elder brothers of the two sides, but enters hardly at all into the working-out of their story. An RTS writer produced *Emily Grey* and *Hartfield or Emily at School* in 1848, both embryonic novels exploring the heroine's development, but she informs the reader that the small incidents of Emily's life were 'not of a nature to be generally interesting', and inserts several pious deaths instead. Such timorous steps nevertheless brought the novel of domestic settings, family life and psychological exploration nearer, and reduced the readers' expectation of romance as the only framework of children's tales.

The Evangelical Romance

Alongside these tentative attempts at the novel there had been, in the first half of the century, many books published and bought for girls which pretended to the status of improving and moral fiction, but which made no attempt to escape from the patterns of romance; Mrs Sherwood's *Susan Gray* (1801), is an example. Their exciting action, and the unblushing authorial control of events which is naturally a part of the form, provoked the distaste and criticism of those concerned with provision for the young as late as 1860, when the Rev. H. Newcomb reprinted Hannah More's criticism of such stories in a handbook for young ladies called *Christian Character*, published by Nelson. Such distrust and severity of tone help to account for the slowness of the RTS in moving to serious fiction, and also the paradox of the well-meaning story-tellers who condemn their characters for reading stories.

The works they attacked were published by commercial firms, less hampered than the societies by hesitant committees: Nelson themselves published religious romances alongside *Christian Character*, and Nisbet, an exemplary evangelical house, led the field, as their circulating library catalogue for 1832, discussed in Chapter 4, makes clear. Both firms expanded their activities in the 1850s by importing material from the USA, and it was initially through Nisbet that the enormously popular romances of Susan Warner came to England, in 1851. Her books, beginning with *The Wide, Wide World* and *Queechy*,[3] were best sellers, and her example was followed by many writers who aimed at the adolescent of all classes. It was eventually accepted by the RTS, as editors sought to select serials to attract such readers to *The Leisure Hour*. The novel for girls, which also developed in the 1850s, grew partly in reaction against these romances, and aimed to correct the sensibility they fostered and to counteract their imperfect, and possibly harmful, moral influence.

The attractions of *The Wide, Wide World* are obvious enough. The interest of the physical details of Ellen Montgomery's life, her little workbox and desk chosen and stocked with her mother's help, her trip on a riverboat to her aunt's farm, and then the full round of American rural life, is commented upon by those modern critics who notice the book at all. The setting is both substantial and meticulous enough to sustain its internal consistency, and far enough removed from the British child's experience to have the attraction of the exotic and picturesque; it provides the Crusoe touch which spices all romance settings from the Indies to the East End. The story is a double romance journey. Ellen is first parted from her ailing mother and her unfeeling father, and sent out alone to battle with various monsters; in particular her aunt's bustling and spartan farm life, to which it is good for her to be subjected, in so far as it represents hard work and a lesson in duty and humility. It also provokes our sympathy, since she is fastidious, as becomes a heroine, and overworked and misunderstood by her aunt, who fails to appreciate her feelings, and is overly proud of her own ways. Ellen has various helpers, who appear with proper fairy-tale promptness: when she is sent away from home, on a riverboat, a gentleman rescues her from neglectful guardians and sets her on the way to coping with the loss of her mother; he turns out in the end to be a friend of her future husband. Then the rough diamond Farmer Van Brunt, who manages her aunt's farm and is to be Ellen's convert, scoops her up and delivers her when she is stranded on the last stage of her journey. Finally there is the minister's daughter Alice Humphreys, who comes to her when she has suffered enough at her aunt's house, and rescues her from spiritual isolation and the danger of growing up in ignorance, becoming her example and her teacher.

Because this is a captured romance these are also the stages on
Ellen's way to conviction of sin and conversion: she loses her mother
so that she may learn to love God best, the first helper showing her
how to set out for this objective and Alice appearing when she has
achieved it, in a very effectively managed scene. The reader is
sympathetic towards Ellen's sufferings, and feels her aunt's unkindness,
which is indeed unjust, coming to a head when she witholds and
opens the little girl's first letter from her mother. Ellen dashes from the
house and up the mountain, where Alice finds her; she bursts into
tears, but her explanation of her state is, quite unexpectedly, a
confession of her own wrong feeling and misbehaviour towards her
aunt. Her conviction of grace is subsequently achieved by means of
The Pilgrim's Progress; Alice dies, which confirms her own goodness
and transfers it to Ellen.

The second journey is the trial of Ellen's new converted identity by
means of the removal once again of the human supports through which
her love is channelled. After her parents' death she is adopted by the
Humphreys family, Alice's father and her brother John, and then
belatedly discovers that she has rich and important relations in Scotland
to whom her mother has committed her; she must set off to fulfil her
duty to the family. The episodes in Scotland seem to throw up a
conflict in the book's moral import. The trial of Ellen's faith and
obedience in some ways resembles that of the pious children among
wordlings which is familiar from the earlier stories, for the aristocratic
relations object to her enthusiastic church-going and devoted bible
study, and also to her fidelity to American republicanism and, most
cruelly of all, to her affection for her 'brother and sister', Alice
and John. But the reader is not allowed to condemn them, in
righteous indignation and in feeling for Ellen, for it is repeatedly
stressed that she owes obedience to their demands, out of family duty.
This is particularly the case in respect of her uncle, who has lost
his own family, and insists that she is to call him father, which she
finds very difficult, and to think and feel as he dictates; all these
demands are made, as we are asked to believe, out of love for her.
His utter selfishness is nowhere acknowledged; it seems to be his
privilege to behave so.

The dilemma of feeling is not resolved, for when John comes to
rescue her from the situation which we are simultaneously told is
perfectly proper for her, he can only do so by propitiating the uncle
and gaining his good opinion, and then going away to await Ellen's
coming of age, when he can claim her as his wife. The reader rebels at

this violation of romance morality, for John is the hero, and the uncle's attempt to rob the heroine of her identity makes confrontation with him an emotional imperative, but we are fobbed off with talk of discipline which did her no harm, and her duty to this seemingly quite spurious family to await the solution of the law. One may conclude that the strongest code the author acknowledges, and to which she subjects her heroine, deals with women not as heroines of romance nor as souls before God, but as the possessions of men — of the dominant male relative, called 'father', first of all, and then of the victorious young challenger, called 'brother' and then 'husband'.

Before this dénouement the book has much to offer the girl reader. Her interest is caught by the domestic settings and personal details, and the romance story urges her on; there are also the beginnings of a novelistic interest in the character of Ellen, of the kind observed in earlier books for girls. The Scottish episode shows the convert in confrontation with the worldly, and in the American part of the book Ellen is taken from her solitary struggles with herself, in confrontation with her aunt and her Bible, to visits and parties where she is part of a group of young people. The testing and developing of the character in the peer group of this kind was to become a central narrative and didactic method of novelists for the young, and Susan Warner handles her group of cousins and visitors well, and sometimes with humour. The quarrel which English writers and critics had with her books was not with this element, but with their evangelical doctrinal bases, and their manner of dealing with emotional and moral subjects as the stuff of fiction. Both the explicit religious teachings of the books and their guidance to readers on social and sexual roles and behaviour were suspect.

Charlotte Yonge intended to do more than echo the remarks of Hannah More about religious tales when she criticised stories in which 'Little children amaze their elders, and sometimes perfect strangers, by sudden enquiries as to whether they are Christians': she found Susan Warner's books had 'the very grave and really injurious effect of teaching little girls to expect a lover in any one who is good-natured to them. Nothing ought to be more rigidly avoided, for it fills the child with foolish expectations and dreams.'[4] The combination of religious and sexual fantasies was precisely their appeal, and the source of their success with a very wide audience. Girls of all classes, untroubled for once by scrupulous explicit placing of the heroine in a duty-ridden role in English society, were able to enjoy an intensely emotional evocation of all they could wish they were: an orphan girl of exquisite sensibility and passionate feelings, who explores exotic places, is heroic under the stress of unfair domestic labour, has a beautiful friend who dies in her arms, transforms men by her influence, inherits a fortune and an aristocratic family, and is going to be carried off and married by her brother-cum-lover at some rather remote date.

Susan Warner's books were officially published in England by Nisbet, who paid her something for the rights and attempted, unsuccessfully, to ward off the pirates who leapt aboard their prize. They reported dolefully to the author that Bohn, Routledge, Wilson and Clarke were all printing cheap editions that undercut theirs, and that ten thousand copies of a pirate edition had been sold at one railway station.[5] All that she and her sister wrote over the next thirty years was snapped up by English publishers, and their books remain among the most common and also the most cheaply and garishly-produced gift and prize publications which have survived from the period. They wrote for their living, and indeed to retrieve the ruined fortunes of the family, but received little from all these English printings.

To many English publishers the religious romance presented itself as a respectable way to profit from the growing popularity of 'sensation' fiction. In 1854 the firm of Thomas Nelson found an American romance with which to rival those of the Warners, and it was even more popular, not to say positively vulgar, in its structure and style. This was *The Lamplighter*, by Susan Cummins; its essentially popular appeal is attested by the fact that it was not only pirated and reprinted widely in England, but was dramatised for the melodrama stage in at least three different versions, two in the year of its importation, and one in 1876. It remained a gift and prize book, despite a very highly coloured prose style and an inclination to mark climaxes not by storms of tears, as happens in the Warner books, but by exciting and often violent action. The story traces once again the struggle which leads to the heroine's achievement of identity, and an idyllic repose in ancestral acres from which she has hitherto been shut out by the forces of evil.

Gerty, her origins shrouded in mystery, is first presented to the reader struggling in the hell of the city, friendless and outcast, and obliged moreover to fight with her darker self, an evil temper, which is externalised as ugliness, making the lost princess appear a 'witch' to her associates. She is rescued from flogging and starvation by the lamplighter, heavily emphasised as a messenger of light, and then assisted in her search for a better self and mastery of her passions by the hero, Willie, and by her antithesis or counterpart, the fair Emily, who is rich, well cared for, saintly, but in physical darkness, for she is blind. Willie is sent away to make his fortune in India, and overcoming her evil nature Gerty tends the lamplighter and all Willie's family on their respective deathbeds; she is then taken into the family of Emily Graham, and becomes the light of her life.

The ascent from the world of spiritual darkness and physical degradation places her in the world of ordinary experience, which is, in the romance fashion, a world of sexuality and violence. Scenes of society rivalries follow, culminating in the reappearance of Willie, apparently engaged to another, and the coming of a mysterious stranger who rescues Gerty and Emily, and also Gerty's rival, from a blazing riverboat. This 'man of sorrows', prematurely grey and obviously tortured, dominates the end of the book; he is not only Gerty's father, but Emily's long-lost childhood sweetheart, whose passionate temper (under cruel provocation) had caused her to be blinded. He recounts this horrifying incident, and the series of gruesome deaths, plagues and thefts that led to his losing Gerty in her childhood, before testing Willie's faith and handing Gerty over to him. Their *éclaircissement* is reached over the lamplighter's grave, in a scene reminiscent of *The Basket of Flowers*, and all are happy ever after: even Emily, represented throughout as feeble, indeed moribund, is married off to her old love and recovers all her strength.

John Rowe Townsend sees the happy ending as 'a cop-out' in which 'promising characters,' especially 'the fierce, impulsive Gerty' become 'beautiful, pious, uninteresting'.[6] He mistakes the romance for the novel. Gerty the lost child is a cipher rather than a character; her transformation into her own antithesis, her apotheosised self, invested with all the qualities of which the waif had been deprived, is the proper pattern of development. What is most remarkable about the book is the extent to which the displacements of and additions to the motifs of romance, which make it acceptable as moral fiction for the young, are in this case so nearly reassimilated to the original, so little Christianised. Even the symbol of the light and its carriers and possessors is connected with love and vitality rather than with moral and religious enlightenment, and the scenes of the interaction of the heroine and her peers — devices added to the romance story for didactic purposes — are here made the setting for contests quite beyond the scope of the demure English houseparties of other writers, in their violence and sexual excitement.

Where these imported examples led, some English writers for the

young followed. The evangelical writers for poor children were not
squeamish about the use of popular story-patterns, and Hesba Stretton,
for example, wrote several romances for the older reader which were
serialised in religious and 'wholesome' magazines; scores of her
imitators in the next generation followed both paths. In the 1850s,
however, the appropriation of this kind of writing to their use was not
yet established, and there were writers who produced religious romances
for young children and for boys. One such oddity was Mrs Charlesworth,
whose range of writing, including stories for servant girls and for the
upper-class nursery, resembles that of a previous generation, but who
managed to throw into *Ministering Children* (1854), some of the
intensity of feeling which captivates the reader who can identify with
Ellen Montgomery and Little Gerty. It is a romance idyll, showing
a harsh social world transformed by Christian charity which flows
through a chain of children, filling their lives with meaning. It has a
curious intensity, which Charlotte Yonge unhesitatingly rejected as
unreal and impractical; despite such condemnation, and the laughter
and parody which it has also provoked, it had imaginative power for
the idealistic child.

A similar sense of the mixture of power and distortion is produced
by the contemplation of the highly emotional romances of Frederick
Farrar, Dean of Canterbury. The intensity with which he describes
both lyrical schoolboy love and friendship, and the lurid sufferings
of the wicked and fallen and weak, strikes us as extreme. Its sexual
connotations seem so glaring that some recent commentators have
been able to descend from the post-Freudian superiority which made
Farrar a laughing-stock at the beginning of this century and recognised
that he did know precisely what he was talking about, and that he was
consciously attempting to guide and control the sexual life of his
readers by admitting its existence and power and discussing it as
openly as possible.[7] He was working quite against the line of
development of moral fiction for boys, which sought to sublimate such
forces much more completely, to avoid the expression of feeling about
religion as well as sex (because these are dangerous triggers for the
irrational and selfish), and to channel physical development and
psychological intensity into the service of less dangerous emotions, such
as patriotism.

The Novel for Girls: the Writers

These variations upon the popular romance were successful in their own right; even the minor *The Three Homes* (1873) sold 28,000 copies before Farrar chose to acknowledge it as his composition; but they were outside the main paths of development of moral fiction. As soon as they were introduced in the 1850s, the main interest in romances of this kind was in their role as fiction for girls, and they were compared with earlier books for young ladies in respect of their religious teaching and moral effect. By the 1880s Charlotte Yonge was admitting as obvious the premiss that 'girls are indiscriminate devourers of fiction', and that 'the semi-religious novel or novelette is to them moralising put into action, and the most likely way of reaching them'.[8] She was referring to girls in Sunday school, but her own novels make it clear that she believed much the same recipe was the best way to serve young ladies.

In the 1850s, this meant that such books became weapons in the two burning controversies of the day: the storm raised between the old evangelical Christianity and the Oxford movement, which carried in its train not only doctrinal debate, but divergences of religious and philanthropic attitude and practice which pervaded every aspect of Christian life; and the question, already touched upon, of the hammering out of new roles for women. The functions of women and the activities of the church and of philanthropic society were obviously closely-related issues in practical terms; and stories for girls, from which beliefs, values and patterns of behaviour could all be imbibed, presented themselves as very important in the debate and resolution of these matters. The romance was firmly aligned with the evangelical party; the novel was to develop in reaction against all that it stood for, offering alternative religious, social and aesthetic values. It drew upon the beginnings of the utilisation of novelistic techniques made by Mrs Sandham and Mrs Hofland, but also upon models outside children's fiction, in the form of the serious novel.

Appropriately enough, the pioneer and acknowledged originator of the attack upon evangelical romance was Harriett Mozley, Cardinal Newman's sister and wife of a keen Tractarian, Tom Mozley of Oriel. The preface to *The Fairy Bower* makes her position clear:

It is to be hoped that the following little Tale may be looked upon as an attempt rather to represent characters as they really are, than to exhibit moral portraitures for unreserved imitation or avoidance. In this respect it may perhaps differ from most publications of the same class, and though it may not possess their poetical beauty, it may perhaps have the advantage over them, that it introduces young persons to those scenes and situations of life which are their actual sphere and trial.

The statement is very reminiscent of prefatory remarks quoted above from Mrs Sandham and Mrs Hofland, and Harriett Mozley goes further than they do in making good her claims to realism of character and setting. A later book for small children, *Family Adventures* (1852), makes the repudiation of 'romantic incidents' the structural framework of the tale, when Aunt Ellen undertakes to tell her niece and her friend (who has the intensely romantic name of Bertha Melmoth) stories which will be very exciting, but include no findings of diamond rings leading to rich old ladies making lucky little girls rich, nor accidents in forests which end in happy marriages. Her stories are all drawn, she says, from incidents of which she has personal experience, happening to children she has known.

In the three-volume tales *The Fairy Bower* (1841) and *The Lost Brooch* (1842) realism of setting, in the 'situations of life' which are the sphere of children and adolescents, is strictly observed, so that even Jane Austen's little bit of ivory seems by comparison a large world full of important events. In *The Fairy Bower* all that occurs is a houseparty of relations at which one little girl tacitly allows herself to be given credit for the decorative invention of another; *The Lost Brooch* is comparatively sensational, for after a good half of the book has described an uneventful seaside holiday, a maid is falsely accused of stealing a small brooch, and cleared of the imputation by the intervention of the accuser's cousin. The three volumes of each novel are filled up with the interaction of three family groups, and while these are drawn in outline from the contrasting families of earlier tales, their detailed treatment ensures that our interest in them is of a quite different kind, and indeed our moral judgements are eventually the reverse of those an earlier tale would have provoked. The conflict between the converted and the unconverted, the strict professor and the worldly connections, is here presented as between the Duffs, headed not by their parents but by their domineering and almost dissenting governess, and the Wards, led by Mrs Ward, who laughs at the idea of her hearing her children say their catechism, and declares that she 'was not brought up under the religious system of the present day'.

No earlier writer makes this explanation of this particular conflict; doing so defuses the moral judgement over which a Mrs Tonna would have waxed self-righteous, and sets the cool, measured tone of

Harriett Mozley's presentation of her characters. She does not, of course, recommend worldly or irreligious behaviour; she does not even refrain from direct comment upon some actions which are to be condemned, finding herself for example unable to pass silently over a conversation in *The Fairy Bower* (the book intended for younger readers) which, she tells us, indicates that 'Mary-Ann shows constantly a very bad spirit [and] Isobella is silly and affected'. But these characters are not therefore Aunt Sallies, set up merely to be knocked down, and while Mary-Ann is an awful warning — it is she who commits the breach of taste and honour and claims another's work as her own — she is understood and cared for by the adults in the novel, and consequently by the reader. Complex moral responses are possible, because the breakthrough has taken place in the novelist's presentation of character, in action and in dialogue, from more than one point of view, and in social and psychological context. Action displays not moral points to be learnt, but morally responsible human beings to be understood.

The change is not a rejection of all the concerns which had inspired the earlier writers. The moralist and educator at work can still easily be discerned, especially in *The Fairy Bower*, for younger readers, in which the parents and the author herself indulge in lengthy discussions of various systems of education, from Pestalozzi to the public schools. The focus of interest and identification is still the little girl, Grace, whose relationships, feelings and behaviour are practically perfect, and against whom all others may be measured; her character may, despite the warning in the preface, be taken as exemplary. She is as intensely sensitive and emotional as a heroine of romance, and her relationship with her mother is as intimate and tender as that of Ellen Montgomery; but her sphere of action is confined quite unremittingly to the world inhabited by her readers, and no romantic story develops — in terms of romance, indeed, nothing at all happens in the book. More important in this effect than the confining of the action is the tonal shift which renders the telling of these everyday events unromantic: almost all the action, the characters and their conflicts, and the moral points which may be deduced from them, are rendered ironically.

The doctrinal point is made more forcibly by *The Lost Brooch* (for older readers) through the ironical and ultimately satirical treatment of the religious system of the Duffs. The evangelical family and their educative and philanthropic theories are systematically taken apart by means of the ironical juxtaposition of its pretensions and their effects upon its members. No one in either novel voices any disbelief or criticism of the Duffs' 'Christian' professions; but the disastrous effect their education has had upon them and their destructive influence on the world around them is the moral substance of the books. Harriett Mozley's quarrel, and that of the new Church party, was with the form taken by the evangelical profession of dedication of the whole of life to God: the inclination, as she saw it, to lower the sacred by handling it familiarly in everyday life and dissipating, and eventually coming to abuse, its power, by associating it with the profane, the trivial, and finally with selfish concerns.

The stories for the young which ladies like Mrs Tonna and Mrs Trimmer pioneered were actual examples of the process she abhorred, attaching great religious importance to the mundane details of life, and dramatising the outward elements of profession which a child might adopt and pretend to understand and feel. The process is shown not only as irreligious, but also immoral, when the Duff children in the nursery are not corrected for their faults, but bought tempting little books in which those faults are corrected, so turning their punishments into rewards. For an attack upon the trivialised and externalised distortion of religious observance, therefore, the mode of parody which she adopted is particularly appropriate, for it exposes the fault through one of the very things in which it was manifest. It is an interesting coincidence that by so doing Harriett Mozley made a significant step forward in fiction for the young, demonstrating the critical tenet that development in an art takes place by means of such parodic transmutations of form.[9]

Harriett Mozley put the novel for the young into the hands of the Church party of the 1840s. Its next practitioner was Elizabeth Sewell, who secured a large readership of young ladies in Britain and America: her novels had sold 68,000 copies by 1863. As in Harriett Mozley's case, she was born into the Church party; one of twelve children in an Oxford and clerical family, she was made 'a Church person' by her brother William's exposition of the *Tracts for the Times*. She found that the religious mode they suggested suited her, largely because it rejected the cant of religious conversation to which she objected, both in life and in literature. In her autobiography she explains that it was this 'literary fastidiousness' which determined her adoption of Church principles, which seems to her a rather ignominious admission. She found herself to be one of the young people who greeted Harriett Mozley's stories with 'special satisfaction' because they 'turned from the texts, and prayers, and hymns, which Mrs Sherwood had introduced into her stories, and yet needed something higher in tone than Miss Edgeworth's morality'.[10] In fact the account she gives of her own religious life in her autobiography indicates another reason for glad acceptance of the revival of the Church and its authority, which she also shared with many of her contemporaries. She was beset by fundamental doubts from about the age of fifteen, and being too intelligent and sensitive to charm them away by the repetition of the cant of enthusiasm, and too honest to convince herself that she had overcome them by the rational means she did apply, the opportunity to turn resolutely away from them, and to rest upon the protective authority of the Church and her duties within and towards it, came as a relief from unbearable nervous pressure. It was not until well into middle years that she dared to confront her inner misgivings again.[11]

One might perhaps see this passive and frightened reaction to the spiritual questioning of the Victorian period as essentially a female response, for it is the reaction of a mind confronted not simply with an intellectual problem, but with one which, if it is resolved in the direction of scepticism, calls into question everything hitherto accepted as the basis and justification of life. Theoretically of course this was also the case for the Victorian man who had been a Christian; but if the divine will and sanction, and the eternal life to come, were removed from his world view, something remained to justify his existence: his work, his influence in the world, the family he had founded and owned. For his female counterpart, especially if she were unmarried, nothing remained; if her duty, which was self-sacrifice and abnegation, served no God and led to no everlasting life, it certainly had no justification in the present. Only the strongest and most secure of their identity — only the George Eliots — could unflinchingly dismiss 'the scrolls of promise', God and immortality, and yet insist upon the sacredness of the remaining scroll, that of duty.[12]

Elizabeth Sewell gives an account of herself as a child, and of her interest in the education of girls in later life, which leads one to make this connection between her fierce adherence to an authoritarian religion and her struggle to accept her female role. She had, she says, a 'very violent temper' as a little child, coupled with an 'early religious taste' which led her to saying prayers and hymns to herself in her cot, for the sake of comforting herself. She went to school at the age of four, in 1819, and had a radical teacher who made them all have boys' haircuts; she indulged 'vague dreams of distinction, kept under from the sense of being a girl'. She felt she had been an unpleasant, irritable, vain child; before she was thirteen years old she had planned a college for girls by analogy with those her brothers were attending at Oxford.

All this rising rebellion and rejection of her destined place in the world was brought under control by subjection to a school system which ingeniously worked on the girls' own sensitivities: the pupils were expected to accuse themselves of any faults they committed, with the result that by the age of thirteen Elizabeth had worked herself into such a state of hypertension and 'strained conscience' that she had several years worth of punishment tasks lined up to do, and collapsed in hysteria. Sent to a more liberal school, religious scepticism set in soon after she had recovered; until the age of seventeen she struggled with it by reasoning, when she was sent for by her family to take up the task of educating her younger sisters. It is no wonder that her elder brother's exposition of a way in which she could rest assured of value and meaning in the life of service opening up before her came as a relief. It was a restoration of the comforting safety of the prayers of the three-year-old in the cot.[13]

It is instructive to compare this pattern of development with that of Charlotte Tucker, outlined in Chapter 4. There, too, the aspiring intellect sought for a way round female dependence and impotence, and found in a very strict evangelical code (one which differed little in practice from the manners of the Church, for she is noticeably sparing and fastidious in her use of the phraseology of profession and the name of God) a way of achieving and expressing her sense of individual worth, and a creative release which she could dedicate to a purpose beyond the narrow limits of the drawing room. The family positions of the two differed in that Charlotte Tucker could work entirely for philanthropic ends, needing none of her earnings, and perhaps more able, therefore, to follow the unusual paths of her particular literary sensibility; Elizabeth Sewell was in the same position as the Warner sisters, needing to earn considerable sums to recoup the family fortunes.

Her father died in 1842, leaving £500 per annum and a house to his wife and four daughters still at home. From 1844, when she was twenty-nine years old, Elizabeth was the breadwinner, and under a 'great pressure of pecuniary anxiety and personal responsibility'. This had, she repeatedly says, the effect of 'crushing any feeling except that of momentary pleasure connected with the success of any of my books'. Even before this happened, she had 'no delight in being an authoress': the pain was apparently compounded of shame at the need to make money and some obscurer feeling of self-indulgence or self-exposure, or the sense that she put herself into an unladylike, immodest position by appearing as a writer. Her first books bore only her brother's name, as 'editor'; she hated people to praise or even speak of her writing to her. Her public face was that of schoolmistress, and she kept and taught in private schools for most of the rest of her life.[14]

Praise of her as an author was extensive in the late 1840s and the 1850s, for she was a considerable figure in more than one literary circle, critically acclaimed not only as a champion of the Puseyite cause, but also recognised as a member of an increasingly important group of women novelists. She was compared with Jane Austen, and linked with the domestic and social problem novelists, especially Elizabeth Gaskell.[15] There is some ground for such comparisons, especially in the novels of her middle and later years; but she herself regarded her writing as 'the outcome of the influence of the Oxford movement', beginning with the question 'which had the primary claim, home, or church services, and works and charity?'[16] Many lesser writers, including those discussed above, also formulated in this way the conflict which is the central issue in the socio-religious definition of female roles under debate in 1844, when Elizabeth Sewell began to write. The difference which gave her writing distinction was perhaps due to the acutely personal way in which the conflict affected her, because of her position, and the deliberate and difficult truce she made between her intelligence and her faith; the result was that her writing 'does manifest an interest in the individual consciousness and its efforts to conform to the world around it — a step beyond the treatment of moral problems in a social context'.[17]

There is no lessening of the didacticism of Elizabeth Sewell's writing on account of its exploration of the individual consciousness, and its gravity is by no means decreased by her objection to texts and hymn-singing infants in fiction. At the outset of her writing career her debt in this respect and in the structure of her tales to earlier writers for children is quite clear. *Amy Herbert* (1844), owes much to Harriett Mozley's *Grace*, being a young teenage girl whose close relationship with her mother is the central fact of her life, until a family of cousins arrives to inhabit the nearby ancestral home. In interaction with them and with a Christmas houseparty which gathers the human material for a set of comparisons, *Governess*-style, between various examples of nature and nurture, Grace's virtues are demonstrated and their source made clear. Her sweet nature is the result of the efficacy of the sacrament of baptism, ridding her of original sin, followed by effort on her own part and loving guidance by her mother. This is the thrust of the Church teaching of the book, stressing the mystic value of baptism at every opportunity, and thus diverging from the low-church belief in the need for individual conversion. The moral lesson is enunciated by Mr Herbert:

> children injure themselves for their whole lives by indulging in what
> are called trifling faults — a little vanity, or a little selfishness, or
> hastiness of temper. If they could only be made to see the infinite
> importance of subduing these feelings early, they would grow up
> with confirmed habits of goodness, which, by the blessing of God,
> would never leave them, however they might be tempted in after-life.

This is the corollary of the doctrinal point, but it effectively reimposes
the restraints which the rejection of Calvinist doctrine might have
relaxed. Amy's life is at least as serious and exemplary an affair as those
of the little Fairchilds, even though she teaches her cousin Dora only
prayers from the prayer book, and makes no impertinent enquiries
about the spiritual health of others.

Laneton Parsonage (1844-7) has a more ambitious structure than its
predecessor, working with three little girls, the twins Ruth and Madeline
Clifford, of the parsonage, and their neighbour Alice, adopted child of
the manor. The contrasts and comparisons between these three show
the beginning of the author's delicate handling of individual
consciousness, for each is explored in sympathetic detail, and certainly
none is cast as exemplar or awful warning. She was not yet confident
enough to rely entirely upon character becoming plot, however, and
took as a further structural principle the illustration of the church
catechism. She felt this a relief from the construction of a story, with
which she had had difficulty in *Amy Herbert*; moreover, she intended
to imitate Mrs Sherwood's stories on the same subject, purging them
of the older writer's text-mongering, but sharing the urgency of her
desire to instruct, and also her capacity to imagine and evoke the
feelings of very young girls. Madeline, shutting herself in the boot
cupboard at school and burying her face in her hands to say her
prayers, in a desperate effort to find the strength to be different from
her friends, is an entirely recognisable little girl. We are equally
convinced of the much greater spiritual dangers of the good child Ruth,
unable to summon up the maturity to see beyond her own achievements
and superiority, and trapped by her self-confidence into an offence
which nightmarishly reveals to her the true limits of her supposed
self-command.

Alice is a more ambitious and rather less successful study of a child
at odds with the paternal generation, and so unable to guide herself
aright; her initial tussles with her guardian, whose regime is only

forbidding because she does not understand that she is loved, are entirely convincing, but she gets so far out of the line of good training and behaviour that she has to be reduced to a proper state by external disasters, including the old standby of fever. The bed of pain and repentance does not, of course, lead in this Church scheme of things to conversion and translation; instead she rises from it in a fit state for confirmation.

Elizabeth Sewell resembles Charlotte Yonge in the greater credibility and interest of her good characters: but the focus upon individual consciousness sees clearly, in her case, only those whose personalities were sufficiently like her own for her to explore their struggles sympathetically. The further removed from grace a character is, the more externally he or she is viewed. Perhaps this imaginative incapacity to bridge distances between herself and her characters was part of the reason for the shift which soon took place in her writing to concentrate upon older protagonists; there are few after *Laneton Parsonage* who do not either begin the book as near-adults, or soon attain that age.

Her most successful novels take the form of quasi-autobiographical accounts of a girl's growth to maturity, told in the first person. In 1853, for example, she published *Experience of Life*, her most 'really popular' work; of it she said that the heroine's 'troubled mind was a record of my own personal feelings' in growing up.[18] The story of the girl, Sarah, begins around her thirteenth year, and the first significant event is her confirmation. She is an infinitely more subtly drawn and developed version of the pious child with worldly relations, for her father is lazy and extravagant, and the whole family tone jars upon her religious and social sensibility. On the day of her confirmation, when she finds it very hard to attain the necessary frame of mind, they have invited lots of people to lunch. She manages to tear herself away — so far is she from confronting them with her own superiority to their shortcomings that she really wants to take part in the festivities — and has lunch alone in her room. She reflects: 'that one slight self-denial I have often thought upon with great gratitude; because I am sure its effects were not slight. It gave me what, I suspect, we all want more than almost anything else at the beginning of life — a consciousness of moral strength.' This stoic conception of the growing consciousness of self is softened by a scene following it in which the reader's sympathy is stirred: Sarah is left alone when her sisters go to a ball, staring at the fireplace and reflecting self-pityingly upon being not only sickly but unmistakably plain; her little sister Hester gets out of bed and comes to find and to hug and comfort her. The pious little girls who escape from wicked dissipation through picturesque illness leading to affecting deathbeds are here transformed into an ugly Cinderella, an unhappy adolescent who has to find some way of coming to terms with her own weakness and her unpopularity in her family.

She has also to contend with overwhelming religious doubt, as her author did, and she takes the same course, crushing the perplexities out of her mind and hurrying on with her duties. She acquires a clear, unselfpitying, sometimes rather astringent view of herself and others: she accepts that it is not only her role to live for other people, but to do so while knowing that she will not find any perfectly reciprocal affection: 'none will ever love me best' she says, and she is right. Looking back on a moment in her eighteenth year, she offers almost incidentally a very perceptive definition of the difference between maturity and immaturity: 'I trusted in the judgement of others, for I had not yet learned to fear that my own might be of equal value.' The kind of verbal skill Elizabeth Sewell shows in the use of the word 'fear' is several times made part of the character of her heroine: she is positively ironic when she pronounces of a lady of insensitive self-satisfaction that 'her remarks were often valuable, though, unfortunately so well-rounded, that they slid down the palate of one's mind without leaving much flavour behind . . .'

The second half of the novel resorts to romance technique, however, and there is a similar defect in *Ursula* (1858). This is a subtle and detailed account of a girl's growing consciousness, set in a very finely detailed milieu; but the dénouement is only achieved by a last volume full of activity and sensation, with Ursula foiling fraud and forgery in France. It is well enough done, and Ursula's coping with sinister French lieutenants and rapacious peasants without speaking a word of their language is entertaining; but it is not much to the point, in thematic terms. To make such a criticism is to make it clear that one has moved into the realm of the novel, and these books do indeed bear critical comparison with the novels of the 1840s and 1850s. The element in them that has kept them from much serious critical consideration is perhaps the terminology of the element of analysis which they contain: the 'reflection and advice' are both explicitly Christian (though in no way offensively so, as the author's horror of cant ensures), and explicitly concerned with women. The combination may account for the writer having dropped completely out of sight.

This is not quite the case with the last author to be considered here, Charlotte Mary Yonge. She has never completely lost her readership, and lip service at least is paid to her in critical surveys of the Victorian novel.

Her genuinely appreciative readers and commentators now are almost always women, however, and while they maintain that this is accidental, the terms of their critical esteem make it clear how this has come to be the case.[19] The fervent response to Charlotte Yonge's most famous book, *The Heir of Redcliffe* (1853), was shared by very many men, including not only John Keble, whose doctrine and patronage were its inspiration, but also younger men such as William Morris, at that time an undergraduate at Oxford, who vowed to take its hero as his model.

The need for a popular and attractive image for the youthful enthusiasts of the Oxford movement to aspire towards has long gone by; what remains is the author's protracted study of family relationships, and the moral ambience in which the study presents itself is an essentially feminine idealism. The books are serious; and their perceptions and judgements about the human condition place at the centre aspects of life which most men have not taken as seriously as most women. They deal with these matters, moreover, in a manner sufficiently accomplished in literary terms to command the reader's response and identification even today, if the reader is a woman, while representing a way of thought and a set of certainties few can now hope for outside fiction. Hence the wistful praise of her books as a healthful escapism, a refuge from a world dominated by male violence, into one which values people and believes in their potential, and their control over what is important in human life.[20] The concomitant restrictions on individual liberty and power provide the conflict in the novels; but the novelist, responding to the emotional and moral needs of the reader rather than to a strictly literary criterion of excellence, frequently violates the artistic integrity of her stories to provide a world in which all is, ultimately, for the best. People are more important than plot. But after all this corresponds to Charlotte Yonge's personal experience: as has been said of her by modern critics, '*things* did not happen to Miss Yonge, but *people* happened'.[21]

Charlotte Yonge came of the same sort of background as Elizabeth Sewell, a solid gentry family with intellectual connections, traditions of service to Church and country and roots in the English countryside. Unlike the older writer, she never had to shoulder the burden of family ruin, and her picture of idyllic happiness amidst a crowd of carefree relations and friends, engaged upon useful work for others, adding Victorian duties to inherited privileges, was never seriously disturbed. Her childhood was solitary, which fostered her reliance upon an imaginative life, while a large and beloved group of cousins whom she visited regularly provided it with material: 'it was natural to dream of other children and their ways and sports till they became almost realities', she wrote, and 'as Scott's yearning for Border chivalry led to his poems, so did my solitude and longing for young companions develop into tales of large families'.[22]

The Oxford movement was in full swing in her early years; and John Keble arrived to be vicar of Hursley, under whose jurisdiction her native Otterbourne came, in time to prepare her for confirmation, in 1837. She was fourteen years old. The influence of the great man, coming fresh from the triumphs of his Oxford career to be a parish priest, was overwhelming, and never lost its grip on her. He gave her idealism a solid intellectual foundation, of a highly selective kind, and a conception of the nature of a churchwoman's duty which pervades her thought and writings. She began to publish almost at once, having already written a set of stories as a French exercise which were published, in 1838, to raise money for a new girls' school to be built alongside the Gothic church which was her father's contribution to the movement. The plan of this book, that of framed tales, is in the *Governess* tradition of writing for girls, and the Melville sisters whose story the framework tells are the first of her imagined families, the one dreamt of as a child; they reappear as the Mohuns in later books. This first effort, devoted to the service of the Church and the education of girls, was typical of her lifelong pattern of writing and publishing, which was always *Pro Ecclesia Dei* and concerned with women, at home or at school.

The family chronicles for which she is remembered are not by any means the sum of her writings. Her first serious duties were, of course, as a Sunday school teacher, and she wrote stories for and about the village children, as well as text books, especially of history, for their weekday use; later the historical writing and the advice about teaching and bringing up children were extended to the uses of the nursery, and the teaching of younger members of the family which devolved upon her as upon the heroines of her novels. Even in the Sunday school tales she shows a propensity to let the people outgrow the books, writing several times about Langley school, which was first drawn from her own experience in 1850. These, and the historical stories which she wrote so abundantly for all classes of young readers, are chiefly remarkable for their proficient use of the conventions proper to them in interaction with the writer's personal preoccupations and methods of embodying the values she wished to convey.

Friarswood Post-office is an example. It first appeared in the Mozleys'

Magazine for the Young, a Tractarian magazine for Sunday schools, in 1858-9. It is in the tradition of the tales descended from deathbed tracts, in that the central figure, Alfred, suffers from a tubercular hip, and dies a pious and improving death in the course of the story, a death which is, to use the evangelical phrase, 'blessed to' those around him. He even comforts himself with prayers and texts; but the Church bias is made clear. He is attended and prayed with by a deacon who comes most opportunely to take charge of the parish, and teaches him not only that he must repent, but that he has a right to God's mercy because he is baptised. The climax of the tale involves them both equally, when Mr Cope takes orders just in time to administer the boy's first communion, having 'received, straight down from the Twelve, the Power from on High', so that 'the Voice of Authority now assured [Alfred] of what he had only been told to hope and trust before'. The communion has a further significance, however, which is woven into the tale to embody Charlotte Yonge's personal inflection of Church doctrine: the sacrament is shared by Alfred's mother and sisters, and by Paul, a boy from the workhouse who has won his way into the family by honesty, intelligence and diligence; Paul's first communion confirms his belonging in the family of God. Alfred's brother Harold however, sits outside on the stairs, excluded by his selfish and thoughtless behaviour, which has led to his confirmation being delayed.

The family group is eventually united at Paul's marriage to sister Ellen, where Mr Cope officiates and Harold, now his devoted servant and follower, is present to giver her away. The family relationships, especially that between the sick boy Alfred and his rough and noisy brother, are a very subordinate part of the story, but they are sketched with a delicacy quite unlike the heavily-pointed style of the average Reward, and the sisters Ellen and Matilda and their mother, even less central to the moral of the tale, are not only given their significance, Ellen especially being Alfred's nurse, but are also very clearly characterised through the scope and limitations of their responses to others inside the family and out. The detail and complexity of their portrayal is not by any means all directed to the principal lesson; but the writer's conception of even the most basic moral and religious teaching included an understanding of personal morality as part of the dynamics of family life.

Similar points could be made about the Langley school stories, both those of the 1850 volume and the revived use of the framework in the 1880s; in the historical tales, also primarily didactic but in a different way, the factual information she conveys is similarly laced with stories

of family duty and the training of young children. It is in two later
tales of upper-class schoolrooms, *The Stokesley Secret* and *Countess
Kate*, that her use of the conventions of story-telling for children
reaches its high point in parodic and comic adaptation, and in the
injection of a novelist's handling of character that are more than worthy
of Harriett Mozley's successor. In both books irony is a major tool, and
it enables the author to create her characters with such affectionate
subtlety that moral antitheses become explorations of immature
sensibility. *The Stokesley Secret* was serialised in the *Magazine for the
Young* in 1860-1, and resembles very closely in its situation *The
Parliament in the Playroom*, by ALOE, published in 1861.

In Charlotte Yonge's story the schoolroom group is left in the charge
of the inexperienced governess, because their mother has been taken
to London to see doctors, and the game they get up is a charitable
enterprise, the saving of all their money for a poor woman. The potential
preciousness of this is dissipated by the form of the proposed gift: they
mean to buy her a pig. The comedy of their preoccupation with the
philanthropic pig is made much of from the first line, which is '"How
can a pig pay the rent?"' The family group, the 'ministering' they
intend, even the moral issues raised, are familiar from the tracts of the
previous fifty years; but they are brought, astonishingly, to life.
The sparkling sense of the reality of these children demonstrates what
a skilled writer, not hampered by a non- or an anti-literary background,
could do with these conventions. The realisation of physical detail,
their holland frocks, the mud-coloured schoolroom paint, and the clear
pale green of the horse-chestnut leaves, has a quite new intensity; the
array of juvenile moral types becomes a collection of individuals viewed
with irony and affection which is communicated to the reader.
Practically for the first time one cares about the moral growth that
the story describes. The largest factor in effecting this change is
Charlotte Yonge's handling of dialogue. She had a very acute ear for
speech, and her characterisation often rests upon it, especially in
respect of her boys. She is capable of using a conversation simultaneously
to discuss a moral issue, further a relationship and comment upon a past
scene; where the moral fabulist made dialogue spell out an explicit
lesson, the novelist demonstrates by it some of the complexities of
human interaction.

In *Countess Kate*, serialised in following numbers of the *Magazine for
the Young*, there is the same shift of emphasis in pointing out the moral:
Kate is a naughty girl, as we are repeatedly told, and yet we sympathise
with her sufferings most heartily. This is achieved by the use once again

of a comic, indeed parodic, relationship between her characterisation and the conventions of children's stories, which shape the whole tale: the book is about the discrepancy between the world outside and the story which she tells to herself. She first appears as an orphan, being brought up in her maternal uncle's poor vicarage in the country, entertaining herself and her cousin with fantasies of wealth and excitement. These are suddenly realised: she is translated to the aristocracy by the death of intervening relatives, and sent to live with Lady Barbara Umfraville and her sister in fashionable London. Her imaginary life-story immediately shifts to a familiar model:

'I know what my aunts will be like; they will be just like ladies in a book. They will be dreadfully fashionable! Let me see — Aunt Barbara will have a turban on her head, and a bird of paradise, like the bad old lady in Armyn's book that Mary took away from me; and they will do nothing all day long but try on flounced gowns, and count their jewels, and go out to balls and operas — and they will want me to do the same — and play at cards all Sunday! "Lady Caergwent", they will say, "it is becoming to your position!" And then the young countess presented a remarkable contrast in her ingenuous simplicity,' continued Kate, not quite knowing whether she was making a story or thinking of herself — for indeed she did not feel as if she were herself, but somebody in a story . . . She went on musing very pleasantly on the amiable simplicity of the countess, and the speech that was to cure the aunts of playing cards on a Sunday, wearing turbans, and all other enormities, and lead them to live in the country, giving a continual course of school feasts, and surprising meritorious families with gifts of cows.

In fact she is as out of place as she imagines, but the result is not glorious: she cannot manage herself, her emotions, or her imagination, and she cannot and will not learn to be ladylike, and at the least opportunity of freedom she turns play into chaos, bringing brackets down from walls by posing on them as Shakespearean heroines, turning a large family of good children into rampaging wild arabs, and finally plunging ignominiously into a lily-pond at the Crystal Palace because she is frightened by thunder. Everything her imagination offers as excitement her aunt sees only as disobedience and lack of propriety and manners, and the narration balances the two views perfectly, so that the reader is able to understand and be amused by both, not only identifying with Kate but also feeling how trying she is, and so comprehending that Aunt Barbara and Aunt Jane have equivalent centres of self, from which things appear differently. The solution satisfies the reader's romanticism, however, bringing together Kate's desired picture of herself and the possibilities of the rest of the world. Another uncle and aunt return from India, heartbroken from the death of their last surviving son; they rebuke Aunt Barbara for the faults on her side, which are pride and lack of love, since she has acted throughout only from a sense of family fitness and duty, and they take on Kate, so that she will be helped to control herself and not to be naughty. This is to be achieved not only by management, but by meeting her need to be important: the story she tells herself about being a ministering child to her sad uncle and restoring love to his life will be allowed to come true. When story and reality come together, the imaginative energy can be channelled into a source of good.

These tales were all material for the use of teachers like herself, and Charlotte Yonge contributed to their theoretical and practical training in other ways too, keeping up a stream of non-fictional writing which offered advice and example for all kinds of schooling in which they might be involved. For them to make successful use of the advice, however, there was a need that their own education should be attended to; and since teaching was seen, by Charlotte Yonge as by Elizabeth Sewell, as a matter of personal giving and example in very intimate relation to spiritual guidance, the cultivation of their own spiritual growth and health was a main part of that education. The Mozley publishing house produced a Church magazine for Sunday scholars, one of the necessary tools of such work for each shade of religious opinion, but they also felt that it was necessary to float a periodical for the upper-class schoolroom, in which the instructors of the Sunday schools might themselves be instructed. This was the *Monthly Packet*, edited by Charlotte Yonge from 1851 to 1890, and prefaced with its purposes:

> It has been said that every one forms their own character between the ages of fifteen and five-and-twenty, and this Magazine is meant to be in some degree a help to those who are thus forming it . . . as a companion in times of recreation, which may help you to perceive how to bring your religious principles to bear upon your daily life, may show you . . . examples, both good and evil . . .[23]

The novels of family life were also for this audience and this purpose.

They drew upon most of the modes of writing so far mentioned in this chapter for their starting points of plot and structure. Charlotte Yonge herself pointed out her debt to Harriett Mozely and Elizabeth Sewell, and through them to Maria Edgeworth and the tradition of writing for girls which goes back to *The Governess*:

> and then came the impulse to literature for young people given by the example of that memorable book the *Fairy Bower*, and followed up by *Amy Herbert*. It was felt that elder children needed something of a deeper tone than the Edgeworthian style, yet less directly religious than the Sherwood class of books; and on the wave of that opinion, my little craft floated.

Looking back to her early work, Charlotte Yonge noted her own constructional shortcomings: 'of arranging my materials so as to build up a story, I was quite incapable. It is still my great deficiency; but in those days I did not even understand that the attempt was desirable.' Instead, she explained:

> My heroes and heroines had arranged themselves so as to work out a definite principle, and this was enough for us all. Children's books had not been supposed to require a plot. Miss Edgeworth's, which I still continue to think gems in their own line, are made chronicles, or, more truly, illustrations of various truths worked out upon the same personages.

This is an acute analysis of the peculiar tendency of her own novels to disregard story or to use it cavalierly, but she was less than just to herself in not mentioning that she drew inspiration for the use of characters as the organising principle in her books from a source which was by no means a weakness, the plotting of Jane Austen. The work from which these prefatory remarks are taken, *Scenes and Characters*, is very close to its author's reading of *Sense and Sensibility*. Its moral is 'that feeling, unguided and unrestrained, soon becomes mere selfishness; while the simple endeavour to fulfil each immediate claim of duty may lead to the highest acts of self-devotion'. The elder sister of the family is Eleanor, and the transmutation from Elinor is only that which Charlotte Yonge's interpretation of the story here would indicate. In her book Marianne is the name of a minor character, but the equivalent of Jane Austen's Marianne is Lilias, who eventually conquers her excess of feeling, which had done damage not by leading her to rash avowals of love but by interfering with the proper education of the younger children, and the work of the parish.

In the case of *The Heir of Redcliffe*, Charlotte Yonge did own to her literary models: Scott and the German romantic tale *Sintram*. Scott was her other favourite author, and she felt that the taste for romance was best satisfied by his high seriousness in its use (though even then, as Lilias discovered, unrestrained indulgence in it could lead to neglect of duties). *Sintram* is often mentioned in her writings; she felt its Gothic gloom and chivalry were religiously inspiring, as a modern romance should be, rather than morally enervating; Guy Morville, the hero of *The Heir of Redcliffe*, takes Sintram as his model, and he became in turn the heroic inspiration of his many admirers.

Since this was the most successful of Charlotte Yonge's books and is the least forgotten, and since it has been admirably described and analysed by Kathleen Tillotson,[24] I refer the reader to that essay rather than undertaking a repetition of it here. The point from it which needs to be stressed most strongly in the present context is that connected with Charlotte Yonge's achievement of mastery of the material with which she was working. Taking a Byronesque hero with an exotic story, a family inheritance that couples an ancestral castle on a wild Northumberland crag with a temperament as tempestuous as the scenery, and an ancient feud with his own kin, she turns the story into an examination of 'the penitence of a truly good man' — a study in the psychology of two young men in domestic circumstances, turning on trivial incident. That this is mastery rather than perversity in the handling of romance is demonstrated by the audacity with which she continues the story at length after the death of Guy, the original heir, creating a new focus of narrative suspense in the waiting for the birth of his child, which will be the new heir if it is a boy.

In this section of the book the second young man, Philip, the other potential heir, is the central figure, and we come to feel for his ordeal of self-discovery. In Guy's lifetime Philip is the object of the reader's dislike, a self-deceiver, pompous and priggish and jealous of Guy, adding to his pain; now a shift of focus is demanded of us, and we are asked to understand that his fate as reluctant inheritor of what he had previously coveted, and for which he did wrong, is far more tragic than Guy's death, which was made happy in his conquest of himself. This capacity to extend the reader's comprehension and willingness to feel with others to include the unprepossessing and unattractive as well as the sympathetically heroic is that which George Eliot reckoned the true art of the novelist.

Kathleen Tillotson suggests that Charlotte Yonge was aware of having surpassed herself in this book, and therefore refrained from adding a sequel, as she was often prompt to do. The extension of the ending of *The Heir of Redcliffe*, allowing the exploration of character to determine the shaping of the story, was an artistic masterstroke, but it was a case in which she scored a success by means of a propensity which often mutes and undercuts the purely literary achievement of her books. The inclination to allow the characters to run away with her, to outgrow the story and then the book and reappear in other tales, was one of the characteristics for which her admirers, the readers of the *Monthly Packet* who sought there 'examples . . . both good and evil' loved her work, but it was the unusual disciplining and containing of it achieved in *The Heir* which attracted a wider readership.

Concentration upon character did not lead her to exclude remarkable incident and extreme situations as rigidly from her domestic world as Jane Austen had done. In her stories retribution for wrongdoing may be death, perhaps the death of an innocent child, which brings the evildoer to agonised repentance in several books. External circumstances sometimes bring drama into ordinary lives, as when Leonard in *The Trial* (serialised in *Monthly Packet*, 1862-4), is wrongly convicted of murder. More important than such occasional sensations, though, is the way in which the sphere of activity of the families described extends beyond the home when the active lives of sailors, soldiers and missionaries are brought into the book. Charlotte Yonge is not only prepared to report conversations between men with no ladies present, but she makes a very convincing job of it: the conversation which is the great strength of her writing acutely records the language of men and boys. The relative freedom with which she used exciting external incident is less important in the effect of her novels than is her use of dialogue, which becomes the tool of the real structural principle of the books, the holding in play of personalities. The working-out of incident is relatively unimportant, and time and again climaxes come upon the reader unexpectedly, or are passed by practically unmarked, as the author, 'rapt in the curious semi-belief one has in the phantasms of one's brain', draws another breath and goes on to what they thought or felt next. It is what is said between the characters that is always important; whole relationships, and thus whole movements of plot, are determined by the nature of the language which people evolve between them and the consequent depth, or failure, of the communication they have.

The Trial (1804) offers an example. Leonard's arraignment for murder takes place even earlier in the book than Guy's death in *The Heir of Redcliffe*, leaving the rest of the narrative to deal with three quite different probations. Tom May hastens to propose to Leonard's sister Averil, who is about to be carried off by her other brother Henry to avoid the disgrace, but she refuses him, because she had never been able to tell the difference between the ironical, over-punctilious courtesy with which he had mocked her pretensions when they first met, and the apparently exactly similar language and manner with which he had addressed her as his love for her grew. He must suffer as he sorts out the personal confusion of pride and real sensibility which had led to his habitual reserve, to her and to his family; she must undergo a harder trial in the swamps of an American settlement, learning to understand him and herself, and obey her brother; and Leonard has three years of bleak imprisonment to test his devotion to the romantic idealism fired by the poetry of Scott, before he is fit for the real battles for the good as a missionary.

As in *The Heir of Redcliffe*, the extension of the expected structure is deliberate, making clear the order of importance in which the author places mere false accusation, however sensational, and real failure of duty, however minor. In the chronicle novels, however, no such artistic justification is felt to be needed: the transposition of families from book to book, generation upon generation, intermarrying as they go, became a habit that was part of the bond of affectionate recognition and comfortable understanding between Charlotte Yonge and her readers; most families figure in several books, interlocking with others who are also met elsewhere, until the individual volumes seem to be parts of the history of a whole pre-existing society, a parallel world.

Novels for Girls: the Teachings

The approved behaviour, which Charlotte Yonge assumes 'children of gentle birth learn . . . they hardly know how', partly 'by the unanimous consent of their story books',[25] differs in emphasis in these writings for girls from the way in which it is presented to boys and to poor children, but little in its essentials. Truthfulness, here as in the boys' books, is the *sine qua non* of childish virtue; the plot of *The Fairy Bower* hinges entirely upon a tacit untruth, which stigmatises Mary-Ann for ever; Alice in *Laneton Parsonage* had told a lie, 'a deadly sin, perhaps the greatest a child can commit'; when Tom in *The Daisy Chain* (1856) learns to 'shuffle' over his lessons in order to avoid being bullied, his father Dr May cannot be told because he 'would be so dreadfully grieved and angry'. Trustworthiness, which is partly dawning maturity and rationality, and partly feeling for others, is stressed, but neither Charlotte Yonge nor Elizabeth Sewell values obedience as a virtue in a child, regarding it rather as a tool in their upbringing with which the capable adult soon provides herself, to the comfort of all concerned. Mrs Clifford in *Laneton Parsonage*, for example, established total control over her girls in their extreme youth, and they say that she 'lets us alone' quite safely thereafter, since 'they had lost the inclination [for disobedience], for their mother's tastes and wishes were their own'.

It is with a similar sense of the essential comfort of all concerned that Charlotte Yonge tells us categorically 'the kindest thing to be done by a child is to teach it self-restraint'[26] and Elizabeth Sewell has her heroine celebrate her first victory over her own inclinations in *Experience of Life*. Charlotte Yonge stresses that all children and all adults benefit from the capacity to control themselves, and cites as evidence the great difficulties that beset dealings with 'persons of the lower classes' who tend to lack such training, however admirable they may be in other respects, and so are at the mercy of their feelings and impulses.[27] The primacy of the need for control is evident in her early novels, when she is usually concerned to advocate certain particular principles, of which this is always the chief. *Abbey Church* (1844), her first novel, is subtitled *Self-control and Self-conceit*; the danger of giving free rein to feelings is shown at length in *Scenes and Characters; Henrietta's Wish* (1850) is subtitled *Domineering*, and concerns the evil consequences of various characters' incapacity to subject their own desires to the unflinching obedience due to their elders.

In her later, fully-developed novels the mastery of the self is still vital, and it is usually presented in terms of the 'unfashionable virtues' discussed by Katherine Briggs[28] as the foci of Charlotte Yonge's 'exceptionally vivid and delicate discrimination on all ethical questions': chastity, humility, resignation, and filial piety. Men are required to show these qualities: Philip in *The Heir of Redcliffe* fails in humility, Guy has it, and achieves resignation; filial piety is the hinge of family relationships, and these are central to the well-being of all Charlotte Yonge's characters without exception. These are virtues of a theocentric universe, which make full sense if one believes that personal circumstances are a direct dispensation from God, who knows what is best for each individual more clearly than one does oneself.

As such, they are presented by Charlotte Yonge as generally desirable; but it is their articulation into a pattern of behaviour specifically for women, or rather for ladies, that is the special business of these novels, and it is the nature and effect of that pattern which is uniquely interesting as moral guidance through fiction.

For girls, self-control was expressed by Charlotte Yonge through the particularly mid-Victorian idea of 'refinement'. Many kinds of behaviour criticised in her novels are due to imperfection in this respect. Its cultivation must begin in early girlhood with physical restrictions: between the ages of seven and twelve, when there is a natural inclination to 'rough, noisy and bouncing' behaviour, which is not in itself a bad thing, the girl must nevertheless be taught 'the lesson of *retenue* and self-control' and forbidden boyish sports, or any physical freedom, with anyone outside her immediate family. At this age, 'refinement . . . can be taught by careful repressive influence';[29] afterwards, it becomes the first responsibility of the young lady in moulding herself, the task she undertakes after her confirmation, and continues until she is twenty-five, during the period of life, in fact, when she is reading *The Monthly Packet* and Charlotte Yonge's novels. A whole chapter of her serialised manual of instruction, *Womankind*, is devoted to its definition, beginning with the assertion that it belongs to man as to woman, and to all stations, but going on rapidly to its consideration entirely in terms of young ladies:

> Real refinement has full play of all its faculties; and its very modesty hinders it from dependence and feebleness . . . All that can be said is, that it is the delicate aroma of Christianity. It shrinks from no task, however painful or disagreeable, that ought to be done . . . It makes no parade of sensitiveness or of decorum, but it silently stands aside from whatever jars on its sense of the fitting . . . All that is tainted with evil, and bears the trail of the Serpent, is evil to it. No undesirable newspaper report, no novel founded on crime and full of questionable situations, are studied by it . . . In those days, when finery, *i.e.* over-refinement, was the danger, there used to be crusades against the use of the term *vulgar*, when it was misapplied to what was merely homely and simple. Now vulgarity, in its true sense of the basely common, is one great danger of our whole society. Bluntness to real delicacy of thought, action, and word, is cultivated, under a supposed notion of liberty; and our women and girls are doing their utmost to throw away all the restraints that authority, hereditary delicacy, and conventionality,

still impose on them; and therewith all true respect. For a man will never respect an inferior copy of himself, in boldness, skill, and loudness . . . She will be no restraint on his bad habits, no curb on the coarseness of his nature . . . Where woman is not refined, man will not be chivalrous.[30]

The link with man's 'chivalry' is perhaps the key to the behaviour that is advocated. Chivalry is a code of behaviour designed to internalise the control of violence and so avoid damaging conflict: the chivalrous man achieves his reward in society by holding in his instinctive reactions, and modifying the use of his strength, which might otherwise lead him to be provocatively aggressive in pursuit of his own desires. It is the masking of power, to fit it to society, by substituting ritualised for direct assertion of each man's claim to dominance. So refinement is the internalising of control of female power, through sexuality; society rewards the lady for restraining instinctive self-assertion, and modifying the use of her capacity to provoke potentially disruptive responses. In each case the approbation for 'manly' or 'feminine' perfection goes to the individual who displays the least outward sign of male or female power. The adverse consequences of the social use of such repression may be greater in the female case, where it seems so much more complete, without even such safety-valves as boys' and men's games were increasingly used to provide. This possibility was explored by many of the rising female novelists of the 1840s and 1850s, including to some extent Elizabeth Sewell; but Charlotte Yonge regarded repression as perfectly natural, and leading only to good effects: 'the kindest thing to be done by a child is to teach it self-restraint'.

The reason she took this view is uncompromisingly set out at the beginning of *Womankind*:

I have no hesitation in declaring my full belief in the inferiority of woman, nor that she brought it upon herself. I believe — as entirely as any other truth which has been from the beginning — that woman was created as a help meet to man. How far she was then on an equality with him, no one can pretend to guess; but when the test came, whether the two human beings would pay allegiance to God or to the Tempter, it was the woman who was the first to fail, and to draw her husband into the same transgression. Thence her punishment of physical weakness and subordination, mitigated by the promise that she should be the means of bringing the Redeemer to renovate the world, and break the dominion of Satan.[31]

In other words, the consequence of the Atonement differs for men and women; for men, Christ brought personal salvation; to women, only one of two kinds of instrumentality in that salvation, either as the mother, or the maiden, the two roles sanctified by Mary. The mother, 'her most natural, most obvious, most easy destiny', is the helpmeet to the husband, and the inspiration of her children; the unmarried woman is also a helpmeet, 'not necessarily of any individual man, but of the whole Body whom Christ our Lord has left to be waited on as Himself' The men of her family have first claim to her services, and after that 'their Lord is ready for their direct, complete, and uneclipsed service in whatever branch seems their vocation'.[32] Married women are provided by history with 'examples of the exemplary woman, whose affections have been a law to her, and have trained her in self-denial, patience, meekness, pity, and modesty',[33] but the unmarried woman may be at a loss for such guiding lights, and feel purposeless, or find herself competing for the position and privileges of a man. It is especially to her that Charlotte Yonge speaks. In *Womankind* she addresses her directly, as 'a daughter of the Church',[34] and makes demands upon her dedication which seem, stated baldly, to be in the last degree unreasonable, doctrinaire and repressive; but in the novels, the imaginative transformation of refinement into an ideal of behaviour and a means of knowing oneself may be as successful as the magic worked in the literary glorification of chivalry.

. Since they are concerned to offer models, the novels do not spend much time upon females who are not of the kind Charlotte Yonge imagined her readers to be. This leads to some obvious exclusions by class, which is much more rigidly stratified in her novels than in Elizabeth Sewell's writing: like chivalry, refinement is partly a concept of caste, which relies not only on matters of taste, culture and values, but also on birth. A novel such as *Beechcroft at Rockstone*,[35] for example, depends on niceties of class distinction for much of its story, turning upon the inherited and learnt refinement of different members of the White family, the product of a marriage of mixed classes, between a young officer, 'one of our own' as Gillian Merrifield says, and a 'southern beauty', half Irish, now gone to seed and become 'the queen of the white ants'. The children demonstrate by their refinement, or lack of it, to which side they belong. The 'peasant' woman may be perfectly refined, in her own station, and Ellen in *Friarswood Post-office* is seen struggling for the exact level of feeling and behaviour in this respect which becomes her place, when her reasons for objecting to going to work in the hayfield are discussed; the matter is in question because she is a step or two above the mere cottager, and it is in the context of such nice discriminations and possible pretensions within the changing and expanding middle classes that the matter is usually discussed.

The stories are also largely confined to exploring the possibilities and trials of the potentially good, and indeed some readers have felt that Charlotte Yonge's great strength as a writer was the capacity to make goodness interesting. There are some characters whose potentialities are limited, however, and these are usually women who transgress the first rule, and fail to perceive and acquiesce in their god-given inferiority. In Elizabeth Sewell's novels these women are selfish and dishonest, though not necessarily consciously so. In *Ursula* there is Mrs Temple, whose imperious and selfish manner is a discomfort to everyone, beginning with her weak husband whom she treats as a slave; Ursula makes her first justified self-assertion when she refuses to wait upon this lady, and from that point in the story they are pitted against each other. Mrs Temple is a mixture, very puzzling to her young and innocent opponent, of the self-seeking and the self-deceived: her parade of piety and rectitude, which recalls Harriett Mozley's Constance Duff, is not hypocrisy, for she does believe herself to be a righteous woman; but her enmity to Ursula springs from her accurate perception that the girl could stand in the way of her attempt to take over her cousin, Mrs Weir, body and soul, for the purposes of her own private comfort. In *Experience of Life*, a more self-conscious version of this type is presented in the mature young lady Horatia Grey, who is not merely overbearing and selfish but is actively seeking riches and position, and therefore legacies and a husband, by means of a display of brilliance and hypocritical goodness. She deliberately blackens the young Sarah in the eyes of the rich members of her family to make sure that she does not come in for any of the gains she is seeking for herself.

Charlotte Yonge's selfish women are less dangerous to her heroines, but still capable of doing great harm. She particularly disapproved of the sort of smug self-satisfaction which she perceived in some girls, who were not obliged to fight for the invaluable self-control, but were 'the placid, easy-going smooth-tempered sort, which dislikes a "fuss" far more than a transgression'.[36] Such girls were not only inclined to let natural refinement slip into a taste for luxury and a distaste for effort, but were tempted by their easy attainment of good conduct to the the sin of pride. Some are shown as simply indolent and self-destructive, as is Emily Mohun in *Scenes and Characters*: 'she ate, drank, and slept, talked agreeably, read idle books, and looked nice in the drawing-room, wasting time, throwing away talents, weakening the powers of her mind, and laying up a store of sad reflections for herself against the time when she must awake from her selfish apathy'. Others find moral rectitude as natural as neatness and fine sewing, until they are old enough for their love of self to lead to dreadful transgression of duty. This is the case with the unfortunate Flora May: intelligent, capable, beautiful, sensible in childhood and unruffled by adolescence, she goes into marriage with the assumption that pleasure and power are her right, and her husband only the means by which they will be attained. Leaving her baby, therefore, with its nurse, she pursues these aims in Society, and makes her husband an MP. The child is habitually quieted with opium by the ignorant nurse, and dies. The death serves to 'rend aside every wilful cloak of self-deceit and self-approbation', and she declares 'I have seemed to myself, and to you, to be trying to do right, but it was all hollow, for the sake of praise and credit.' She survives, and accepts the penance not only of genuine service to her foolish husband, who cannot act for himself or for her, but also of a second child who is an even less rewarding object of care in a worldly view, for she is subnormal.

The unselfish woman, the potentially happy and successful helpmeet, was not of course presented as free from error. One may indeed sometimes feel a tension in the approbation of the mother by these spinster writers which leads them to sentimentalise about her and at the same time to condescend to her, or criticise her failings harshly, because she has the easier path marked out for her by nature. The criticism is normally confined to the girls whose destiny is to *become* mothers, since achieved maternity demands submission which is beyond critical appraisal. The girl whose path is the obvious one has temptations, and may be shown succumbing to them to some degree. These are the pretty, soft, sexually attractive young things towards whom most unmarried lady writers of the period found it hard to be entirely charitable.

In *Ursula* Elizabeth Sewell has Jessie, for example, who is a great trial to the narrator simply because she is the chosen wife of Roger, Ursula's beloved brother. She is a very young and rather silly girl whose head is slightly turned by the adulation of men, and who puts herself and Roger through agonies by her flightiness, for she continues to encourage another man until her wedding, thus giving his upstart associates a means to press her to admit them to the better society of the village. This pressure and her fear of her husband are enough to bring about physical collapse, and Roger's outraged sense of her betrayal hurts him so deeply that their relationship is never the same again, and he turns back to his reliance on his sister. Averil in Charlotte Yonge's *The Trial* is never as aberrant as this, but she is not quite up to the level of refinement represented by the May family before her trial, because she does not come of a good family, and has been educated expensively at a boarding school. She demonstrates her unfitness for the role of wife by failing to subordinate herself to her ill-bred and unreasonable brother, and spending her time instead exercising her great musical talent in impressing the congregation and choir, so neglecting to make Henry's home pleasant to him of an evening.

If these naturally beautiful and usually submissive young ladies avoid the dangers of their attractiveness, however, they may be allowed a sort of perpetual girlhood, an innocence which passes unsullied into gentle and still-innocent motherhood without any intervening need to take responsibility for themselves or to encounter the world. Hester in *Experience of Life* has this happiness, for Sarah stands between her and hardship, and all she has to do is make the right choice between her suitors; Blanche May and Violet in *Heartsease* are both child-brides who never lose their 'infant' innocence. Violet suffers from her husband's family and their pride, but she is never tormented by internal failure or conflict on her path to the dignity of motherhood; Blanche is treated by her family and her husband as a sort of delightful child, whose seriousness is comical and adorable, as if she had never passed out of the stage of 'attractive kitten-like grace' which causes, according to *Womankind*, an unfortunate tendency for grown persons to pet very little girls, leading them into 'coquetry'. Blanche is unpolluted by the affection showered on her all her life, marries at the age of seventeen a man almost as young and innocent as she is, and serenely passes on to motherhood.

These girls are related to the heroines of romance who are often set up as paragons of feminity in opposition to masculine, assertive women who oppress them, or compete with them. In *The Wide, Wide World* little Ellen chooses to admire and imitate the perfectly ladylike Alice Humphreys, to the chagrin of her rough, efficient, independent Aunt Fortune; in such romances as Hesba Stretton's *The Clives of Burcot* the conflict is a direct one, between the lovely young bride Rhoda and her fierce mother-in-law Mrs Ashworth, a self-made woman who has raised herself and her illegitimate son from their degraded position to material prosperity. The difference between the two modes is in the demands made upon the girl: she is in romance the wandering heroine, wearily active, caught up in adventures and in preservation of her innocence; in the calmer regions of the domestic novel she has only to become a mother.

The mothers whom we meet in their prime are the repositories of all promise for their children; their peculiar cross is that of physical suffering, and their most sanctified position is 'on the sofa'. This is obviously a consequence of their biological function, which is often demanded of them to an alarming extent, surviving families often numbering up to a dozen; it is perhaps an indication that they suffer from, rather than enjoy, their fulfilment. The most morally impressive mother-figures of all are confined to their sofas without ever experiencing childbirth, thereby reproducing the pattern of the Virgin Mary as closely as possible: Margaret's exemplary life and death in *The Daisy Chain* is the obvious example, and Averil takes her place when she survives her trial and becomes Tom's wife on her deathbed, reviving for a few years of 'a sofa life', which is nevertheless 'the family centre'. Many plots begin or are furthered by the absence or incapacity of the mother in consequence of illness, and it is in this state that she most effectively fulfils her function of moral influence upon her children. The sofa is the final expression of the passivity of her role. Courted, married, put upon a pedestal, she is finally immobilised by her female function: living not only for her family but vicariously through them, she is the source and symbol of their consciences, their embodied super-ego, and so necessarily a still centre in their lives, giving them stability by her moral weight.

Elizabeth Sewell and Charlotte Yonge differ in their exploration of the implications of this position. Elizabeth Sewell finds that the conditioning which leads women to remain in dutiful obedience to their husbands in inappropriate circumstances can be psychologically destructive, however theoretically correct it may be. The mother of the heroine in *The Earl's Daughter* is revealed in the course of the story to have fallen into a mental decline leading to acute depressive illness because she felt that she was at odds with her husband and rejected by him, and therefore that she was a failure; she spends her last years in the obsessive repetition of the burial service. There is a link here, perhaps, with the exploration of 'passion' and its connection with madness which occurs in the sensation novels of the period, which are often concerned specifically with the problem of repression, and the proper role of women. Charlotte Yonge deals with passion and its management in quite other senses, and the psychological and physical conditions of woman's lot as wife and mother trouble her little: they are the consequences of the Fall, and therefore perfectly natural.

The less obviously natural position of the maiden receives much fuller treatment; her path is more difficult to discern. The central problem is the necessary departure from passivity. An active life is constantly presenting the need for decision and choice, and each decision is potentially wrong, selfish or undutiful, since every activity is potentially bad, as well as perhaps potentially good, so that no objective judgement is possible. Elizabeth Sewell sets down that 'it is not *what* we do but *why* we do it, that is of consequence', for we must 'work for Him to whom nothing is great and therefore nothing can be little'.[37] Some find their way comparatively easily by coming as near as possible to the position of a mother, without suffering its supreme achievement and its incapacitating consequences: they remain in their family situation, tending young and old, and filling the rest of their time with similar ministrations to others, without desiring anything different.

Those without the opportunity for vicarious mothering are in great danger of becoming cut off from feeling for others, selfish and unwomanly, so that their lives are a distortion unpleasing to themselves and everyone else. This is the fate of Mrs Weir's daughter Millicent in *Ursula*, who is well-meaning enough, but has failed in her duty to her mother, partly by Mrs Weir's own neglect, and is incapable of helping anyone, however she might wish to. Her attempts to manage and teach in the village are resented as interfering and rude — Ursula as a child is frightened of her loud voice and abrupt manner, and hates her — and her mother's weakness and illness is a torture to her, for she is not only incapable of nursing, but makes matters worse by her clumsiness and noise. Her dress and manner are uncouth, and she is led astray and almost robbed by sharpers, because they flatter her supposition that she can manage her own affairs like a man. Ursula, too, has to make her way as a maiden for much of the book, and her relationship with Millicent is instructive to her, and ultimately one of some affection on both sides, so that Millicent comes to rely upon the younger woman, whom she has always tried to bully, and to speak to her a little about her own unhappiness. Sarah has a better model to emulate, and a source of much good advice, in her Aunt Sarah, who guards and guides her at every crucial point in *Experience of Life*.

Aunt Sarah has her eccentricities which include a way of organising her life and everyone else's which brooks no interference, but this is partly a device to make it possible for her to protect Sarah's interests when the rest of the family, including the rich Uncle Ralph, are against her. The old lady's positiveness and independence are respected, for they are entirely selfless and dedicated to God and the good of others, and so become a permissible exercise of influence and power. She is able to teach younger women by precept and practice: the young Lady Rivers learns her parochial duties from Aunt Sarah's great ledger of the poor. and her instruction to her niece is firmly and practically expressed: 'Look to yourself, and never be a burden', she says, and work both for your own living and for others. The large, happy supportive family is not her picture of the ideal scene for such a life, and she says that 'large families are trials', urging Sarah to do her duty by hers, but to attempt self-preservation within it. It is by her example of ceaseless concern for those around her while sustaining herself by her private piety that her niece is able to come to terms with her own destined life of service, and her more troublesome inner struggles with religious doubt.

Ursula is nearer to Charlotte Yonge's concept of the maiden type, though she does eventually marry; she is shown in the course of the story struggling with the temptations which beset many of Charlotte Yonge's maiden heroines. Aunt Sarah's advocacy of independence and self-protection would be wasted on her, for too great a reliance on her own abilities and deserts is her great temptation, and the set of mind which makes her perception and pursuit of her duty most difficult. Allied to it is the passionate nature which makes her prone to answer back and to strong feeling, which she has to learn to moderate, for it is unwomanly. She fights her way through much opposition to a position of respect in her brother's household and in the community, winning a tight control of herself and working out the expiation of her youthful sin of pride and possessiveness towards her brother, before her author lets go of her sufficiently to marry her to the rather insignificant John Harvey.

Charlotte Yonge is particularly hard upon her maiden heroines because they are often partially self-portraits; she understands their temptations fully and enters into them. Her expectations are high, since she gives them the gift of intelligence and creativity which she has herself, and values highly as being the talent she has from God for His service. The failures of her clever, imaginative, passionate girls are her own, seen in the light of her dedicated self-examination, and therefore seen as far as possible without mitigation. Countess Kate, unhandy, gawky, wildly running and screaming with laughter, selfishly absorbed in imaginative aggrandisement of herself, is not in control of her body or mind; but she is a child, not well looked after, and she is forgiven. Rachel in *The Clever Woman of the Family* (1965), tries to be a maiden, with aspirations as undisciplined as Kate's to being important through her teaching and philanthropy; she is taken in by an unscrupulous man, and is to blame for the death of a bright and promising child, the lacemaker's apprentice Loveday, whom she intended to patronise. Rachel is prostrated by the mischief she has caused and deeply shamed by the fall of her pride in her own abilities, and she is only rescued by marriage.

In contrast to Rachel's abortive attempts to assert herself and lay claim to wisdom Charlotte Yonge sets up several other ladies. Mrs Curtis, the mother of the family, makes a comical fuss and lacks cleverness and education, but has rightness of feeling, proceeding from her sacrosanct maternal status. Rachel never manages to emulate her, however hard she tries to do right, while good feeling comes in the course of nature even to the feeble young girl Fanny, Lady Temple, when she becomes a mother. On the other side of the portrait of Rachel stands, or rather sits, for she is another invalid, the truly wise maiden, Ermine Williams, who is a respected writer to whom Rachel's intellectual pretensions are transparent. Rachel does not know of her fame and is very inclined to hector and condescend, but Ermine tries to help and guide her with a forbearance the reader does not share, for we feel both more sympathetic towards and more annoyed with Rachel, in her callow enthusiasm.

This conflict between the professed tenor of the characterisation and its literary impact is not unusual in the portraits of this type in Charlotte Yonge's work. It springs partly from her hard dealing with herself, but more strongly from her insistence upon the inferiority of her heroines to men, and their need of male guidance, which is difficult to accept when they seem either so capable, or of such superior sensitivity to the men around them. It is a discrepancy of intention and effect which has something in common with the confusions which arise in books for the poor child that show exemplary obedience and subservience to masters who are unworthy of it. The message there is that the poor, in carrying out the functions of their station, do their duty to God, which does not depend upon whether others do theirs; but the story has its own assertion of logic and justice, and the better the story, the more strongly this is felt. The same applies to the women in these books. In Charlotte's fullest picture of the maiden, Etheldred

May, however, the character is so strongly imagined and drawn that the author, having shown her growth to her full moral stature, must allow her to dominate the book. She becomes in the end a heroine worthy of consideration in the tradition of Jane Austen, without losing her didactic function, the creation of a fully serious artist capable of transcending the limitations of her chosen form while remaining true to its purpose.

6 THE END OF THE CENTURY: CHANGE AND DECAY

All the kinds of writing that have been discussed went on being produced up to and beyond the end of the nineteenth century; some of the writers considered here were still productive in the last years of the century, and their lead was followed by very many others. From the time the Education Acts of the 1870s began to take hold, however, the production of fiction for children took on a different complexion; the conditions under which children were reading changed, and there was also a shift in the emphasis of the cultural messages which were to be passed on to them.

The acquisition of the skills of reading and writing came increasingly to be taken for granted, as an expected part of the childhood experience. The majority of even the least privileged had some experience of schooling; more and more working-class children had parents who could read and write, and not since their grandparents' time had the possibility of learning to do so seemed a remote and desirable prize. From the other point of view, reading was no longer felt even by the most reactionary to be a dangerous tool, which could be offered sparingly as an inducement to conformity, and must be channelled and controlled. The Sunday schools now had little to do with teaching reading; day schools controlled by sectarian groups no longer felt they held the reins and could dictate their terms for the dispensation of education. Board schools were supposed, in theory at least, to be set up as a right of the people wherever any body of population needed one.[1]

The result of wider spreading literacy was to increase the demand for children's books, and also to change their nature. Schools and other prize and present buyers could no longer hope to attract their readers simply by the promise of learning the skill, nor to control them by offering them anything they wished them to believe embodied in fiction: the fiction had to have an obvious and immediate appeal, if only in the form of a glittering binding. The entry into the field of more publishers, and of writers drawn to the composition of children's fiction by motives of profit rather than philanthropy, hastened this change, and it affected the books offered as educational and improving fiction at a deeper level than their gilt outsides. The values which even the RTS and the SPCK sought to pass on to children through their stories

191

changed, whether in response to these specific challenges, or to those of a changing society; and the didactic traditions of writing for children, which had had an independent life for the best part of a century, eventually merged with the literary and other traditions to form one mainstream of juvenile fiction.

The changing state of publication in the field is easily detected in the lists of the societies. The RTS made major changes in their appeal in the 1850s (see Chapter 3) and continued to try to keep up with broadening taste, especially in their books for the young. In 1879 they began to publish the *Boy's Own Paper*, which was in the van of adventure story publication, serialising not only W.H.G. Kingston and Ballantyne, their successor Henty, the latter-day evangelical boys' writers like Gordon Stables, but also the remarkably un-Christian Talbot Baines Reed school stories and the scientific wizardy of Jules Verne.[2] The SPCK introduced boys' writers, including Kingston, Gordon Stables and George Manville Fenn, and some of the new professionals, like E. Everett-Green, as well as pursuing their own particular line of development, in the direction of improved literary quality aimed at a more highly educated readership, with notable historical novelists like Austin Clare, and the works of Mrs Ewing and Mrs Molesworth. By the early years of the twentieth century the RTS had become so shy of the effect of the word 'religious' in their title that they issued books like T.B. Reed's stories in volume form as from 'the office of the *Boy's Own Paper*'.

The commercial publishers also rose to the challenge of the 1870s. Nelson, who had been producing school stationery and textbooks for some time, expanded that side of their enterprise to supply the new Board schools, and also added to their children's fiction lists; the publishers who had previously dealt in a few children's books only as a sideline, like Macmillan, also added to their operations. Macmillan had published a few selected authors, such as Charlotte Yonge, Charles Kingsley and Thomas Hughes, and a few weighty textbooks; now they brought out a series of biographies of 'English men of action', and added some lesser children's authors to their lists.

One publisher in particular, Blackie and Sons, only entered the school book and juvenile market after the 1870s Acts had expanded it, and they brought a new attitude to the publishing of children's fiction. They produced as their first Rewards in 1882 two books by Henty, *Facing Death* and *Under Drake's Flag*, but soon included a very wide spread of books under the same heading, ranging from Henty and Manville Fenn to a whole series of George Macdonald's works, which they published from 1886 onwards, romance writers like Annie S. Swann, and professional entertainers like Bessie Marchant. Their wide-ranging list crystallised after 1894 as Blackie's School and Home Library, which became Blackie's Library of Famous Books. The range of this is surprising: *The Pilgrim's Progress* is there, *The Basket of Flowers* and *Tom Brown's Schooldays*, *The Little Duke* and *The Lances of Lynwood*, as well as *Sandford and Merton*, Scott, Marryat, Cooper, Ballantyne and Maria Edgeworth, and also Louisa Alcott and Susan Coolidge's Katy books, *The Lamplighter*, a solid chunk of voyages and biographies and, to crown it all, selections from *The Spectator* and *Northanger Abbey*. Gladstone sent a postcard hoping that the books would not be *all* secular, and although they are not, his alarm is understandable: the balance of instruction has swung decisively away from the explicitly religious. The oldest books included are rationalist rather than evangelical; the weight in the selection is supplied by non-fiction calculated to inspire emulative heroism which is directed at earthly forms of achievement.[3]

These changes in the didactic pattern of writing and publishing for children spring, one must presume, from changes of emphasis in what society regarded as desirable. Just as reading itself had ceased to be thought of as potentially dangerous, so amusement for children, even poor children, was no longer distrusted as it had been as automatically breeding disrespect and idleness. The Sunday schools laid themselves out to provide leisure activities; books for the poor ceased to be regarded as the implements of a forcible social manipulation and, perhaps because society was coming to regard all education and culture in a rather different light, there was no longer a feeling that the best products of the arts and literature needed careful handling and introduction to a wide audience, lest they should somehow cause a socially undesirable result.

Perhaps more important still, for educators will always seek to impress their values upon those they bring up, the notion of what it was actually desirable for the average child to value and strive for had undergone a change. The heritage of literature became more available because it was a part of the achievements of the nation, and it was now to these, rather than to any more abstract ideal, whether religious or social, that appeal was increasingly made. Publishers who broadened their lists for children to include adult literature and the new, less morally and spiritually demanding stories for the young beside their older didactic fiction were reflecting these changes, partly directly, and partly by responding to the demands of their purchasers.

Sunday schools wanted not only their old message dressed more attractively, but also any 'wholesome' book which would command the attention of the more sophisticated and well-supplied readers who were now their scholars; buyers of presents for their own children met from them a similar rejection of naive form and unpalatable moral demands, and had changing ideas themselves about what were the values they wished to pass on. The huge new market for which the publishers were all competing, the Board schools, had a distinctive new blend of ideas, some of which were not only modern, rejecting the paternalist assumptions of the old National schools, but actively radical in tendency. The chief example of this trend is the London School Board, and a survey of their prize and library selections in the twenty years from their inauguration, in the early 1870s, makes these changes very clear.[4]

The board believed in competition as a motive for effort, and instituted a complex system of medals, certificates, cards and prizes to reward conduct and attendance, and performance in examinations; at the same time, in 1874, they set up a library system which was also to be used as 'a means of rewarding good conduct and attendance'. The books they selected for these purposes began with the expected choices, the classic Rewards and prizes: *Jessica's First Prayer, The Pilgrim's Progress, Robinson Crusoe, Swiss Family Robinson,* Marryat, Ballantyne, Kingston and ALOE, even *Evenings at Home* and Maria Edgeworth. From the first, however, they also included romances like *Uncle Tom's Cabin, The Wide, Wide World* and *Black Beauty*, fairy tales and toy books for infants, Scott's poetical works as well as some of his novels, *Gulliver's Travels* and a selection of Goldsmith: entertainment and art were to be offered. There were also a number of books which urged the Board school child to get on, to do well and to rise in the world.

The catholicity of selection was even more marked when they began to compile the list of library books, in 1877-8. Of the 600 or so titles from which libraries of 200 were to be chosen for a school the majority were fiction, headed by ordinary Rewards (11 by ALOE, 9 by Hesba Stretton) and adventures (31 Ballantynes, 13 Marryats, 11 Mayne Reids, 9 by Kingston; the predominance of Ballantyne is partly because he had offered the board a special deal if they bought direct from him in bulk). The time-spread from *Evenings at Home* to the latest Susan Warner importations is repeated here, and the extension in the direction of fantasy and fairy tale is taken much further, including several collections of traditional tales, the Alice books, *Mopsa the Fairy* and *The King of the Golden River*. If these cultivated literary tastes, they could then be satisfied by a substantial selection of adult novels, including much Scott, *Don Quixote, The Vicar of Wakefield*, 21 volumes of Dickens and two of Lever, even three by George Eliot; there were also Lamb's *Tales, Tales from Chaucer*, Wordsworth, and the *Ingoldsby Legends*. More utilitarian aspirations were to be fostered by eight volumes of the works of Smiles, and numerous stories based on his philosophy.

The spreading of the net continued in the next prize selections, which included Hesba Stretton's *In Prison and Out, Silas Marner*, Tennyson, and Mrs Molesworth's *Carrots* and *The Cuckoo Clock*: these last were so popular that a stock of 2,000 copies was used up within a year and had to be reordered. Old books, *Sandford and Merton* and some of Harriet Martineau, began to be transferred to older readers at this point, indicating their growing difficulty for the young. The new authors begin to appear as they begin to write: Henty enters the lists decisively.

The selection process was continuous and careful: two members read and reported on each book offered by the publishers, and a decision was made in subcommittee. The bias of the choices made and the comments of the readers reveal their principles of selection. As the 1890s advanced, there was a growing inclination to cut out tract-like Rewards, with comments like 'An average Story; rather fitter for a Sunday School Prize than for the Board' or, in December 1891, 'Not recommended; we already have too many of these cheap little tales', which sweeps away twenty titles at one blow. It was delivered by the Rev. A.W. Jephson, who also pronounced thunderously upon a group of sentimental romances by Maud Jean Franc 'I do not like these books: the tone is bad, the teaching of the narrowest, and the style inferior.'[5] The later, imitative writers in the mode fared less well than its originators. A late and rather difficult work by Hesba Stretton, *An Acrobat's Girlhood*, was approved, while the works of 'Pansy', the American tract-writer Isabella Alden, were rejected wholesale, and the enormously popular L.T. Meade, who produced every kind of story, was found wanting every time she was considered.

It is not always clear why a book is passed by the readers. Emma Marshall's *Eastward Ho!* (1890), for example, is a very mechanical handling of old themes in which the story of an heiress, like Countess Kate, who rebels against her parting from her cousins by running away, is mixed with elements of Mrs Walton — she is taken in by travelling basket-makers in a caravan — and of the street arab romance, by means of a cousin who works among the poor in the East End. The working-out of the tale is very wavering, and fails to mix the ingredients in more than a token way, and it is eked out with three, long, interpolated stories which are a shameless device to get the book up to length. This Jephson approved as 'suitable for a Prize', apparently because it was 'well printed and illustrated'. Quality of production was often important; popular romances like *The Lamplighter* which could be had very cheaply were only acceptable in editions with good print and paper, several books of natural history or travels were approved for their lavish illustration although they passed the usual limit of expense, and when Henty's *Out on the Pampas* went up in price, it was decided that it should still be bought.

As the cheapest and most old-fashioned moral tales were dropped, more and more literature was approved: *Deerbrook*, *Wives and Daughters*, *North and South*, *Mary Barton* and *Villette* were selected for prizes in 1891; in the previous year *The Yellowplush Papers* were approved, and pupil teachers were bought an introduction to Dante. Careful discrimination was exercised at all levels, choosing, for example, a good book by Mrs Ewing, *A Flat Iron for a Farthing*, and rejecting one of her failures, *We and the World*; in another case a number of books encouraging self-help and an adventurous spirit were read, and several Nelson volumes with such titles as *Youthful Diligence* and *Notable Workers in Humble Life* were rejected, along with a book on the boyhood of Luther and a life of General Gordon, when others called *Great Explorers* and *Eminent Women* were approved, along with lives of Nelson, Mungo Park and General Grant. The implication would seem to be that the scholar was to be encouraged to aim high: not only were the best models to be offered to him, but the best books were to be sought for him, well printed, well illustrated, and well written, in their various ways.

This is not to say that moral teaching and the passing on of values had ceased to be a matter of importance in children's fiction; rather that the bias of the attitudes thought desirable had shifted, and that one of the new values to be passed on to the mass of English children was value for money. Many of the old books were still popular; but their successors had to do more than reproduce old formulae to be acceptable to the up-to-date Board school selectors. Some writers did not realise, or perhaps did not wish to accept, that changes in the attitude required had taken place, and very many still attempted to teach an evangelical Christianity and a social morality which belonged to an earlier period; the cheap publishing houses like Partridge were content to profit from their work and from the purchasing power of the many equally old-fashioned buyers in Sunday schools up and down the country. The SPCK, never as responsive to change as the RTS, still published quantities of these little books, alongside newer ventures, and brought upon themselves the wrath of Walter Besant, who denounced the Church for its exploitation of its 'literary handmaids'.[6] He wrote for the Society of Authors, and his indignation is that of the professional who sees his own status and wares devalued by other workers being treated as of little worth; and the successful popular writers even of children's books were now adopting his professional approach to their work.

The effects of such an attitude when applied to fiction with a moral purpose were briefly considered in Chapter 6, with reference to Ballantyne's work; but he felt it necessary to claim a Christian calling to write for boys, and excuse his prosperous business enterprise as philanthropy; the discrepancy in his books between the seriousness of purpose which he claims, and which might justify his manipulation of his readers, and the lightweight and easy morality with which he flatters them, nevertheless undermines his work. The writers who were of the professional generation, who felt themselves sufficiently dignified by their success without need to annex the respect due to the missionary, are in some ways less open to suspicion: they could make their moral points openly and unselfconsciously, and had in any case nothing to say that was not already familiar to their readers. There are very instructive differences between the imperialist assumptions of Henty's books, for example, addressed to a public well used to the spectacle of British domination, and what Kingston preached to suspicious emigrants and businessmen.

Henty had a very simple code, which he summed up in addresses to boys in the early years of the twentieth century. True heroism, he said, consists in truthfulness and unselfishness; everybody is capable of influencing others, and should therefore be responsible and Christian. The last seems rather an afterthought, and he was indeed far from evangelical, arguing not only for the equal value of Catholicism but for toleration of any religion, including that of the Aztecs. He also announced, perhaps superfluously, that 'to inculcate patriotism in my books has been one of my main objects'.[7] Henty's imperialism suffers from no sudden doubts about the legitimacy of violence; his conviction of English superiority is visited with no qualms about the failure of most Englishmen to live up to their Christian profession, and his racial generalisations make a simple dichotomy between 'us' and 'them', untroubled by any Christian conviction that all men are equal. In *With Lee in Virginia* (1890) he enunciates with approval the argument for slavery as a kindness to feckless black races, which would surely have caused Kingston, and generations of evangelical crusaders, to ostracise him completely.

His championship of the doctrines of Smiles is as uncomplicated as his championship of England, operating again on the assumption of a simple scale from poverty to prosperity which it is best to strive to ascend. His lower-class heroes therefore shed their accents and their allegiances, as in the incident in *Facing Death* (1883) where a collier lad uses the cultivated voice he has been secretly learning to quell a strike; he goes off to fame and fortune, shedding the girl who has loved him all along. Kingston's attempts to suggest the value of working-class identity and solidarity, however incoherently expressed in such a tale as *True Blue*, are subtleties beyond Henty's brief. The root change is the shift from a belief in a life filled with meaning by its relation to the hereafter to a satisfaction with an idealised, narrowed version of the present state: Gordon Stables called Henty a 'stiff, dogmatic old pagan'.

The effect of this upon his writing, however, is strengthening rather than destructive, for the simplicity of his beliefs and the single-mindedness of his exploitation of them as a source of income led him to take the business-like creation of fantasies for boys to its logical extreme, evolving a perfect formula and writing to it with no variation of ingredients. He was hugely successful; Blackie estimated that at least 25 million copies of his works had been sold, all, as A.J.P. Taylor succinctly puts it, 'tales of adventure such as have been told from the beginning of time. Developed characters would get in the way of the narrative. All the reader wanted was a slightly idealised version of himself — moral integrity combined with physical prowess, quick in mind and body, and success guaranteed after the occasional setback.'[8] Guy Arnold, Henty's latest commentator, has pointed out that where the hero is not an English boy, the books were less successful, however well written and researched; Henty realised this and usually played the game strictly by the rules. The fact that it was a game was obvious not only to him, but also to his readers; Professor Taylor recalls that 'even the most devoted admirers of Henty's books found them comic as well as exciting: they were too good to be true, but very good . . . all the same'. Henty had moved, in fact, to a sophisticated level of popular art, where it operates by setting up, through the familiarity of the conventions employed, a state of willing participation, a complicity, which uses humour to share the control of the game between the writer and the reader. In such a situation the sharing of values is likely and their reinforcement possible, but the teaching and passing on of them by the magic of art is not nearly as straightforward as it might appear.

No doubt many purchasers of Henty's books did expect that boys would learn from them, as the reviews quoted by the publishers suggested, 'the doctrine of courage and truth, mercy and lovingkindness, is indispensable to the making of an English gentleman', and that 'determination and enthusiasm can accomplish marvellous results. How far they were prepared to transfer such notions from the deliberately sought and fostered fantasy world into their own lives is, I think, questionable; their remoteness from what was actually expected of the reader was surely a part of their appeal. Modern critics who suggest that Henty's idea of India may have influenced the making of imperial policy surely over-simplify the role of popular culture in determining behaviour: even civil servants are more intelligent than to think the equivalent of melodramas and western movies a reliable source of practical information.[9] The part such images and their language play in determining modes of feeling is much more complex. The reader's deep satisfaction in the fantasy Henty offered was probably much more primitive, and less admirable, than the doctrines he professed to teach, for he channelled the emotional depths which he stirred by his tale-telling into a glorification of success, and of success, in the end, by means of force.

On a superficial level, Henty's lessons were about history. His version of the active life appropriate to a boys' writer was as a war correspondent, a job he first undertook in the Crimea, and so his favourite settings are military, rather than naval, battles or scenes of exploration and settlement. He presented his readers with accounts of British military history, concentrating upon the imperial wars and campaigns of his own century, seen through the eyes of a young and glorious participant. The history comes in as guilelessly as the useful information inserted by his predecessors, in chunks of exposition and lists of names, with plans and maps to back it up. Like the sailors' jargon and sea battles of earlier generations, and even their expositions of the workings of steam engines and the making of salt, it may well have been perfectly acceptable and interesting to its readers: again Professor Taylor affirms that it was so, and that by comparison with text-book history of the time Henty was 'exciting, almost intoxicating'. His work was often praised for being a painless way of teaching history, and no doubt often bought and given as presents and prizes for that reason. But history is not actually like the naming of ropes or the processes of mechanics, it is not a simple collection of facts to be passed on quite neutrally, incapable of inflection; and in the interaction of history made lively and interesting, moral attitudes unexplored and taken for granted, and the powerful ritual of the repetition of an effective story-telling formula, Henty had evolved an instrument of influence of no small proportions. On the other hand, the nature and direction of the influence may not have been any more closely chanelled towards inspiring imperialism than Gothic melodramas inspired banditry and a belief in ghosts: the final comment from the enthusiastic reader A.J.P. Taylor is that he 'regarded Henty's imperialism and most of his morality as very great nonsense'. The form has been perfected, and had, perhaps, triumphed over any intended application of it to the purposes of its creator.

A similar emptying of meaning might be said to have taken place in the final development of the conventions launched by the evangelical writers for the poor, the nursery child and for girls in the mid-century. An instance is the converted infant with power to bring the most hardened hearts to God, originating as far back in time as Mrs Sherwood's Little Henry. This stereotype had a final burst of life in which the child's converted state was replaced by something impossible in Calvinist theory, a state of childish innocence and perfection. Trailing clouds not of glory but of angelic curls and mispronounced endearments, these prodigies and their tales became very popular. The type developed from Florence Montgomery's *Misunderstood* (1869), a book intended for adults, but soon given to children, and reached its full elaboration in *Little Lord Fauntleroy*, by Frances Hodgson Burnett, published in 1886, after which this child was the model of infant beauty in fiction and even in the dressing and treatment of some real children, for years. The precocious religion of their predecessors is still present in the language of these infants, as they lisp questions about angels; the power of their deathbeds to convert adults is transformed into a capacity to turn ferocious dogs and hardened aristocrats and burglars to jelly by their innocent purity and great personal beauty. Eventually they are exempt not only from original sin, but from morality, and their very naughtiness is made a part of their appeal – they are not held responsible for their actions.

Mrs Molesworth's *Carrots*, in 1876, has as its hero a child who precipitates family chaos by finding and keeping a half-sovereign, thinking it a special sort of sixpence. He is rescued from the threat of a whipping, all is explained, and his elder brother, who has failed to be compassionate towards him, is the more severely reprimanded; Carrots is merely told to be quite sure another time that what he takes is really his own. The incident is turned to sentiment in a scene where he is upset by being given sugar in his tea when he is not having sugar so as to save up for a toy, and so the sugar is 'not his own'. Earlier children denied themselves for the poor, not for hoops; Carrots does not even have to learn about money by the exercise, since it is made up to the necessary amount by an adult without his knowledge.

The story motifs in use were still those of earlier books: there was a beginning of the idea of the child who is misunderstood rather than at fault in romances like *The Wide, Wide World*; Carrots's mother is ill, as often happens in earlier tales, and so he and his sister have to be left with a rich aunt while she goes abroad to recover; but she does recover, there is no retributive death, and no need to separate the child's heart from earthly affections. The love of his mother, indeed, comes to be entirely substituted for his adherence to the love of God. Little Lord Fauntleroy is brought to England from America and set down amidst relatives who resent and reject him as were Ellen Montgomery and all the righteous children in their families of worldlings; but he converts his grandfather to good behaviour — which is signalised by the old man's acceptance of the boy's American mother — by no struggle or endurance of ill-treatment on his own part, but by his assumption that the old man is as innocent and good and kind as he is himself. The issue is one of kindliness, not godliness; and the child is not a responsible agent, but acts in simple ignorance. He has to be brave, and stand by his mother, remembering to go and see her even when he has just been given a pony. He has no struggle to be good, no idea of influencing others; the explanation of his power is 'really a very simple thing, after all — it was only that he had lived near a kind and gentle heart, and had been taught to think kind thoughts always and to care for others . . . he was always lovable because he was simple and loving. To be so is like being born a king.'

Other motifs and story-patterns underwent a similar process of structural hardening coupled with moral softening. Henty had evolved his own unvarying formula from the story-patterns of adventure; other professionals were more versatile, taking a series of story-patterns and exploiting each in turn, as counters to be moved about at will in the creation of bright and attractive patterns to catch the eye. L.T. Meade is a good example.

Elizabeth Thomasina Smith, *née* Meade, was a professional writer and journalist, producing about 250 books and editing a periodical for girls, *Atalanta*. She began to write in the mid 1870s, and started with arab tales, published by Shaw, one of the cheap religious specialists. One of the first was *Lettie's Last Home* (1875), which begins strictly according to formula with the evocation of pathos from street names: 'Lettie's address was Green Alley, Ivy Court . . . a miserable court in one of the worst London localities . . .' The book continues in a similar manner, quoting texts and calling upon the Friend of the People; Lettie's drunken mother has killed all her other children, and now takes to baby farming. Lettie vows to stand between the 'dear, larfin' little kid' and all dangers, chiefly embodied in her mother. The child pines, and Lettie asks a neighbouring barber about death and its aftermath: 'Be the berryins up or down?' She is taken by a Quaker bootmaker to hear a sermon which assures her that death is not the end, and exclaims 'I'll never be feared no more. Oh Lord Jesus Christ! Lord Jesus Christ!' The author has some sense of unease about this, and adds rather lamely 'this instant change might have seemed unnatural to some, but in Lettie's case it was not so', before sending the child off to repeat the lesson for us in quaint words to the barber's wife. Lettie should have taken warning, as Charlotte Yonge points out: in these books it is 'very dangerous to be too good',[10] and sure enough she saves Charlie by returning him to his real mother just in time, and is beaten to death by her own parent. Her example automatically causes the conversion of the barber, marked by his refraining from blinding his canary.

The auxiliary pathos of animals is also invoked in *Scamp and I* (1877). Here little Flo, who is kept honest by the memory of her mother and kept barely alive by mending old boots in a cellar, is comforted by a mongrel which escapes from drowning and then from becoming sparring partner to a fighting mastiff only to be smashed over the head with a sledgehammer defending Flo from robbery. Neither he nor any of the several kind ladies who have taken pains to rescue and tend the little girl is able to save her life: 'Yes, Flo was going to God . . . What a bright lot for the little tired out London child! . . . He loved this fair little flower, and meant to transplant it into the heavenly garden.' On the way, moreover, Flo experiences perfect earthly felicity as she lies in the London Hospital — the Queen visits the wards, and smiles at her. After that she can only be made happier by going '"To live up in the gold streets wid Himself"'. Other motifs from the waif tale are arrayed in the background of her story. Her brother and his friend are arrested for picking pockets on Derby Day; the brother is educated with great success in the reformatory, and the friend is restored to his mother, converted by a sermon in the jail, and 'thus all are doing well' at the end, especially the dead. She produced several other such stories, such as *The Water Gypsies* (1879) which is about canal children; they all alternate childish pathos and physical horrors, for L.T. Meade combines the romance of the early waif tales with the horrors which entered with the reformist zeal of Hesba Stretton.

After the 1870s L.T. Meade left the waif stories for tales of other kinds, distributed to a range of appropriate publishers, from Cassell and Chambers to the RTS, and in each she produced a kind of efficient exaggeration of the formal qualities of the original, packing in its exciting incidents and touching characters, while coarsening, slurring or simply dropping its moral intention. *Beyond the Blue Mountains* (1893), is an allegory deriving from *The Pilgrim's Progress* through ALOE, in which four children, named for prettiness after flowers, set out to reach their parents in the land beyond the Blue Mountains. Two leave as instructed, follow the king's map, stay at the appointed inns, encounter Faith, Hope and Charity, and arrive with little trouble, while the other two let themselves in for one danger after another by laziness and greediness, in the boy, and fastidiousness and weakness in the girl. Both journeys are made interesting, for the author has a knack of creating pretty fairies and hideous hags, but little of the imagery not taken directly from *The Pilgrim's Progress* enforces any moral or scriptural point, and the vital talisman — Christian's scroll of promise — is ludicrously represented by Primrose's old brown hat, which saves her from the wicked fairies and the little dark men; she even rescues others by means of their homely headgear:

'There was a wonderful power in my old hat', she said to herself; 'it must have been because mother trimmed it; perhaps the mothers of the other children have also trimmed their hats. Poor and shabby and ugly as they look they can hurt the wicked sisters here — they are all afraid of them. I am sure I know the reason why: some mother's love has touched them . . . Perhaps if I put *all the hats* on my head I may be able to float to the ground.'

The author is not often bathetic and must have felt the image was a powerful one; her strongest force for good is clearly the love of a mother, rather than that of the individual for God, or the Saviour for his flock. It is not asking much of a little girl to remember that her mother loves her.

There is a similar easy way out in *Four on an Island* (1892), L. T. Meade's Crusoe story, where the children encounter various dangers, and must work hard, but never go short of anything, thanks to a well-preserved ship they happen to find, and are rescued by their father who arrives in a steamer in the nick of time and with the minimum of fuss. The return of the father similarly brings *Cave Perilous* (1898) to an easy ending, without sorting out any of the moral and social complications which the early part of the story seems to suggest. It concerns a miller's children, whose mother is shot by the Chartists in a bread riot. They save their father's capital by shifting all the corn and flour to a secret cave, taking with them their servant and ample provisions and evading the starving throng. The brother is vengeful, and the sister sorry for the rioters, but any working out of their responses is swamped by their adventures in the cave, where they are eventually trapped in a hidden recess, and only found by their father having an intuition that he should go and look for signs of them on the hilltop; he sees their smoke, and digs them out, and the story comes to an end.

One of L.T. Meade's most popular books was *A World of Girls* (1886), a school story derived from the old *Governess* mould in that it brings together contrasting girl characters under the wise tuition of Mrs Willis. The school is the small, intimate, family-like group approved by Elizabeth Sewell, about to pass over into the large, more anonymous swarm of girls in the boarding school which is the setting for twentieth-century girls' school stories. This tale may be compared to the school section of *Laneton Parsonage*: the centrally contrasted girls are Hester, a clever, ladylike, proud child who is our point of view at the beginning of the story, and Annie, a wild, red-haired 'gypsy' who means very well and loves Mrs Willis as her 'mother-friend', having been left in her care by a father who has disappeared. They are versions of the Clifford girls; Ruth, who commits the greater sin through relying upon her own rectitude, and Madeline, who knows and fights against her own weaknesses.

Elizabeth Sewell informs us that 'all great exhibitions of feeling are to be dreaded', but the feelings of all in *A World of Girls* are expressed in the most extravagant terms, not least in the case of Mrs Willis, in her emotional relationships with her charges. The minute incidents of the *Laneton Parsonage* school, where the importation of French novels is the major crime, are exchanged for a plot including not only cruel practical jokes with the belongings of others, for which Annie is unjustly suspected, and midnight feasts in the fields, for which she is really responsible, but a climax in which gypsies steal Hester's little sister, and Annie, with the aid of a walnut juice disguise and her magical way with dogs, bends a gypsy mastiff to her will and snatches the child back from their cave hiding-place. She lies dangerously ill after this exploit, suffering not for her disobedience and unreliability, which caused the child to be taken, but from being misunderstood and insufficiently loved. All is put right when her father returns to claim her. Hester's selfishness and dislike of Annie are condemned as very wrong, but Annie's failings in propriety, honesty and self-control, which would have brought a Charlotte Yonge heroine dreadful disgrace and probably permanent punishments, are represented as the sufferings of a passionate spirit wronged and suspected. A new character is introduced into the pattern to bear the disgrace, Susie, a lazy child who turns out to have perpetrated the tricks that caused the trouble, quite motivelessly, and is too shallow and impervious to cause the reader a moment's concern as she is expelled.

This was an enormously successful book, and set up a new pattern of school stories, and also of heroines who are wild and wilful and do dreadful things because they need love, or alternatively because they love too well to think of anything else before they act. Other situations in L.T. Meade's work in which they appear include that of the neglected family in *The Scamp Family* (1907), where Nora and Snowball, aged thirteen and eight, are wildly given to 'naughtiness' because they have only a selfish great-uncle to care for them. Taken into the motherly care of a neighbour they improve and grow to adore her, but break out one day and ramble in the London fog, with dreadful consequences to Nora's health, for she catches double pneumonia, and Snowball's budding conscience, which causes her to repent and demand to be caned, to help her keep down the 'black thing' inside her. Snowball is saved physically from the fog and a rapacious old woman, and morally from her wickedness, by a saintly lower-class character imported from waif romance, called Blind Joe.

An even more extreme example of the shifting of the moral base occurs in *Miss Nonentity* (1900), in which a girl at a public day school for girls presumes on her ability to win a scholarship for £40 to engage a specialist doctor, who saves her father's life. To travel to London to see him she steals a sovereign from the missionary box; to pay him, when she discovers that she will not get the benefits of the scholarship in cash, she sells a pearl ring she has accepted as a gift from the uncle of a schoolfellow. Her mother is too stern for her to confide in about this problem or about the prank she plays — going to a party in this same schoolfriend's fine dress and jewellery, to relieve her feelings of anxiety. About this she says that her 'mother, poor darling, wouldn't understand'. Her little sister, and a wildly improbable misogynist professor who is a friend of her father's, sort out all the complications for her; her mother concedes 'you did wrong that good might come', and adds that 'your great mistake, dear, was in not trusting me'. She has dashed about the country alone, taken valuable gifts from an older man of whom her mother disapproves, stolen, lied and burnt her mother's account book, and she is told 'the action of that dear little Miss Clare was magnificent'.

If there is anything which L.T. Meade does appear to offer as positive guidance of her own, it is a message addressed to girls which directly contradicts the notion of 'refinement'. Attacking most strongly girls of the 'mother' type who are weak and clinging, and representing their dependence as immoral selfishness and empty-headed frivolity, she advocates 'girls with stuff in them . . . who can act'. In the desert island story the leader of the party is thirteen-year-old Bell, who repeatedly saves the lives of the others by her ability to swim, fish, climb trees, shoot straight and keep up morale by toughness and cheerfulness, while at the same time making a comfortable home with two mugs, some turtle's eggs and a half-knitted worsted stocking. Her brother Ferdinand, who is to blame for their marooning because he disobeyed his father's orders about going out in boats, feels dispirited by his guilt and eventually renders himself quite useless by falling down a hole; he says Bell is the true leader, but she keeps up his spirits by giving him the man's share of the food and attention. Bell falls ill (thus demonstrating to the party how indispensable she is), as a result of the silly and weak behaviour of the little girl Rachel; but she 'got better, of course'.

For older girls this strong female character becomes Mollie, who 'owned that greatest badge that any woman could wear, the Red Cross, bestowed upon her by the sovereign of the land'. She proclaims that she will go to South Africa, speaking 'with a thrill of enthusiasm in her voice', because the war there 'will do us a great deal of good . . . our army wants active service again. We need to test our strength.' Mollie appears in *A Sister of the Red Cross* (1900); the story is concerned with the contrast between her noble bravery — which strikes one as rather monstrous — and her sister's selfish cowardice, when they are both in Ladysmith during the seige. The old reproach of the strong-minded girl, that she is incapable of womanly tenderness as exemplified in nursing, is turned on its head, and it is the pretty, clinging, loving Kitty who burns her officer fiancé's leg in trying to bathe it, and falls asleep when a dying private wants her to write a letter for him.

This new woman is perhaps L.T. Meade's equivalent of Henty's boy heroes, and like them she is rather a reflection of current ideas, shaped into the image of themselves most appealing to readers, than an attempt to demonstrate an ideal to which they might with difficulty aspire. Even this image is not by any means always present in L.T. Meade's books, however, and often they have no vital moral life at all, but are a series of efficiently-managed, brightly-written variations upon the motifs and conventions of story-telling for girls. Conventional writing is not necessarily to be criticised simply because it uses well-known formulae, but any protracted reading of L.T. Meade leaves one with a sense of distaste bordering upon indignation at the writer's attitude to both reader and material.

It arises, I feel, from the fact that one cannot but be aware of the meaninglessness of the conventions to the author herself. Her rate of production, around six books a year, meant that she developed methods of putting together stories from given motifs, characters, incidents and emotions, used as counters to be moved about at will; they call for responses in the reader which are just as easy and undemanding. She uses only accepted, expected ideas and raises feeling which is only to be enjoyed; there is no questioning or challenging of the reader, morally or intellectually, and certainly no attempt to change either the individual or society by her work. There is perhaps no reason why a writer must do these things; but to turn the conventions, stories and figures which a century of religious and social campaigners had filled with a power to evoke compassion and difficult self-examination into such an empty game is, in literary and moral terms, insulting, even outrageous. If the writer's first priority is to sell his works, then the manipulation of the reader's responses, into which a didactic writer enters because he has a personal commitment to influence him in ways in which he believes himself, becomes essentially cynical. He loses the moralist's excuse without acquiring the justification of the artist for intruding upon and handling the reader's inner life. The result is the discrediting of the forms, and the gradual devaluing of and disbelief in even their strongest manifestations.

A century of searching for didactic form for children's fiction, then, came to an end in the professional use of the forms, and the loss of meanings they were to have conveyed. Naive or narrow-minded, well-meaning or repressive, socially indignant, self-satisfied, smug or desperately in earnest, the first generations were conscious of literature chiefly as a tool — a two-edged tool — and they were anxious that its power, newly unleashed upon the children, should only be used to direct them to God and to their duty in that station of life to which it had pleased Him to call them. They sought and found ways of capturing the strength of story-telling from the lowest levels of popular romance to the latest refinements of the serious novel and used it to convey and reinforce their messages. But tale-tellers as well as poets find 'one has only learnt to get the better of words/For the thing one no longer has to say', and that the knowledge drawn from earlier experience imposes a pattern which falsifies the present.

In the 1888 London School Board elections the Rev. Stewart Headlam announced on the hustings his intention of educating the children of the people to give them ideas above their station, and he was elected; in 1883 a Glaswegian Sunday school teacher began to graft militarism onto the Sunday school movement by founding the Boys' Brigade, which by 1910 had become an official cadet force; in 1907 the Boy Scouts were founded, with an ideology of 'Imperialism, social Darwinism, and the cult of national efficiency';[11] Girton, the Girl Guides and even the suffrage movement changed the aspirations and expected attitudes of girls. Thus, while Primitive Methodist Sunday schools could still be found buying prize copies of Fox's *Book of Martyrs* and latter-day versions of the *Token for Children*, others were offering *Alice in Wonderland* and the latest Henty.

In the hands of L.T. Meade and her many peers and rivals, the formulae of didactic fiction, the allegories, romances, historical tales and stories of adventure, became items in the equipment of the professional entertainer; and naturally becoming worn and threadbare with use, they were gradually rendered transparent, until their emptiness was the most obvious thing about them. Some were made to live again briefly by parody and burlesque or by adaptation to the new messages; but the real afterlife of Victorian moral fiction has been as a part of the development of a living tradition of writing for the young, the place where the most basic manoeuvres of that tradition were first worked out. Whenever a children's writer tells the story of the journey of romance, or focuses a view of the world through the eyes of a child, or attempts to bring history to life or to explore adolescent feeling, the nineteenth-century educators and moralists have been there before, and either by assimilation or reaction, their methods are influential still.

NOTES AND REFERENCES

The place of publication is London, unless otherwise noted. Quotations in the text which are taken from the stories discussed are not normally annotated, and earliest available editions are used, without indication of their putative dates. Victorian children's books were produced in many editions and in huge numbers, and very cheaply; surviving copies are often undated and cannot be assigned a provenance with any certainty; even famous books may be represented in most collections only by later editions, for they were by nature extremely vulnerable. In cases where alteration and significant variation can be seen to have occurred, for example in the case of the revisions made by W.H.G. Kingston discussed in Chapter 4, the editions used have been indicated in the text.

Chapter 1: Notes and References

1. 'Christopher Columbus only discovered America: I have discovered the Child.' Victor Hugo, quoted by Priscilla Robertson, 'Home as a nest: middle class childhood in nineteenth-century Europe' in Lloyd de Mause (ed.), *The History of Childhood* (New York, 1974), pp.407-31; see also Philippe Aries, *L'enfant et la vie familiale sous l'ancien régime* (Paris, 1960), translated as *Centuries of Childhood* (1962).

2. For these various experiences of education see P.L.R. Horn, *The Victorian Country Child* (Kineton, 1974); Brian Simon, *Studies in the History of Education, 1780-1870* (1960); John Hurt, *Education in Evolution: Church, State, Society and Popular Education 1800-1870* (1972).

3. For changing attitudes to education at this time see also F. Musgrove, 'The Decline of the Educative Family', *Universities Quarterly*, vol. 14 (1959-60), pp.377-404; R. Johnson, 'Educational Policy and Social Control in Early Victorian England', *Past and Present*, 49 (1970), pp.96-119.

4. T.W. Laqueur, *Religion and Respectability: Sunday Schools and Working Class Culture 1780-1850* (New Haven and London, 1976), p.25.

5. This is the view of Laqueur on the effects of the Sunday schools on the working-class culture; for a different view, which argues that the Sunday school movement was an agent of bourgeois moral imperialism, to be seen in the context of developing class struggle, see E.P. Thompson, *The Making of the English Working Class*, rev. edn. (Harmondsworth, 1968), pp.411-16; Simon, *Studies in the History of Education*, Ch. 1.

6. SSU report quoted in A. Broadbent, *The First Hundred Years of the Sunday School Association 1833-1933* (1933), p.18; W.H. Groser, *A Hundred Years' Work For the Children* (1903), p.127.

7. *Gentleman's Magazine*, vol. 57, part 2 (1787), p.948; Groser, *A Hundred Years' Work*, pp.92, 175. For discussion of numbers in the Sunday schools, see Laqueur, *Religion and Respectability*, pp.44-6.

8. For the debate within the Sunday school movement, see Groser, *A Hundred Years' Work* and W.H. Watson, *The First Fifty Years of the Sunday School* (1873); and also the preface to *The Sunday School Teacher* (the journal of the Sunday School Union), vol. 1 (1868) and *The RTS Reporter* (May 1871), p.101; for the challenge of other youth movements and activities, see J. Springhall, *Youth, Empire and Society, British Youth Movements 1883-1940* (1977).

9. *Sunday School Repository*, vol. 2, no. IX (January 1815), pp.19-22.

10. *National Society Monthly Paper* (1857), p.115.

11. See *School Board for London Minutes of Proceedings*, vol. 3 (1872-3), pp.668-9; ibid., vol. 5 (1874-5), p.56.

12. Eleanor L. Sewell (ed.), *The Autobiography of Elizabeth M. Sewell* (1908), pp.12-13.

13. *Sunday School Repository*, vol. 2 no. IX, pp.19-22, and no. XI (July 1815), pp.99-100.

14. For the Sunday school library grants system, see W.H. Watson, *The History of the Sunday School Union* (1853); for reports of the success of libraries see, for example, *The Sunday School Teacher*, vol. I (1868), p.132, and vol. II (1869), p.422; for reports of their failure, see ibid., vol. IV (1871), pp.139-41, and vol. IX, new series (1895), p.66. Charlotte Yonge's comment is from *What Books to Lend and What to Give* (1886).

15. See for instance the history of the juvenile publisher Thomas Nelson outlined in Ch. 2.

16. Flora Thompson, *Lark Rise to Candleford* (1945), where she discusses the response of tender-hearted village women to pathetic Sunday tales. Other testimony to the reception of moral fiction and prize books may be found in Robert Roberts, *The Classic Slum* (Manchester, 1971), p.139; Michael Home, *Winter Harvest* (1967), p.79, and many other memoirs.

17. On nineteenth-century literacy, how it should be measured and why it was felt to be so important, see Lawrence Stone, 'Literacy and Education in England 1640-1900', *Past and Present*, 42 (February 1969), pp.69-139; E.G. West, *Education and the Industrial Revolution* (London and Sidney, 1975); and Daniel P. Resnick and Lauren B. Resnick, 'The Nature of Literacy: An Historical Exploration', *Harvard Educational Review*, vol. 47 (August 1977), pp.370-85. On the reading of stories, see Aidan Warlow, 'Alternative Worlds Available' in M. Meek, A. Warlow and G. Barton (eds.), *The Cool Web, the Pattern of Children's Reading* (1977), pp.97-102.

18. C.S. Lewis, 'On Stories', reprinted in *The Cool Web*, pp.76-90, p.87.

19. One of the best is still F.J. Harvey Darton, *Children's Books in England*, 2nd edn. (1958); see also Gillian Avery, *Childhood's Pattern, A Study of the heroes and heroines of children's fiction 1770-1950* (1975), and Margaret Nancy Cutt, *Ministering Angels* (Broxbourne, 1979).

20. Bob Dixon, *Catching Them Young I: Sex, Race and Class in Children's Fiction* (1977).

21. The argument of, for example, George Henry Lewes, *Principles of Success in Literature* (1865).

22. G. Genette, *Figures, I* (Paris, 1966), pp.159-60.

23. V.Y. Propp, *Morphology of the Folk Tale*, trans. L. Scott, rev. edn. (Austin and London, 1968).

24. Northrop Frye, *The Secular Scripture, A Study of the Structure of Romance* (Massachusetts and London, 1976).

25. Frye, *The Secular Scripture*, p.54.

26. It is in my evaluation of this use of romance that I think I part company with Professor Frye's conclusions: he holds that the indoctrination of the reader with the values of his culture, be they Marxist or Christian, by the use of 'cliché

mythology' in popular romance, is likely to be vicious or evil, and cites Ballantyne's *Coral Island* — and also its anti-romance, Golding's *Lord of the Flies* — as examples of the danger of mythologies expressed in popular romance. He distinguishes these books as 'not stupid', but will not admit them as social mythology, the expression of 'the area of serious belief' (ibid., p.170). I feel this is to deny the function of the popular or the children's writer because it deals in the affirmation of faith, which the critic, even when he admits the need for belief itself, rejects, because his intellectual training will not allow anything but repudiation of that which bypasses the intellectual.

27. ibid., p.166.

28. Bruno Bettelheim, *The Uses of Enchantment, the meaning and importance of fairy tales* (1976).

29. See Arthur N. Applebee, *The Child's Concept of Story* (Chicago and London, 1978).

Chapter 2: Notes and References

1. See Ch. 1, n.17.

2. William Jones, *The Jubilee Memorial of the Religious Tract Society, 1799-1849* (1850), p.11.

3. For broadside publishers, see Leslie Shepard, *The History of Street Literature* (Newton Abbot, 1973), pp.48, 89-91; for description and examples of penny histories, see Victor E. Neuburg, *The Penny Histories, a Study of Chapbooks for Young Readers Over Two Centuries* (1968).

4. *The Christian Spectator*, no. 8 (July 1839), pp.114-15.

5. British Library, 1077 g 37.

6. Letter of 7 June 1822, quoted in T. Grimshawe, *A Memoir of the Rev. Legh Richmond*, 9th edn (1828), with an introduction by Edward Bickersteth, p.335.

7. Grimshawe, *Memoir*, p.299.

8. Ibid., p. 246-7.

9. Ibid., p. 297.

10. The Janeway tradition persisted for longer without modification in the USA, and was still being imported by old-fashioned believers in Britain in the latter part of the century: in 1867 a collection of deathbed memoirs by the American minister the Rev. E.P. Hammond, *Children and Jesus*, was published in England, and in 1879 a copy of it was given as a prize by the Primitive Methodist Sunday school in Oakham.

11. Preface to the catalogue of the SSU depot attached to the *Annual Report*, year ending 1 May 1824.

12. Jones, *The Jubilee Memorial*, pp.125-7, 147-8, 193-7.

13. Ibid., p.135.

14. This point is discussed below, pp.44-5. The very noticeable degree to which a relationship with readers was struck up through their contributions and correspondence in this and later nineteenth-century magazines for the young is one of their most striking features. It continued until the end of the century, occurring in, for example, the *Girls' Own Paper*, which the RTS began to publish in 1880: see the extracts from this periodical reprinted in Wendy Forrester, *Great Grandmama's Weekly, a celebration of the 'Girls' Own Paper' 1880-1901* (Guildford, 1980).

15. RTS *Annual Report* (1840), p.109.

16. RTS Catalogue (1845), p.10.

17. RTS *Annual Report* (1849), p.127.

18. RTS *Annual Report* (1851), p.119.

19. See R.K. Webb, *Harriet Martineau, a Radical Victorian* (1960), p.107.

20. For an example of the elementary reading books which began to appear during the first phases of renewed interest in schooling, see Thomas Burgess, *The Salisbury Spelling Book* (1786), described by T.W. Laqueur, *Religion and Respectability: Sunday Schools and Working Class Culture 1780-1850* (New Haven and London, 1976), pp.210-12. New sets of primers and spelling books appeared with each phase of nineteenth-century thinking and legislation about education, and providing as they do sure, if meagre, evidence of what their readers were being taught, they have been the subject of detailed analysis: see J.M. Goldstrom, 'The Changing Social Content of Elementary Education as Reflected in School Books in Use in England, 1808-1870', unpublished PhD thesis, University of Birmingham, 1968.

21. Sarah Trimmer, *Reflections Upon the Education of Children in Charity Schools* (1792), p.8.

22. Report of the Standing Committee of the SPCK, delivered at a special meeting on Monday 21 May 1832; from the MS Minute Book, 1829-34, pp.284-6. For the controversy, which was connected with a struggle between lay and clerical members for control of the society, see George Rochfort Clarke, *Reports on the Discussions of the Monthly Meetings of the Society for the Propagation of Christian Knowledge* (1833-8, 1839).

23. SPCK, MS Minutes of the Proceedings of the Committee of General Literature, 1839-47.

24. There were children who could read these books without being troubled by their message, since they were not themselves destined to be servants; to them the verisimilitude and fascinating detail were very enjoyable, and the difficulties of the unfortunate employers seemed comic: see 'Hints on Reading', *Monthly Packet*, no. XV (March 1852), p.239, for favourable comment on Mrs Adams.

25. See Margaret Nancy Cutt, *Mrs Sherwood and Her Books for Children* (1974).

26. There are several examples of these reactions reprinted in Lance Salway (ed.), *A Peculiar Gift, Nineteenth-Century Writings on Books for Children* (Harmondsworth, 1976), pp.84-6, 96-7, 463-78.

27. See the Rev. J.A. Wallace, *Lessons from the Life of the late James Nisbet, Publisher, London, a Study for Young Men* (Edinburgh and London 1867). Wallace was Nisbet's son-in-law, and his book is a very flowery example of the genre of pious biography intended to be 'useful', in the evangelical sense of aiding conversion and devotion; it is necessary to read carefully between its lines to get any sense of the real power which Nisbet and the early evangelical generation at large certainly possessed. A rather more revealing example of the kind is *Three Days at Turvey in Bedfordshire . . . In the Summer of 1847* (1848), written by 'a clergyman's son' whose evangelicalism is at odds with a transparent yearning for saints to worship. The book is a naive account of his relic-hunting trip to his idol's home parish, and records his declaration, made to a phlegmatic parish clerk, that 'Mr Richmond is *my hero*'. (p.115).

28. *Union Magazine for Sunday School Teachers*, vol. 1 (1844), pp.65-9.

Chapter 3: Notes and References

1. See for example Dickens on the subject of Brittania, Hoxton: 'Two views of a Cheap Theatre', in *The Uncommercial Traveller* (1861).

2. See Anne Renier, 'Christopher von Schmid's "A Basket of Flowers"', *Signal*, supplement no. I (1972), which is a bibliographical checklist of editions.

3. Robert Roberts, *The Classic Slum* (Manchester, 1971), p.139.

4. For the controversy over the 'frauds on the fairies', see Lance Salway (ed.), *A Peculiar Gift, Nineteenth-Century Writings on Books for Children* (Harmondsworth, 1976), pp.111-67.

5. For the biography, see Agnes Giberne, *A Lady of England: the Life and Letters of Charlotte Maria Tucker* (1895), and Margaret Nancy Cutt, *Ministering Angels*, (Broxbourne, 1979), pp.75-98.

6. Giberne, *A Lady of England*, p.95.

7. Ibid., p.93, letter of 24 May 1853.

8. Lance Salway in *Signal*, 7 (January 1972), p.9, commenting on Emma Marshall's assessment of ALOE, from her *Women Novelists of Queen Victoria's Reign* (1897), reprinted there.

9. An exception is Annie Keary, whose story curiously resembles Charlotte Tucker's; she produced memorable allegories, including *Little Wanderlin* (1865) which was a Sunday school prize awarded to my sister in 1944.

10. Charlotte Yonge thought allegories of little 'use to anyone: they do not teach us to act, nor to think'; but she admired those of two other male children's writers, 'the two little volumes by the Bishop of Oxford, and Mr. Adams's four beautiful parables' being in her opinion 'quite as many as it is desirable to impress on the mind of a child while it is at school'. ('Hints on Reading', *Monthly Packet*, vol. II (1852), pp.236-9.)

11. This, and several following quotations concerning Sara Smith and her family and transactions with publishers, are taken from her MS 'log books' for the years 1859-71, preserved in the Shropshire County Library.

12. This is one of the books about whose intense popular appeal have anecdotal evidence: a Shropshire farmer's wife, born in the 1930s, told me that her mother had read it over and over again to her as a child, and both were always deeply moved by it. The appeal seems to have been the setting of the romance story in the village where she herself lived but in the heroic past, the same combination of reality and fantasy that inspired the author.

13. Minute of the RTS committee meeting, 27 March 1866.

14. See Flora Thompson, *Lark Rise to Candleford* (1945).

15. *R.T.S. Reporter*, 2 March 1868, p.18.

16. Cutt, *Ministering Angels*, pp.143-8.

17. Details from the log books.

18. Cutt, *Ministering Angels*, p.167.

19. The phenomenon has also been observed more recently: see Charles Causley's poem 'Timothy Winters'.

Chapter 4: Notes and References

1. *Sunday School Teachers' Magazine and Journal of Education*, 4th series, vol. 11 (1860), p.45, and vol. 16 (1865), p.50.

2. William Rogers was the joint founder of the City of London Middle Class School; this remark, made in 1863, is quoted in J.R. de S. Honey, *Tom Brown's*

Universe, the development of the Victorian public school (1977), p.54.

3. David Newsome, *Godliness and Good Learning, Four Studies on a Victorian Ideal* (1961), q.v. for a full account of Arnold's intentions and ideals.

4. See Patrick Scott, 'The School and the Novel: *Tom Brown's Schooldays*' in Brian Simon and Ian Bradley (eds.), *The Victorian Public School*, (Dublin, 1975), pp.34-57. The following paragraph is largely drawn from his analysis of the book.

5. See Simon and Bradley (eds.), *The Victorian Public School*, especially T.W. Bamford, 'Thomas Arnold and the Victorian Idea of the Public School', pp.58-71, and G. Best, 'Militarism and the Victorian Public School', pp.129-146.

6. See J.A. Sutherland, *Victorian Novelists and Publishers* (1976), p.131.

7. See Newsome, *Godliness and Good Learning*, Ch. 4. The ideal is 'manliness' still, but to Arnold it was opposed to childishness, while to Kingsley it is the opposite of effeminacy.

8. Accessible summaries of ideas on the development of British imperialist attitudes may be found in C.C. Eldridge, *England's Mission, the Imperial Idea in the Age of Gladstone and Disraeli 1868-1880* (1973), and the same author's *Victorian Imperialism* (1978).

9. See Edward Salmon, *Juvenile Literature as it is* (1888), p.14.

10. Martin Tupper's most famous work, which had huge popular success, was *Proverbial Philosophy* (1838), which he followed with a proto-Smilesian exercise in which he composed a sonnet and an essay on 70 great men, published in 1839; he wrote very many ballads on such topics as industry and Protestantism. On the myth of self-help, see E.J. Hobsbawm, *Industry and Empire*, The Pelican Economic History of Britain, vol. 3 (1969), p.121.

11. Newsome, *Godliness and Good Learning*, p.222.

12. See M.R. Kingsford, *The Life, Work and Influence of W.H.G. Kingston* (Toronto, 1947).

13. Contemporary statements of this nexus of motives are not hard to find; see for example Carlyle's prophesy in *Chartism* (1839), that to the English people 'two grand tasks' were assigned, that of conquering the earth for the use of man, and sharing, in peace and democracy, the fruits of that conquest. A less abstract vision was that of Edward Gibbon Wakefield in *A View of the Art of Colonization* (1849), where he restated the Benthamite analysis of the usefulness of colonies in absorbing surplus capital and manpower so persuasively as to convert James Mill, Malthus and Nassau Senior.

14. See W.K. Lowther Clarke, *A History of the S.P.C.K.* (1959), pp.165-9.

15. Kingsford, *W.H.G. Kingston*, p.142.

16. William Scoresby, *The Artic Regions and the Northern Whale-fishery* (1820, RTS edn 1849); M.M. Willey, 'Peter the Whaler, Plagiarist', *New Colophon*, vol. 2 (1949), pp.29-32. Willey shows that Kingston took long passages from this original, without, apparently, understanding that the author's view of such a proceeding would be that he was making the facts provided by the non-fictional writer as widely available as possible.

17. See P.B. Gove, *The Imaginary Voyage in Prose Fiction* (New York, 1941). Kingston claimed Peter was 'in every respect, a real character' and that the wreck on the iceberg is reproduced in the book 'exactly as he described it'; the appeal of the 'true' story is evidently important in his conception of his purpose in writing.

18. Editions after 1900 were numerous, the last appearing in 1948.

19. See Richard Faber, *The Vision and the Need, Late Victorian Imperialist Aims* (1966), pp.15-16, where he analyses the motives which lead to imperial expansion.

20. Kingsford, *W.H.G. Kingston*, p.179. He adds that Kingston was following rather than leading the trend of popular feeling in his imperial ambitions; but see Eldridge, *England's Mission*, on the spread of popular feeling for Empire, in

the 1860s.

21. SPCK Tract Committee minutes, 12 October 1877.

22. Kingsford, *W.H.G. Kingston*, p.190.

23. These were published by Griffith and Farran, and are interesting in that they are an instance of deliberate writing for the semi-literate reader. Advertisements stated that 'the object of the series is to supply the cottagers and humbler classes of England, whose knowledge of reading and whose vocabularies are limited, with books in large clear type composed of words the meaning of which they understand, sentences which the eye can take in with ease . . . so that they may obtain amusement and beneficial instruction without the labour which a large number of works at present put into their hands demands'. The *Ragged School Magazine* approved, confirming that the language was 'terse Saxon terms . . . level to the capacity of the humblest'.

24. See E.S. Turner, *Boys Will Be Boys*, new rev. edn (1975), pp.74-5, 88-9, and Louis James, 'Tom Brown's Imperialist Sons', *Victorian Studies*, vol. XVIII (September 1973), pp.89-99.

25. Kingsford, *W.H.G. Kingston*, p.197.

26. Elizabeth Reid and Charles H. Coe, *Captain Mayne Reid, His Life and Adventures* (1900),

27. See Eric Quayle, *Ballantyne the Brave* (1967), for these details of his life.

28. See Quayle, *Ballantyne the Brave*, p.133, where he reprints a letter of Ballantyne's to his sister-in-law about his submission to a divine calling to write for boys.

29. James Bowman, whose earlier story *The Island Home* (1851) Ballantyne used extensively in writing *Coral Island*, was a more capable literary artisan, and framed his tale in a manner deliberately suggestive of earlier stories. The preface claims that the narrative is from a manuscript discovered in a model ship on the high seas, and the tale begins as if previous pages were missing, with the casting away of the boys, and ends without returning them to civilisation. The first chapter includes a discussion of the proper conventions of the Crusoe tale. Ballantyne's chief apparent innovation in the story, the omission of an adult mentor to guide the boys and moralise the tale, is taken from Bowman; but he was neither sufficiently perceptive to copy Bowman's structural sophistication, nor sufficiently the naive artist to replace it with effective popular story-telling.

30. See Salmon, *Juvenile Literature*, p.14, where Dickens tops the list of authors.

31. Ibid., p.148.

Chapter 5: Notes and References

1. See P. Thomson, *The Victorian Heroine, a Changing Ideal 1837-73* (1956), Ch. 1, and on the education of women, Ch. 2; see Lee Holcombe, *Victorian Ladies at Work, Middle-Class Working Women in England and Wales, 1850-1914* (Newton Abbot, 1973) for the surplus of women and its results; and Anthea Zeman, *Presumptuous Girls, Women and their World in the Serious Woman's Novel* (1977), pp.30-1.

2. Charlotte M. Yonge, 'Children's Literature in the Last Century', *Macmillan's Magazine* vol. XX (May-October 1869), pp.229-37, 302-10, 448-56, p.449.

3. Susan Warner published for part of her career as 'Elizabeth Wetherell'; in later years she sometimes wrote in conjunction with her sister Anna.

4. Charlotte M. Yonge, 'Children's Literature', p.309.

5. Anna B. Warner, *Susan Warner ('Elizabeth Wetherell')* (New York and London, 1909), pp.357-8.

6. John Rowe Townsend, *Written for Children*, rev. edn (Harmondsworth, 1974), p.77.

7. See for example Gillian Avery, *Childhood's Pattern, a study of the heroes and heroines of children's fiction 1770-1950* (1975), p.182.

8. Charlotte M. Yonge, *What Books to Lend and What to Give* (1886), p.10.

9. See Victor Erlich, *Russian Formalism, History-Doctrine* (The Hague, 1955), p.226, on parody and change in formalist theory.

10. See Eleanor L. Sewell, *The Autobiography of Elizabeth M. Sewell* (1908), pp.57-8, 62.

11. Ibid., pp.37-8.

12. See F.W.H. Myers, *Century Magazine*, vol. 23 (November 1881), pp.62-3.

13. See Sewell, *Elizabeth M. Sewell*, Chs. 3-5.

14. Ibid., pp.75, 80.

15. See Shirley Foster, 'Elizabeth M. Sewell: a biographical and critical study', unpublished PhD thesis, University of Liverpool, 1974, p.68; K. Tillotson, *Novels of the 1840s* (Oxford, 1954), pp.134-5.

16. Sewell, *Elizabeth M. Sewell*, pp.75, 80.

17. Foster, 'Elizabeth M. Sewell', p.79.

18. Sewell, *Elizabeth M. Sewell*, p.115.

19. See for example *A Chaplet for Charlotte Yonge* (1965), the tribute produced by the Charlotte Yonge Society, an association of distinguished, female critics, declaring the absence of men from their ranks to be a regrettable accident (p.13).

20. See for example M. Mare and A. Percival, *Victorian Best-Seller, the World of Charlotte M. Yonge* (1947), p.5.

21. Ibid., p.12.

22. Preface to Charlotte M. Yonge's *Scenes and Characters*, added in 1886; also 'Lifelong Friends', *Monthly Packet* (December 1894), pp.694-7, p.695.

23. Introductory Letter to *The Monthly Packet of Evening Readings for Younger Members of the English Church*, vol. I (January 1851), pp.i-iv.

24. K. Tillotson, 'The Heir of Redcliffe' in G. and K. Tillotson, *Mid-Victorian Studies* (1965), pp.49-55.

25. Charlotte M. Yonge, 'Womankind', *Monthly Packet*, vol. 17 (January-June 1874) (serialised January 1874-June 1877), p.122.

26. Ibid., p.121.

27. Ibid.

28. Charlotte Yonge Society, 'Charlotte Yonge's Ethics: Some Unfashionable Virtues', *A Chaplet for Charlotte Yonge* (1965), pp.20-30.

29. Yonge, 'Womankind', *Monthly Packet*, vol. 17, pp.120-1.

30. Yonge, 'Womankind', *Monthly Packet*, vol. 19 (January-June 1875), pp.175-6.

31. Yonge, 'Womankind', *Monthly Packet*, vol. 17, pp.24-5.

32. Ibid., pp.27-8.

33. Ibid., p.28.

34. Ibid., p.29.

35. Serialised in *Monthly Packet*, January 1877-December 1888.

36. Yonge, 'Womankind', vol. 17, p.394.

37. In *The Earl's Daughter*.

Chapter 6: Notes and Reference

1. See David Rubinstein, 'Socialization and the London School Board 1870-1904: aims, methods and public opinion' in P. McCann (ed.), *Popular Education and Socialization in the Nineteenth Century* (1977), pp.231-64; on pp.254-6 he discusses the change in parental attitudes as Board schools came to be accepted, and notes that by 1899 the need for education had come to be taken largely for granted.

2. See E.S. Turner, *Boys Will Be Boys*, new rev. edn (1975), pp.88-9.

3. See Agnes C. Blackie, *Blackie and Son, A Short History of the Firm, 1809-1959* (London and Glasgow, 1959), Ch. 3.

4. For the radical element on the London School Board, see Rubinstein 'Socialization and the London School Board'; the following details concerning the board's prizes are all taken from the *School Board for London Minutes of Proceedings* vol. V, 1874-5, et seq.

5. Jephson was one of the clerical members of the board who aligned himself with the radicals, though he was not a socialist; he had indeed joined the board in order to defend Church schools from its encroachments, but rapidly decided that the Board schools served the children well and deserved to be supported. He remained one of the board's most active members until he resigned in 1906, disgusted with the bureaucracy, penny-pinching and neglect of educational goals which he felt resulted from the transfer of control of London education to the LCC. See A.W. Jephson, *My Work in London* (1910), pp.124-42.

6. Walter Besant, *The Literary Handmaid of the Church* (1890); for the society's answer, see W.K. Lowther Clarke, *A History of the S.P.C.K.* (1959), pp.186-7.

7. See G.A. Henty, 'True Heroism: A Talk with the Boys', *Home Messenger*, vol. XII (1903), and the *Boy's Own Paper* (December 1902), quoted in Guy Arnold, *Held Fast For England, G.A. Henty, Imperialist Boys' Writer* (1980), pp.20 and 67.

8. Quotations from A.J.P. Taylor are taken from his review of Guy Arnold's book. *Held Fast for England* in the *Observer*, 13 April 1980, p.38.

9. See Mark Naidis, 'G.S. Henty's Idea of India', *Victorian Studies*, vol. VIII (September 1964), pp.49-58, and Louis James, 'Tom Brown's Imperialist Sons', *Victorian Studies*, vol. XVIII (September 1973), pp.89-99; James suggests some of the ambiguities which must, in my opinion, qualify all modern views of the attitudes and effects of popular writing of the past.

10. Charlotte M. Yonge, 'Hints on Reading', *Monthly Packet*, vol. II (March 1852), p.237; the same critical jest about the pious slaughter perpetrated by writers for children had been made by Catherine Sinclair in her *Modern Accomplishments* (1836), where the heroine says that she learnt from *The Child's Companion* and *Early Piety* that it must be 'impossible for any religious child to survive, and that it would be condemning myself to death if I became truly pious'.

11. J. Springhall, *Youth, Empire and Society, British Youth Movements 1883-1940* (1977), p.59.

BIBLIOGRAPHY

What follows is a simple alphabetical listing of some critical and historical works relevant to the study of Victorian children's books, intended as an introductory guide for students. It includes all such works referred to in the text (except those concerned only with literary theory), and others which have been found useful in the course of research. No worthwhile attempt to list the works of the writers for children who have been discussed could be made in such short compass, but see index entries for the stories which are mentioned in the text.

The place of publication is London, unless otherwise noted:

Allen, W.O.B. and Edmund McClure, *Two Hundred Years, the history of the Society for the Propagation of Christian Knowledge 1698-1898* (1898)

Applebee, Arthur N., *The Child's Concept of Story* (Chicago and London, 1978)

Aries, Philippe, *L'enfant et la vie familiale sous l'ancien régime* (Paris, 1960)

Arnold, Guy, *Held Fast For England, G.A. Henty, Imperialist Boys' Writer* (1980)

Avery, Gillian, *Nineteenth-Century Children, heroes and heroines in English children's stories 1780-1900* (1965)

—— *Childhood's Pattern, a study of the heroes and heroines of children's fiction 1770-1950* (1975)

Bamford, T.W. *Thomas Arnold* (1960)

Barlee, E., *Pantomine Waifs, or, a plea for our city children* (1884)

Battiscombe, Georgina, *Charlotte Mary Yonge: the story of an uneventful life* (1943)

Bettelheim, Bruno, *The Uses of Enchantment, the meaning and importance of fairy tales* (1976)

Besant, Walter, *The Literary Handmaid of the Church* (1890)

Blackie, Agnes C., *Blackie and Son, A Short History of the Firm, 1809-1959* (London and Glasgow, 1959)

Blackie, W.G., *Sketch of the Origin and Progress of the Firm of Blackie and Son* (privately printed 1897)

Broadbent, A., *The First Hundred Years of the Sunday School Association 1833-1933* (1933)

Charlotte Yonge Society, *A Chaplet for Charlotte Yonge* (1965)

Coveney, Peter, *Poor Monkey, The Child in Literature* (1957)

Craik, Dinah M., *A Woman's Thoughts About Women* (1858)

Cunningham, Valentine, *Everywhere Spoken Against, Dissent in the Victorian Novel* (Oxford, 1975)

Cutt, Margaret Nancy, *Mrs Sherwood and Her Books for Children* (1974)

——, *Ministering Angels* (Broxbourne, 1979)

Dartt, Robert, *G.A. Henty, A Bibliography* (1971)

Darton, F.J. Harvey, *Children's Books in England*, 2nd edn (1958).

Davies, Brian, *Social Control and Education* (1976)

Dixon, Bob, *Catching Them Young I: Sex, Race and Class in Children's Fiction* (1977)

Eldridge, C.C., *England's Mission, the Imperial Idea in the Age of Gladstone and Disraeli 1868-1880* (1973)

——, *Victorian Imperialism* (1978)

Faber, Richard, *The Vision and the Need, Late Victorian Imperialist Aims* (1966)

Fleming, Sandford, *Children and Puritanism* (New Haven, 1933)

Forrester, Wendy, *Great Grandmamma's Weekly, a celebration of the 'Girls' Own Paper' 1880-1901* (Guildford, 1980)

Foster, Shirley, 'Elizabeth M. Sewell: a biographical and critical study', unpublished PhD thesis, University of Liverpool, 1974

Fry, T., *Domestic Portraiture* (1833)

Giberne, Agnes, *A Lady of England: the Life and Letters of Charlotte Maria Tucker* (1895)

Goldstrom, J.M., 'The Changing Social Content of Elementary Education as Reflected in School Books in Use in England, 1808-1870', unpublished PhD thesis, University of Birmingham, 1968

Gove, P.B., *The Imaginary Voyage in Prose Fiction* (New York, 1941)

Green, Martin, *Dreams of Adventure, Deeds of Empire* (1980)

Green, Roger L., *Tellers of Tales*, rev. edn (1969)

Grimshawe, T., *A Memoir of the Rev. Legh Richmond*, 9th edn (1828)

Groser, W.H., *A Hundred Years' Work For the Children* (1903)

Harrison, Brian, 'Religion and Recreation in Nineteenth-Century England', *Past and Present*, 38 (1967), pp.98-125

Healey, Edna, *Lady Unknown, the Life of Angela Burdett-Coutts* (1978)

Hibberd, Dominic, 'Where there are no spectators: a rereading of *Tom Brown's Schooldays*', *Children's Literature in Education*, 21 (Summer 1976), pp.64-73

Hobsbawm, E.J., *Industry and Empire*, The Pelican Economic History of Britain, vol. 3 (Harmondsworth, 1969)

Holcombe, Lee, *Victorian Ladies at Work, Middle-Class Working Women in England and Wales 1850-1914* (Newton Abbot, 1973)

Home, Michael, *Winter Harvest* (1967)

Honey, J.R. de S., *Tom Brown's Universe, the development of the Victorian public school* (1977)

Hope, Ascott R., *A Book About Boys* (Edinburgh, 1868)

Horn, P.L.R., *The Victorian Country Child* (Kineton, 1974)

Hurt, John, *Education in Evolution: Church, State, Society and Popular Education 1800-1870* (1972)

James, Louis, 'Tom Brown's Imperialist Sons', *Victorian Studies*, vol. XVIII, (September 1973), pp.89-99

Jephson, A.W., *My Work in London* (1910)

Johnson, R., 'Educational Policy and Social Control in Early Victorian England', *Past and Present*, 49 (1970), pp.96-119

Jones, M.G., *The Charity School Movement, a Study of Eighteenth-Century Puritanism in Action* (Cambridge, 1938)

Jones, William, *The Jubilee Memorial of the Religious Tract Society, 1799-1849* (1850)

Keary, Eliza, *Memoir of Annie Keary* (1883)

Kingsford, M.R., *The Life, Work and Influence of W.H.G. Kingston* (Toronto, 1947)

Laqueur, T.W., *Religion and Respectability: Sunday Schools and Working Class Culture 1780-1850* (New Haven and London, 1976)

Lawson, John and Harold Silver, *A Social History of Education in England* (1973)

Lowther Clarke, W.K., *Eighteenth-Century Piety* (1945)

——, *A History of the S.P.C.K.* (1959)

McCann, P. (ed.), *Popular Education and Socialization in the Nineteenth Century* (1977)

Mack, E.C., *Public Schools and British Opinion Since 1860* (New York, 1941)

Maison, Margaret M., *Search Your Soul, Eustace, a survey of the religious novel in the Victorian age* (London and New York, 1961)

Mare, M. and A. Percival, *Victorian Best-Seller, the World of Charlotte M. Yonge* (1947)

Marshall, Emma, 'A.L.O.E.' in *Women Novelists of Queen Victoria's*

Reign (1897) (reprinted as 'All for Love, and No Reward', *Signal*, January 1972)

Mause, Lloyd de (ed.), *The History of Childhood* (New York, 1974)

Meakin, A.M.B., *Hannah More* (1911)

Meek, M., A. Warlow and G. Barton (eds.), *The Cool Web, the Pattern of Children's Reading* (1977)

Mumby, Frank A. and Ian Norrie, *Publishing and Bookselling*, 5th edn (1974)

Munby, G.F.W., *The Life of Legh Richmond* (1894)

——, and Thomas Wright, *Turvey and Legh Richmond*, 2nd edn (Olney, 1894)

Musgrove, F., 'The Decline of the Educative Family', *Universities Quarterly*, vol. 14 (1959-60), pp.377-404

Naidis, Mark, 'G.A. Henty's Idea of India', *Victorian Studies*, vol. VIII (September 1964), pp.49-58

Neuburg, Victor E., *The Penny Histories, a Study of Chapbooks for Young Readers Over Two Centuries* (1968)

Newsome, David, *Godliness and Good Learning, Four Studies on a Victorian Ideal* (1961)

Quayle, Eric, *Ballantyne the Brave* (1967)

——, *R.M. Ballantyne: A Bibliography of First Editions* (1968)

——, *The Collector's Book of Children's Books* (1971)

——, *The Collector's Book of Boys' Stories* (1973)

Reid, Elizabeth and Charles H. Coe, *Captain Mayne Reid, His Life and Adventures* (1900)

(RTS) anon., *The Story of the R.T.S.* (1898)

Renier, Anne, 'Christopher von Schmid's "A Basket of Flowers"', *Signal*, supplement no. 1 (1972)

Resnick, D.P. and L.B. Resnick, 'The Nature of Literacy: An Historical Exploration', *Harvard Educational Review*, vol. 47 (August 1977), pp.370-85

(Richmond, Legh) 'a clergyman's son', *Three Days at Turvey in Bedfordshire . . . in the summer of 1847* (1848)

Rivington, Septimus, *The Publishing Family of Rivington* (1919)

Roberts, Robert, *The Classic Slum* (Manchester, 1971)

Salmon, Edward, *Juvenile Literature as it is* (1888)

Salway, Lance (ed.), *A Peculiar Gift, Nineteenth-Century Writings on Books for Children* (Harmondsworth, 1976)

Sandison, Alan, *The Wheel of Empire* (1967)

Sangster, Paul, *Pity My Simplicity* (1963)

Sewell, Eleanor L. (ed.), *The Autobiography of Elizabeth M. Sewell* (1908)

Shepard, Leslie, *The History of Street Literature* (Newton Abbot, 1973)

Simon, Brian, *Studies in the History of Education, 1780-1870* (1960)

Simon, Brian and Ian Bradley (eds.), *The Victorian Public School* (Dublin, 1975)

Smith, Naomi Royde, *The State of Mind of Mrs Sherwood* (1946)

Spinghall, J., *Youth, Empire and Society, British Youth Movements 1883-1940* (1977)

Stone, Laurence, 'Literacy and Education in England 1640-1900', *Past and Present*, 42 (1969), pp.69-139

Sutherland, J.A., *Victorian Novelists and Publishers* (1976)

Thompson, E.P., *The Making of the English Working Class*, rev. edn (Harmondsworth, 1968)

Thompson, Flora, *Lark Rise to Candleford* (1945)

Thomson, P., *The Victorian Heroine, a Changing Ideal 1837-73* (1956)

Tillotson, K., *Novels of the 1840s* (Oxford, 1954)

Tillotson, G. and K., *Mid-Victorian Studies* (1965)

Townsend, John Rowe, *Written For Children*, rev. edn (Harmondsworth, 1974)

Trimmer, Sarah, *The Oeconomy of Charity* (1787)

――――, *Reflections Upon the Education of Children in Charity Schools* (1792)

Turner, E.S., *Boys Will Be Boys*, new rev. edn (1975)

Tweedie, Rev. W.K., *The Early Choice* (1855)

Wakefield, Edward Gibbon, *A View of the Art of Colonization* (1849)

Wallace, Rev. J.A., *Lessons from the Life of the Late James Nisbet, Publisher, London, A Study for Young Men* (Edinburgh and London, 1867)

Warner, Anna B, *Susan Warner ('Elizabeth Wetherell')* (New York and London, 1909)

Watson, W.H., *The History of the Sunday School Union* (1853)

――――, *The First Fifty Years of the Sunday School* (1873)

Webb, R.K., *Harriet Martineau, a Radical Victorian* (1960)

West, E.G., *Education and the Industrial Revolution* (London and Sidney, 1975)

Wilkinson, Rupert, *The Prefects, British Leadership and the Public School Tradition* (1964)

Willey, M.M., 'Peter the Whaler, Plagiarist', *New Colophon*, vol. 2 (1949), pp.29-32

Yonge, Charlotte M., 'Children's Literature in the Last Century', *Macmillan's Magazine*, vol. XX (1869), pp. 229-37, 302-10 448-56. *What Books to Lend and What to Give* (1886)

Zeman, Anthea, *Presumptuous Girls, Women and their World in the Serious Woman's Novel* (1977)

INDEX